# Walking Together Forever
## The Broad Street Bullies, Then and Now

Jim Jackson

*Foreword by Ed Snider*

www.SportsPublishingLLC.com

ISBN: 1-58261-389-3

All photos courtesy of the Philadelphia Flyers Archives unless otherwise noted.

Publishers: Peter L. Bannon and Joseph J. Bannon Sr.
Senior managing editor: Susan M. Moyer
Acquisitions editor: Scott Musgrave
Developmental editor: Regina D. Sabbia
Art director: K. Jeffrey Higgerson
Dust jacket design: Joseph Brumleve
Project manager: Jim Henehan
Imaging: Heidi Norsen
Photo editor: Erin Linden-Levy
Vice president of sales and marketing: Kevin King
Media and promotions managers: Nick Obradovich (regional),
        Randy Fouts (national), Maurey Williamson (print)

Printed in the United States of America

Sports Publishing L.L.C.
804 North Neil Street
Champaign, IL 61820

Phone: 1-877-424-2665
Fax: 217-363-2073
Web site: www.SportsPublishingLLC.com

*To my Father*

*They really are great guys, Dad. Really!*
*I only wish you could have met them.*

# Contents

# Foreword

Back in the 1930s, baseball's St. Louis Cardinals earned the nickname "The Gashouse Gang" for their on the field excellence coupled with their off the field antics and togetherness. Then in the 1970s along came the Broad Street Bullies, hockey's own "Gashouse Gang."

They were the closest group of guys on a team that I have seen before or since. The 1974 and 1975 Stanley Cup Champion Philadelphia Flyers exemplified the word team in the best way possible. They ate together. They drank together. They played together. It was just wonderful.

None of us will ever forget coach Fred Shero's words on the blackboard during the 1974 Stanley Cup Finals: "Win today, and we will walk together forever." Those were prophetic words, indeed. Members of those championship teams were close then, and in many ways are still close today. The bond that developed on their way to the Cups was a strong one. It remains unbroken.

Despite being created in 1967, the Flyers developed a rich tradition in a very short period of time thanks largely to the strong ties of those teams. To this day, the majority of the members of those teams reside in and around the Philadelphia area. It should be no surprise then that the Flyers' Alumni ranks right at the top of the NHL teams and in all of sports, for that matter.

Helping to continue that bond is the relationship those teams have with the fans of the Delaware Valley. It was unique as well. No one in this area has ever forgotten them.

The two parades are symbols of the feeling the people of the Philadelphia area had for those teams. In my mind, there's never been anything like it anywhere, for any team, at any time. The first year, there were two million people at the parade, without exaggeration. It was mind-boggling. Everybody wore Flyer shirts.

It was interesting that the apologists reasoned that the only reason so many people showed up was that it had been a long time since the city had witnessed a major sports championship. In my mind, I knew that those were not football fans coming out for that reason. I thought all along that they were Flyers' fans.

The next year 2.3 million people attended the parade. The apologists had nothing to say at that point! In later years, when some other teams in the city won championships, there were maybe 250,000 people along the parade routes. To me, that tells you what a special place those Flyer teams had with the fans of this area.

In fact, Philadelphia is a great hockey city. It has been ever since the Flyers captured the fans' imaginations with their Cup runs.

Thirty years later, the Broad Street Bullies and their legend are still revered in Philadelphia. This book is a nice way for Flyer fans, and even hockey fans in general, to relive some of those glorious moments of yesteryear. I'm sure the fans will enjoy catching up on what their heroes have been doing with their lives since the Cups.

After reading this book, I think they will find that Shero's famous quote holds very true. The bond among the players and with the fans remains strong. They are indeed, "walking together forever."

—Ed Snider
*Chairman, Philadelphia Flyers*

# Preface

After more than a decade as a play-by-play voice of the Philadelphia Flyers, I suppose it's time to make a confession. As a youngster growing up in the small upstate New York city of Utica, I was not the biggest fan of the Flyers. In fact, I was a diehard supporter of those dreaded New York Rangers!

Back in the 1970s, my father and I used to grow weary of those "Broad Street Bullies" beating up on our "Broadway Blueshirts." One of my favorite players was an unassuming defenseman named Dale Rolfe. When the Flyers' Dave Schultz pummeled him in a much-ballyhooed fight, I was enraged. When Gary Dornhoefer used to park his body in the way of Ranger goaltender Eddie Giacomin's view, I was more than a little annoyed. When Bobby Clarke used to make the perfect pass at just the right time or score the key goal, I was frustrated. Finally, when Bernie Parent made a spectacular save on Rod Gilbert or one of the other Rangers, I was heartbroken.

Yes, back then, you could have included me along with so many of the hockey fans outside of Philadelphia who had the opinion that the Flyers and their aggressive tactics were the bane of the sport's existence. It got so bad that even when the Rangers weren't the opposition, my father and I would pull for the teams going against the Flyers. So, I suppose, it might seem a little strange that 20 years later in 1993, I was suddenly a big fan of the Orange and Black. Then again, when an organization chooses you to broadcast their games and fulfills your lifelong dream of calling play by play in the NHL, your opinion tends to be affected! When I accepted the job, one of my duties was to look to the heavens where my since deceased dad was sure to be looking down. Of course, I had to ask his forgiveness. Surely even he could understand I had to go where the bread was going to be buttered.

In the ten or so years I have been involved with the Flyers organization, I have gained a deep appreciation for the pride and tradition of this franchise. In fact, those very same people I saw as villains as a youngster, I now see in a vastly different light. It is impossible not to. First of all, it did not take me long to take note of the love and passion that hockey fans of the Delaware Valley have for the players who were part of the

Flyers two Stanley Cup clubs. So many of the members of those teams settled in the Philadelphia area, so it is quite obvious there is a bond that goes both ways, never to be broken. They will always be legends in this town.

They came along at a time when the Philadelphia sports landscape was rather barren. The NFL's Eagles were in what seemed like a long-term dry spell. The NBA's 76ers were the league's laughingstocks. Baseball's Phillies had yet to begin their rise to consistent contention. Sports fans gravitated to the newest sport in town, the one played on ice. This group of Flyers was the perfect tonic, not only because they were winners. Just as important, they so gloriously represented the blue collar, no-holds-barred attitude that Philadelphians swear by to this day. In my time in this city I've come in contact with many of the principals of the Cup teams. One of them I work for (Bobby Clarke). Another I work with (Gary Dornhoefer). One has sold me my insurance (Orest Kindrachuk). Another has provided me transportation to games in New York (Dave Schultz). One I have covered as a broadcaster (Bill Barber). Another I have filled in for as a host on his radio show (Bill Clement). In getting to know these guys, it has become obvious to me there is something special about this group. They were teammates 30 years ago and in many ways, they remain teammates today. Oh, some have moved away and there have been disagreements among members of the group the way there are disagreements in any family. However, there remains a connection or a link among them even so many years after their moments of glory. The head coach of the championship teams was Fred Shero. He proved to be a visionary of sorts when during the 1974 Stanley Cup Finals with the Boston Bruins, he wrote on the locker room black-board, "Win together now and we walk together forever."

It is my hope that the following pages do justice to the journeys that the "Broad Street Bullies" traversed from their championship days in 1974 and 1975 through the trials, travails, and triumphs of their lives ever since, journeys that in many ways, have indeed seen them "walk together forever."

Even my father, wherever he is, can appreciate their stories. I hope!

# Acknowledgments

My name goes on the cover of this book, but in reality, there should be dozens of other names along with it. Without the help of so many people, this project would not have had a chance. This is my attempt to show at least a little of the gratitude I have for everyone who has helped.

I will start with the cooperative people at Sports Publishing, who contacted me about writing a book and had enough faith in this rookie author to get the job done. Developmental editors Kipp Wilfong and Gina Sabbia guided me along during this fascinating process.

I have to thank the entire Philadelphia Flyers organization from chairman Ed Snider for supplying the foreword, to president Ron Ryan for giving me the go-ahead, to Zack Hill, Joe Klueg, Jill Lipson, Kevin Kurz and the public relations staff for answering my many questions.

Joe Kadlec is an original Flyer. Through the years, he has served in many different capacities with the Flyers. He tells me no one has seen more Philadelphia Flyers games in person. Well, I thank him for his help in tracking down some of the old Flyers and for lending me some of his vast array of pictures.

Speaking of photographs, the Flyers' Archives Department, headed by Kerrianne Brady, has been a lifesaver for me. Most of the pictures in this book were found and organized by Kerrianne and her assistants, Katie Lynch, Joseph Heller, Matthew Giddings, and Amie Morrisey. There is no way I could have pulled this off without their help!

Photographer Len Redkoles also deserves special mention. Len helped me get the guys together for the picture that appears on the cover of this book and also provided me with various other pictures from his collection. He is a class act and a great photographer.

I must credit and praise Jay Greenberg for his book *Full Spectrum*, which was a guide for me in tracing Flyers history. If you are a Flyers' fan and haven't read that book, you've missed out on a great account of the glorious past of this franchise.

Of course, I must thank the very people this book is about. The members of the Flyers' championship teams were all very accommodating to me as I scheduled interviews with them and pestered them for pictures. Ed Snider has said they are simply a great bunch of guys and that assessment was substantiated during the course of putting this book together. It's not difficult to see why they were able to produce such magic back in their days as players.

Finally, and most importantly, I have to thank my family. I wrote this book during the course of the hockey season, so the result was very little time spent with my wife, Bernadette, daughter, Deanna, and son, Johnny. When I wasn't preparing for a game, I was writing. So, I owe my family a ton for dealing with my relative absence from their lives.

Thanks to all...I hope you are happy with the finished product!

# The Bullies Are Born

I t's doubtful that even the heartiest of Philadelphia Flyers' loyalists realize
that the names Jack Chevalier and Pete Cafone have to be considered
important when it comes to determining the actual origin of the Broad
Street Bullies. Most fans would say that honor would fall to men with names
like Snider, Clarke, and Parent.

However, Jack Chevalier and Pete Cafone cannot be ignored. Chevalier
was the beat reporter covering the Flyers for the *Philadelphia Bulletin* in the
early 1970s. Cafone was a headline writer at the *Bulletin*. Their combined
efforts led to the official birth of "the Bullies."

The Flyers were in their sixth season of existence in the National Hockey
League. A rather consistent pattern was developing with the club during the
1972-73 campaign. The Flyers were becoming the terror of the league. In
town after town, they would leave their mark with physical play that often
resulted in fisticuffs. The likes of Dave Schultz, Bob Kelly, and Andre Dupont
were transforming the image of the Flyers from expansion wannabes to tough
opponents that no team relished facing.

In late December and early January of that season there came a particularly rough string of events. On December 29 in Vancouver, after a fight had
broken out on the ice, a fan reached over the glass and yanked Flyer forward
Don Saleski's hair, triggering a bench-clearing melee in which more than one
Flyer punched the fan and several marched into the stands.

The next night in Los Angeles, Schultz pummeled the Kings' Terry
Harper into submission and another group of fans became aware of the growing swagger of the boys from Philly. On January 2, the Flyers pounded the
Flames in Atlanta as their intimidating tactics clearly aided in the victory. The
night ended with veteran winger Gary Dornhoefer giving referee Wally Harris
the choke sign. Clearly this club was taking no prisoners and enjoying it.

From his perch in the press box, Chevalier was taking notice. He had followed the Flyers in their early years and could discern their team personality

**This famous *Philadelphia Bulletin* headline gave a group of hockey players an identity.**

emerging as his story the next day as recounted in Jay Greenberg's *Full Spectrum* explained:

> "The image of the fightin' Flyers is spreading gradually around the NHL and the people are dreaming up wild nicknames. They're the Mean Machine, the Bullies of Broad Street and Freddy's Philistines. Living up to their reputation, the Flyers learned last night that winning on the road can be easy and profitable fun. They swaggered into the Omni, ordered the Atlanta Flames up against the wall and fleeced them for a 3-1 win."

Originally, Chevalier had used the term "Blue Line Bandidos" instead of the "Bullies of Broad Street" when he wrote the story. However, on the flight home from Atlanta, he changed his mind and called in the change. Cafone was back in the office and it was his headline that read: "Broad Street Bullies Muscle Atlanta."

Thanks to the combined efforts of Chevalier and Cafone, a gritty and talented group of hockey players had that necessary element that any legendary team attains, a catchy nickname. Officially, the Broad Street Bullies were born in the early morning hours of January 3, 1973.

Of course, it is much more involved than simply the name. The Philadelphia Flyers of that era would go on to win two Stanley Cups and even more incredibly the imagination and support of the entire Delaware Valley. They remain to this day, some 30 years later, as revered as a team can be in a particular city. Stories of their accomplishments and exploits, both on and off the ice, are still recounted with pleasure so that even the later generations of hockey fans have grown to recognize and admire them.

So, while Chevalier and Cafone can take credit for the name, we need to look deeper to find out just when this group became truly special. When did the Philadelphia Flyers become synonymous with all of those attributes a blue-collar city like Philadelphia could fully relate to? When were the "Broad Street Bullies" as true Stanley Cup contenders first a reality?

· · · · ·

Obviously, there could not have been the Broad Street Bullies without the birth of the Philadelphia Flyers franchise itself. Credit for that goes largely to Ed Snider. In the early 1960s, Snider's fascination with the game of hockey began with the help of two incidents.

Snider saw his first hockey game at Madison Square Garden. He remembers being interested in Rangers goaltender Gump Worsley and the action on the ice. A couple of years later he was leaving a 76ers-Celtics game at Boston Garden when he noticed a long line at the ticket window. When told it was a line for the remaining tickets for the last-place Bruins' next game, he was impressed.

When the National Hockey League decided to expand from its "Original Six" teams in 1967, Snider saw his opportunity to act on his new-found passion. He decided to attempt to build a new arena in South Philadelphia and apply for entry as one of the six teams being added to the league. In the process, he risked practically everything he had.

"I was young and full of enthusiasm," Snider recalls in Ross Sports Productions' *25 Years of Pride and Tradition* video. "I had seen hockey and loved it. I had seen its success in the six cities that had it. But I didn't realize the history of hockey in Philadelphia or in other places. Maybe, if I had, I wouldn't have gone through with it."

The only other NHL experiment in Philadelphia came back in 1930. However, the Quakers lasted all of one season. Minor league teams with names like the Arrows, Rockets, and Ramblers had come and gone. It was a checkered history at the very best. Oblivious to this, Snider pressed on despite obvious ambivalence from the financial community as he sought backing.

"When we first wanted to borrow the money, we were going around to all of the banks," Snider remembers with a chuckle. "One banker fell asleep while were giving our presentation. Another one told us, 'I don't think soccer is going to make it in this town.' I mean they weren't even listening to us!"

Snider, though, would not be denied. He found some financial support and put everything he had on the line. Then he made a convincing presentation to the NHL. On February 9, 1966, Philadelphia officially became one of the six NHL expansion teams.

"I was a nervous wreck," Snider admits. "I had signed for all kinds of things. If it didn't succeed, I was history."

Things happened quickly. The Spectrum was designed, constructed and opened for business in less than a year's time. Veteran hockey man Bud Poile was named the team's first general manager, and Keith Allen arrived from a successful stint in junior hockey out west to be the Flyers' first coach.

That first year, some pieces of the puzzle for later championship glory were already acquired. In addition to the leadership of Snider and Allen, Bernie Parent, Ed Van Impe, Joe Watson, and Gary Dornhoefer were on hand at the very beginning. Little did any of them know as they saw a half-filled building on most nights early in their inaugural season and then were forced to play home games in Quebec after the Spectrum roof blew off, that Stanley Cup success was just six years away.

• • • • •

With a team in place, now an identity was necessary. The Flyers' first two visits to the playoffs would provide the seeds for growth of what eventually became a legendary reputation for the club.

By most accounts, the Flyers' first season was a success. Allen took his group of other teams' castoffs and won a division title, despite having to play a month's worth of games on the road due to the roof problem at the Spectrum. In addition, as the season went along, attendance steadily increased as the team began to gain acceptance in Philadelphia.

However, Ed Snider also remembers that first year for how it ended. The St. Louis Blues took on the Flyers in the first round of the playoffs and in a seven-game series, physically took it to their smaller opponents. The owner took notice.

"St. Louis just outmuscled us and brutalized us," Snider recollects in *25 Years of Pride and Tradition*. "I will never forget the fight at the Spectrum when the Blues' Noel Picard sucker punched Claude Laforge. I mean he just came up from behind him and Laforge [who was all of 5' 9" and 165 pounds] went down in a pool of blood. I wasn't used to that type of thing. I basically made up my mind at that time that while we might not be able to come up with the great skaters, the great shooters and the great talents right away because we were an expansion club, we could come up with guys who could beat up other guys if that's what was necessary. I didn't want a Philadelphia Flyer team intimidated ever again."

The following season, the Blues once again took care of the Flyers in the first round, this time with a sweep. Allen was the coach, soon to become general manager, and he, too, recognized what was going on.

"They just kicked the hell out of us," Allen recalls. "Noel Picard and the Plager brothers come to mind for how they worked us over. We realized right then we had to get more muscle or we weren't going to be very successful. The next draft, we tried to fix that problem."

In the fifth and sixth rounds of the 1969 draft, the Flyers selected Dave Schultz and then Don Saleski, respectively, two forwards with some size. In 1970, Bob Kelly, known for his rambunctious style of play, was picked in the third round. While these players would not arrive on the scene for a couple of years, it was clear the direction the Flyers were headed. The Bullies had at least been conceived.

• • • • •

With a developing identity, the Flyers needed a leader. He would arrive in that same 1969 draft. After some internal debate, the Flyers selected Bobby Clarke out of Flin Flon, Manitoba, with their second-round pick. The only reason the prolific junior scorer wasn't picked earlier was that teams were afraid of his diabetic condition. The Flyers took a chance, and did it ever pay off!

"At the end of his very first practice session," recalls Allen in *25 Years of Pride and Tradition*, "it was obvious he was our best player. You knew it right away. He just did so many things well. He was so competitive. You knew that if anybody was going to take us to the promised land, this was the kid." Clarke led by example. His determination was legendary. His desire to win contagious. "A big part of what developed into our never wanting to give up in a game is a testament to Bobby Clarke," says former Flyer defenseman Tom Bladon. "It didn't matter whether it was a game or a practice, he went 100 miles an hour. I know there were times when everybody was dragging like when we practiced a day after a game. There was Clarkie going all out. We would think, 'Jeez, if he can go like that, what's stopping me?'"

**Bobby Clarke, a youngster from Flin Flon, Manitoba, became the franchise focal point.**

Clarke was and is, for that matter, all about the team. You certainly do not have to tell Ed Snider.

"When the WHA started, guys were defecting from the NHL," Snider explains. "Bob came in to see me and told me he wanted to sign a contract. We discussed a deal and agreed on a five-year contract. Bob told me he wanted to sign for a certain amount. Well, the amount was low. I told him there were guys who couldn't carry his jockstrap making a lot more with the WHA. He told me he didn't care. He wanted to win a Cup, and if he signed for this amount, we could probably sign the rest of the guys we needed to. I've never forgotten that."

Clearly the Flyers had their leader.

•   •   •   •   •

Slowly it was coming together. But who was going to mold the players into championship material?

Keith Allen had coached the team through its first two seasons. Vic Stasiuk was the bench boss for the following couple of seasons, one resulting in a four game sweep in the first round of the playoffs and the other a heartbreaking loss on the final day of the regular season which kept the Flyers from even getting into the postseason.

**Fred Shero was brought in to put the pieces together.**

A new bench boss was needed. Out of the New York Rangers' farm system stepped 45-year-old Fred Shero, the bespectacled coach with impressive minor league credentials. He came with the reputation of being a players' coach who was willing to experiment with new trends. He also was thought to have an aloof nature about him.

"Freddy Shero was perhaps the only coach that could handle our team at the time," claims Bill Barber in *25 Years of Pride and Tradition*, who would join the club one year after Shero. "He let everybody be himself. He never took away our character. He never took away our fun."

"He was a very bright guy," says Don Saleski. "He was ahead of a lot of coaches of that era in terms of game plans and running a team. He also had a great sense of how to lead. He rarely yelled at us. When he did speak sternly, he certainly got our attention."

His calm demeanor came in handy in his first year. The Flyers, for the second time in three years would lose in their final game of the season to miss the playoffs, this time on a late goal by Gerry Meehan in Buffalo. But instead of panic, Shero and the Flyers handled the potentially devastating setback properly. Thus the loss didn't have an everlasting effect.

• • • • •

Most of the final pieces to the puzzle came together in and around the 1972-73 season. An impressive crop of young players arrived on the scene. Bill Barber burst upon the NHL stage with 30 goals as a rookie. Another first year player, Tom Bladon, led Philadelphia defensemen with 42 points. Rick MacLeish blossomed into a major scoring threat, scoring 50 goals, 49 more than he had the previous season. Orest Kindrachuk and Jimmy Watson would arrive late in the year as two more youthful ingredients. Recent veteran acquisitions Barry Ashbee, Andre Dupont, Ross Lonsberry, and Terry Crisp all performed their rolls effectively.

"We could feel ourselves coming," says the 1972-73 Hart Trophy winner as the NHL's Most Valuable Player, Bob Clarke in *25 Years of Pride and Tradition*. "All of a sudden, we had some of the top young players in the game on our team. We also felt we were extremely well coached."

As the season moved along, the team's confidence grew. They played especially well at home, and Schultz began to open eyes with his raucous style of play. He pummeled Keith Magnuson in one memorable scrap at the Spectrum. Then came the aforementioned series of wild games as the calendar turned from 1972 to 1973, and the Flyers' identity, so long in developing, became cemented.

It fed upon itself. As other teams heard about the Flyers' fistic exploits, they were expected to answer the challenge. As a result, especially on the road, the Flyers found themselves answering the bell time and time again. With the likes of Schultz, Kelly, and Dupont leading the way, they reveled in it! The Broad Street Bullies were now very much a reality!

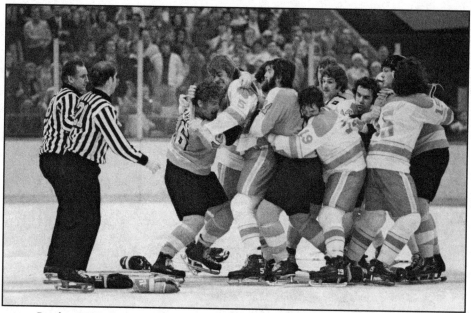

By the 1972-73 season, the Flyers' reputation was being earned on a nightly basis.

As the Flyers' reputation grew, the ice seemed to open up for their skill players. Clarke, MacLeish, and Barber took full advantage. Now, not only were teams respecting the Flyers' toughness, they were finding out this team could play the game. Still, a playoff series victory was necessary before the Flyers could truly be taken seriously.

The Minnesota North Stars provided the Flyers with the opposition in the first round of the 1973 postseason. With the series tied at two games apiece, Gary Dornhoefer carried the puck down the left wing in overtime, cut to the middle and beat Cesare Maniago as the big forward sprawled to the ice. It was the key goal, propelling the Flyers to a six-game series win, their first playoff triumph in franchise history.

When they arrived home for Game Three of their semifinal match-up with Montreal tied at a game apiece, the Philadelphia crowd was in a total frenzy.

"In all my years in hockey, I have never heard an ovation like the one they gave us that night," remembers Dornhoefer. "They gave us about an eight-minute standing ovation. I could have been right next to you skating on the ice and I would have had to yell as loud as I could for you to be able to hear me. That's how deafening it was. It was unbelievable. I will never forget it."

The Flyers would eventually lose the series in five games. But to a man, they felt they were ready to take the next step. Veteran defenseman Ed Van Impe vividly recalls the moments after the Flyers had been eliminated.

"Most of the time after you lose a playoff series, there's a period of time when you feel bad," he explains. "I can remember getting on the bus right after that game to go to the airport. Here were all of these young guys on the team actually upbeat. They could hardly wait for training camp to start! I thought to myself, 'Jeez, that's four or five months away, let's get some rest.' But these guys really believed we were ready. Their enthusiasm was contagious."

Less than a month later, the Flyers would reacquire goaltender Bernie Parent in a trade with Toronto. He had been traded in a deal that helped the Flyers get Rick MacLeish two years earlier. After a stint in the World Hockey Association, he was ready to come back to Philadelphia to work his magic.

It isn't clear exactly when the Flyers became the Stanley Cup hopeful Broad Street Bullies. It was really a series of events beginning with the formation of the team itself. Building an identity and adding a leader like Clarke and a coach like Shero were key developments. When in 1972-73 the pieces seemed to be falling into place, the excitement naturally followed.

What is clear is that by the summer of 1973, the Flyers themselves knew they were on the verge of something special.

# Hoisting the Cup

To get an understanding of the bond that developed between the Flyers and their growing legion of fans in the Delaware Valley, one must think back to the major sports landscape in 1973. Quite simply, there was a void that needed to be filled.

The beloved Eagles were in the process of enduring one of their longest stretches of futility. They hadn't had a sniff of the postseason since winning the NFL Championship back in 1960. They had not been able to register a winning season since 1966. A long line of coaches and quarterbacks had come and gone, and yet the Eagles still resided at or near the bottom of the standings, year in and year out.

Baseball's Phillies were experiencing a similar downtrodden era. Their last good shot at a pennant had ended in the disastrous collapse of 1964 when they blew a six-and-a-half-game lead in the final two weeks of the season. It would precipitate a rapid decline for the franchise. The Phillies' last winning season was also back in 1966, before falling all the way to the bottom of the National League East from 1971 through 1973.

The NBA's 76ers laid claim to the last championship for a Philadelphia team. Led by Wilt Chamberlain and Hal Greer, the Sixers knocked off the San Francisco Warriors to give Wilt his first crown back in 1967. It was all downhill from there, however. Playoff disappointments would follow in 1968 and 1969. By 1972, the Sixers were out of the playoffs altogether. In 1972-73, they would set league records for ineptitude by going 9-73! Oh, how the mighty had fallen.

Into the sports breach stepped a group of Canadians playing a sport the city of Philadelphia was just beginning to understand and appreciate. But that learning process had not taken long. A big reason for that was what seemed to be an instant identification between the fans and the playing style of the Flyers. The connection was distinct.

"We brought everything here," popular Flyers winger Rick MacLeish says now. "The 76ers followed. The Phillies followed. Even the Eagles eventually followed. But we started everything in getting the sports turned around, a bunch of guys from Canada."

It was a perfect match. In essence, these raucous, take-no-prisoners Flyers came along at precisely the right time for a city hungering to reestablish its sports excellence. As the 1973-74 NHL season commenced, their time had come.

• • • • •

As obvious as the match between the Flyers and their fans was, just as unlikely was the match between the team and the woman who became the symbol of their success in their glory days. Kate Smith was a prominent radio and television star from the 1930s through the 1960s, who by the 1970s was more frequently seen on the concert tour. This isn't a likely resume of someone who would become, at least in the minds of Flyers' fans, the all-important "seventh player" for the team. But so it was.

Smith's association with the Flyers actually began in the team's second season. Spectrum president Lou Scheinfeld was looking for a way to spice up the pregame ceremonies. He had been upset that some fans had been taking the national anthem for granted. He figured by playing another patriotic song the fans would miss the anthem and then have more respect for it. After testing many songs in an empty Spectrum, he decided to go with Smith and her rendition of "God Bless America." Little did Scheinfeld or anyone else know at the time what this decision would start. Flyers owner Ed Snider was among those who thought Scheinfeld's idea was crazy. But after playing the recording of Smith's rendition, the Flyers scored three goals in a 3:42 first period span on their way to a 6-3 win over Toronto. Two games later, Kate's recording preceded a 4-0 win over Pittsburgh. By the time the 1973-74 season dawned, the Flyers had posted a remarkable 28-3-1 record in games following "God Bless America." She had become the Flyers' very own good luck charm!

On October 11, 1973, the time had come for Smith to appear live at the Spectrum. The 67-year-old legend had sung for presidents, emperors, kings and other heads of state. Now she sang for 17,077 crazy fans and a team that she had become permanently associated with. The Flyers snuck her into the Spectrum that night for the season opener and the cheers that greeted her caught even the longtime star by surprise.

"The cheers went right through me," she said according to Jack Chevalier's *The Broad Street Bullies*. "I've played before larger crowds, but I've never received a greater ovation. It was fantastic and I'm sorry that is such a mediocre word."

Bernie Parent would make sure the lady's live debut at the Spectrum would be a successful one as he blanked the Leafs 2-0 and the Flyers got their season underway with a smashing performance. Smith's tape would be played

**Kate Smith, the Flyers' very own good luck charm during the glory years, sings the national anthem.**

eight more times that season; all of them wins before a rather important return engagement in May.

Smith passed away in 1986, but to this day, when the tape of her "God Bless America" rendition is played before a Flyers' game (now only on rare occasions and usually in tandem with current anthem singer Lauren Hart), there is a special electricity in the crowd. Just as the fans haven't forgotten any of their playing heroes, they haven't forgotten the team's good luck charm, either!

•     •     •     •     •

Kate Smith wasn't the only advantage the Flyers had when they played at the Spectrum. Their following was as enthusiastic as any in the NHL, and it paid off handsomely. The Flyers would compile an impressive 28-6-5 home ice record in 1973-74. They would lose only once in their last 16 games in Philadelphia.

Among the 17,007 that filled the Spectrum on a nightly basis were some clearly recognizable regulars such as Dave Leonardi, known by everybody simply as "Sign Man." He would bring his array of flashcards with some nifty sayings and display them at precisely the appropriate time. It became a habit of television camera operators to seek him out in his seat location behind one of the goals when something noteworthy happened in a game. There was also the group that became known as "Schultz's Army." Hard hats like those worn in combat by soldiers became the headwear of the day for these ardent supporters of the Flyers' policeman. More than anything, though, it was the noise made by the fans who packed the house night in and night out that helped carry the Flyers to their remarkable home ice record. "They were the greatest fans in the world," says Bill Barber in Ross Sports Productions' *25 Years of Pride and Tradition* video. "We had a hard-working team. They were a hard-working group of people who paid to go watch us play so hard. So there was an almost immediate bond that complemented one another's lifestyle."

It was a bond that would last well beyond the players' days on the ice.

• • • • •

"They live together. They work together. They drink together, and they fight together."

Those are the words of Fred Shero in Jack Chevalier's *The Broad Street Bullies* describing his teams. It's a simple statement, but it does capture what the championship Flyer teams were all about. As much as they developed into a tight-knit unit on the ice, they became very close off the ice as well.

"When we would go out, it was never just two or three guys," relates Flyers backup goalie Bobby Taylor. "There would be 12 to 14 guys, if not the entire team at least, starting the night together. Everybody did everything together. We sort of had this rule that after a game on the road, every player had to be there, at least for a half hour or so. They didn't have to stay all night, but at least show up for a half-hour to 45 minutes. We all bit into it, but it wasn't very difficult because we all liked each other anyway."

Many times the boys would party into the night. The Broad Street Bullies did develop a reputation for being just as fun off the ice as they were rambunctious on it. This is a group that the myth says when an airport terminal gate was closed one time, decided to jump en masse onto the baggage conveyor belt and take the ride inside!

There were the impersonations by Bill Clement, the hilarious verbal sparring between Bob Kelly and broadcaster Gene Hart, the constant ribbing of everyone and on and on. "Every club had four or five characters," says Terry Crisp, who had arrived in Philadelphia having already played with three other NHL clubs. "But on the Flyer clubs, we had 18!"

Many of the stories aren't necessarily fit for print. Suffice to say, this was one wild bunch!

• • • • •

As much fun as they had away from the rink, when it came time to play, these Flyers were ready. Building on the confidence they had gained the year before, riding the spectacular goaltending of Bernie Parent, and with youthful additions like Jimmy Watson and Orest Kindrachuk adding even more depth, the Flyers rolled through the 1973-74 regular season. They won their first four games and then lost their next three. But from that point on, the Flyers would lose consecutively only once more. Meanwhile, they would put streaks of three or more wins together nine times. With the exception of Bill Barber, whose point total rose modestly from 64 points to 69, all of the big guns offensively saw their numbers slip from the previous season. However, it simply was in indication that this club was better balanced.

"This is the best team I've ever seen in hockey for discipline and desire," Fred Shero told the *Sunday Bulletin*. "I don't think I've ever seen any better or ever will."

The result was a franchise-record 50 wins and 112 points, topped only by the Boston Bruins (113). The Flyers won a division that included an original six NHL team (Chicago) for the first time and headed into the playoffs a supremely confident bunch.

The first-round opponents, the Atlanta Flames, provided little resistance. The Flyers would outscore the Flames 17-6 in a four-game sweep. In fact, the Atlanta nightlife gave the team more problems than did the Flames (see Fred Shero's chapter).

The semifinals would be a different story. The New York Rangers were judged by many to be as strong a contender as any team for the Stanley Cup. With eight players having scored 20 goals or more, led by Rod Gilbert's 36, a defense anchored by Brad Park, and the acrobatic Eddie Giacomin in goal, the Rangers were loaded.

Each team won on home ice through the first six games of the hotly contested series, leaving a berth in the Stanley Cup Finals hinging upon a deciding game at the Spectrum. On the way, the Flyers lost all-star defenseman Barry Ashbee to a career-ending eye injury in Game 4. The tone for Game 7 was set when Schultz pummeled New York defenseman Dale Rolfe in the first period and no Ranger came to his aid. The Flyers outshot New York 37-19 in building a 3-1 lead through two periods of play.

However, things got dicey in the third when Steve Vickers got away from Gary Dornhoefer and beat Parent to bring the Rangers within one goal. But Dornhoefer would make amends by popping home a rebound just 12 seconds later for what eventually turned out to be the game-winning goal in a 4-3 triumph. The Flyers had become the first expansion team to defeat an original six club in a playoff series. More important, they were on their way to the Stanley Cup Finals to face the Boston Bruins.

"We made it on guts and determination," claimed the goat turned hero Dornhoefer in the *Evening Bulletin*. "These guys wanted it real bad. But now we're an awfully tired hockey club. I worry about our legs. Whatever we got left, we'll give Boston all of it."

"You work for this all of your life," Joe Watson told the *Philadelphia Inquirer*. "Like American boys want to be in a World Series or a Super Bowl. Well, a Canadian boy wants this!"

· · · · ·

The Finals would provide the Flyers with their ultimate obstacle. These were the Stanley Cup Champions of 1970 and 1972. The Bruins of Bobby Orr, Phil Esposito, Ken Hodge, and Wayne Cashman. The Bruins had been the bane of the Flyers' existence, especially in Beantown. Since winning their first ever game at Boston Garden, the Flyers had gone 0-16-1 covering six and a half seasons. It had become their own personal house of horrors. Now, with the Bruins owning home-ice advantage, the Flyers had to find a way to win at least once in Boston or forget about the Stanley Cup.

Game 1 was a tense affair that wasn't decided until Orr ripped a shot through a crowd in front of Parent with just 22 seconds remaining in the third period. The 3-2 verdict gave the favored Bruins the series lead, but oddly enough, the Flyers a great deal of confidence.

"After the game, they pulled the bus inside Boston Garden for us," recalls Taylor. "I can still remember clearly as we got on that bus and waited to move on out that we came to the realization that we could beat that team. We knew that they had to play real hard just to beat us by one goal. We all said to one another, 'We can beat these guys!'"

Game 2 would prove their beliefs to be well founded, although it was anything but easy. The Bruins jumped out to a quick 2-0 lead in the first period and still led 2-1 going into the final minute of the third period. That's when Rick MacLeish set up Andre Dupont for a slap shot that beat Boston goalie Gilles Gilbert with just 55 seconds remaining. Instead of going down two games to none, the Flyers had forced overtime.

In the extra session, both teams had their chances, but Parent and Gilbert were outstanding. Finally a little more than halfway through the first overtime, Schultz intercepted a Carol Vadnais clearing pass and fed Bill Flett in the slot. The guy they called Cowboy was not in shooting position so he dished to Clarke, who was cutting in front of the net. Gilbert stopped his first shot, but Clarke got the rebound and flipped it home. His subsequent victory dance is an image that will never leave any true Flyer fan.

The six-and-a-half-year Boston Garden jinx was swept out the window by one of the most dramatic goals in Flyers' history. What had been a determined belief that they could win the Cup had been upgraded to supreme confidence that they would take the cherished prize.

"I don't see how anybody could have doubts about us now," Clarke beamed after his heroics. "We know we can beat them."

They would need more of that courage as Dornhoefer joined Ashbee, Kelly, and Clement on the injured list when he separated his shoulder in

**Bobby Clarke's jump for joy after his overtime winner in Boston is an image stamped indelibly in the minds of Flyers' fans.**

Game 3. However, Shero's brilliant strategy of directing the puck toward Orr so that he would get pounded consistently began to pay dividends as the superstar slowly but surely wore down. The Flyers cruised to 4-1 and 4-2 wins at the Spectrum before the Bruins staved off elimination with a 5-1 victory in Boston in Game 5.

The stage was set on May 19, 1974. Who else to get the festivities started that day but the Flyers' grand lady as she come to be known. Kate Smith made her second live appearance to sing her song in Philadelphia, and it was the beginning of a classic afternoon of hockey.

The goaltending of both Parent and Gilbert made sure this would be a low-scoring affair. Rick MacLeish's tip of a Dupont point shot late in the first period gave the Flyers a 1-0 lead. It was a lead they would never relinquish. Parent turned back shot after shot in a display Snider has called "the greatest game in goal" he has ever seen.

"I was numb at the time," Parent recalls in *25 Years of Pride and Tradition*. "Especially in the last ten minutes of the game. I was so keyed on winning that game that I forgot to even get nervous."

He would stop everything the Bruins fired his way that glorious day. As time wound down, Orr had fired the puck all of the way down the ice and Joe Watson went back behind Parent's net to get it. In the press box, Gene Hart uttered his now legendary call, "Ladies and gentlemen, the Flyers are going to win the Stanley Cup! The Flyers win the Stanley Cup! The Flyers win the Stanley Cup! The Flyers have won the Stanley Cup!"

The players mobbed each other on the ice and were joined by several hundred fans making their tour with Lord Stanley's silverware a cumbersome one, not that anybody minded at that point. The culmination of so many dreams for these players had arrived.

"Until you experience it, you really don't know what winning a Cup is all about," says Ed Van Impe, one of four original Flyers [Dornhoefer, Joe Watson, and Parent being the others] still around for the crowning glory. "There have been a lot of great individuals that were tremendous players, even Hall of Famers, who have never won a Stanley Cup. To me, it was the ultimate. Until you get to the top of that mountain and have that feeling of your dream coming true, you really never understand."

The sports enthusiasts of the city of Philadelphia understood, though. Their championship drought was over and with their other teams at that point struggling, this title was like an oasis in a huge desert for them. As a result, the fans went crazy, piling into the streets in a spontaneous celebration. Roads were blocked and the city came to a standstill, all in honor of their new heroes.

• • • •

If ever there was confirmation that something special was going on between this team and the people of the Delaware Valley, the day after the Cup triumph was it. Philadelphia police expected a couple hundred thousand people to line the route for a parade of the champions from the Spectrum to Independence Hall. They had the correct number, but their decimal was in the wrong place!

Police estimated more than two million people took in the parade that has become part of legend. And it was an enthusiastic throng. Many of the Flyers, riding in open convertibles, had difficulty maneuvering through the streets to get to the reviewing stand. In fact, Clarke and Van Impe never did make it to the ultimate destination.

Everybody, it seems, has a story from that parade. Tom Bladon decided the best way to get to Independence Hall was by foot. He jumped from his slowly moving car and jogged most of the way, barely getting noticed by the fans whose attention was on the cars. MacLeish ended up with a bruised arm from reaching out of his car to shake the hands of crazed fans. Don Saleski had the sleeve of his safari jacket ripped right off. It was just one of the problems he had.

"My car overheated and stalled to begin with," Saleski recalls. "My wife and I made it to the reviewing stand and it was a little scary there were so many people. Anyway, as the ceremony got underway, I reached down into one of my pockets and low and behold I found two joints! In the other pocket, I found a couple of pills of some kind. Some fans had slipped them in my pockets! I looked at my wife and she told me to throw them underneath the

**An estimated two million people witnessed the now-famous parade honoring the 1974 Stanley Cup champs.**

bleachers we were standing on. Here's Mayor Rizzo honoring us, and I've got pot and pills I'm trying to get rid of!"

The festivities got the best of some of the players. Upon his introduction, Orest Kindrachuk flashed the peace sign with a both of his hands and promptly fell backwards into the awaiting arms of some of his teammates. In general, though, it was a great time for all. Ed Snider summed up the feeling of the day when he told the crowd, "They deserved the title. They've worked hard. We've got the number-one team in the world in the number-one city in the world."

A group of guys from Canada had made everything seem right again in the city of Philadelphia.

# Validation

W hile there was lots of celebrating after the 1974 Stanley Cup, there would be no resting on any laurels. Keith Allen took care of that. The general manager was busy just five days after the Flyers had hoisted the Cup.

Allen dealt Larry Wright, Al MacAdam and a first-round draft pick to the California Golden Seals in order to acquire winger Reggie Leach. On the surface, it was a bold trade for a team that had just reached the pinnacle because it was going to change the chemistry of the team. Three days later, Bill Flett was traded to Toronto to make room for Leach, who had put up incredible numbers as a junior linemate of Bobby Clarke's in Flin Flon.

"The legendary coach and manager Jack Adams used to say you have to move people before their production falls off in order to keep your team on top," Allen explains. "I tried to remember that. Besides, I thought Leach had never played with a good team and had a chance to be a star, especially playing with Clarke."

Allen wasn't through. He would add veteran defenseman Ted Harris and backup goaltender Wayne Stephenson to the mix before the next training camp began. Allen was clearly thinking about 1975 instead of looking back at 1974.

"He was maybe the best general manager of his day," said Fred Shero years later in Ross Sports Productions' *Stanley Cup II* video. "He knew exactly what type of players we needed and what they could afford to get. I don't think we could have possibly won the Cups without him."

Nicknamed "Keith the Thief" by Bill Fleischman of the *Daily News*, for his repeatedly shrewd trades, Allen seemed one step ahead of everyone else when it came to building and maintaining a championship-caliber team.

*Inquirer.* "They don't take time to consider why a team like ours keeps winning. It's no secret. The answer is plain enough to see, if only they would bother to look. It's about discipline and self-sacrifice."

Plenty of both would be needed in the semifinals against the upstart New York Islanders. They had just become the second team in NHL history to erase a three games-to-none deficit in winning a playoff series when they came back to knock off the Penguins. When a Gary Dornhoefer shot caught Parent on the knee during warmups for Game 1, knocking him out of action, the Flyers had to figure it was a bad omen.

In true Flyer fashion, they responded by suffocating the Islanders and protecting substitute goalie Wayne Stephenson with diligence. The result was a convincing 4-0 win that only further exemplified this teams' resolve to overcome adversity.

The Flyers would win the next two games, one on an overtime goal by Clarke and the other with Parent back between the pipes only facing 14 shots in a 1-0 decision. In Game 4, they overcame a 3-0 deficit to tie the game at 3 before seemingly winning it on a Leach goal at the third-period buzzer. But after consulting with the timekeeper, referee Dave Newell ruled the goal had come a split second too late and it did not count. Instead it was overtime. The Flyers were confident they would find a way, but instead it was New York's Jude Drouin getting the goal and extending the series.

Most everyone thought the Islanders' win was only delaying the inevitable, but a shocking 5-1 New York win in Game 5 (the Flyers' first loss on home ice in the 1974 and 1975 playoffs) and a 2-1 verdict in Game 6 suddenly had the series going to a seventh and deciding game.

With the Islanders on the verge of making history again, the Flyers rose up and put an end to their run. After originally being scheduled for the Finals opener, Kate Smith was hurried in for the all-important Game 7. With the crowd still buzzing after she sang her song and then received flowers from Ed Westfall and the Islanders, Dornhoefer blistered a slap shot by Islander goalie Glenn "Chico" Resch just 19 seconds in. Just over two minutes later, MacLeish had scored, starting his hat trick, and the Flyers were on their way to the Finals for a second straight year with a 4-1 win.

"The only reason we won is because we worked hard," a battered Dornhoefer told the *Daily News.* "All of us. If we had even a few guys cheating, the Islanders would be in the finals and not us."

•   •   •   •   •

Standing between the Flyers and their Cup of vindication were the Buffalo Sabres. In only their fifth year of existence, the Sabres had shot into contention behind the famed French Connection Line and a solid group of forwards. The Flyers were confident, though, because they were unbeaten in their last nine games against Buffalo and had never lost to them at the Spectrum.

Sure enough, the Flyers took care of the Sabres in Games 1 and 2 in Philadelphia. Backed by outstanding goaltending by Parent, the Flyers knocked off Buffalo 4-1 and 2-1. When they took an early 2-0 lead in Game 3 at the sweltering Buffalo Auditorium, a sweep seemed quite probable. But then the warm temperatures caused a persistent fog to envelope the arena. A surreal atmosphere developed with Buffalo forward Jim Lorentz flagging down a live bat with his stick to add to the spooky nature of the proceedings. Players were asked to skate around the ice to dissipate the fog on numerous occasions. A funny thing happened during all of this. The Sabres climbed back into the game and the series.

A Bill Hajt goal in the third tied the score at four and forced overtime. Two exhausted teams were battling the heat, the fog and each other. Eventually, Rene Robert snuck the puck past Parent late in the first overtime to get Buffalo their first win. When they followed that up with a 4-2 decision in Game 4 it appeared the fog had turned the series around on Freddy "The Fog's" team.

"It's two out of three now, and the home-ice advantage isn't nearly as important now," Lorentz told the *Daily News*. "Where both teams are now, you lose one and your back's to the wall."

He proved prophetic, but not as he intended. It was Philadelphia that took charge scoring three early goals on their way to a 5-1 win in Game 5. The Sabres were the team with their proverbial backs to the wall as Game 6 com-

**The fog gave the 1975 Stanley Cup Finals a surreal atmosphere.**

menced in Buffalo. A tight, tense game turned on a goal by Bob Kelly on a wraparound, beating Roger Crozier early in the third period.

Given a rare shift with Clarke and Leach, Kelly went behind the net, stole the puck, stepped in front, and beat Crozier to earn himself a five-dollar bill.

"The best part of scoring that goal," Kelly explains in Ross Sports Productions' *25 Years of Pride and Tradition* video, "was that I got five dollars. It sounds corny, but after practice, Freddy used to have this competition where we would have to come out from behind the net and try to score. The player who won would win five dollars. So after I scored the goal in Buffalo, while everybody was congratulating me, I looked over to Freddy and said, 'Hey Freddy, that's five bucks you owe me!'"

Later in the third, Kindrachuk deserved at least a five-dollar bill when he sacrificed his body, taking a huge hit from monstrous defenseman Jerry Korab, while delivering the puck to Bill Clement for a breakaway on Crozier. Clement cut in on goal and scored to more or less put away the Flyers' second Cup.

"As I got the puck, all I could see was five-hole," recalls Clement. "I held, held and held and as he backed in, I took a little chip shot that went right between his legs. I was so close to him [that] by the time I shot my stick hit his pads on the follow-through. Honestly, it was so easy and I was under such control, I didn't think it would count! I figured there must have been a whistle and he let up. Really! When I got back to the bench, I was still in shock that it counted!"

But indeed, it did stand and moments later as Clarke jumped for joy after winning a face off in his own end, the Flyers had completed their mission. A second straight Stanley Cup had proven once and for all that this team was much more than a one-hit wonder, that they were worthy of being considered true champions.

"I'm happier this year than I was last year," Shero told the *Philadelphia Inquirer*. "We proved it wasn't a fluke."

The celebration, taking place on the road, was, as a result, more subdued than the year before. However, there was a special air of satisfaction and accomplishment this time around. The Flyers had proven their point!

•  •  •  •  •

Philadelphia outdid itself for the parade after the second Cup. This time, 2.3 million people took in the festivities, about 300,000 more than had shown up the year before. It was, once again, a Flyers' love fest. The people of the city paid tribute to a group of hockey players who had become their heroes and forever would be.

Things went more smoothly this time around. The only glitch was because of natural causes. Parent had to stop the procession for five minutes when he jumped off his truck and knocked on the door of a household on

**Bobby Clarke and Bernie Parent were able to hoist the Cup for a second straight year.**

South Broad Street to ask if he could use the bathroom! Permission was granted.

This time, the parade ended inside JFK Stadium where over 100,000
fans were waiting. It was the perfect salute to this tight-knit group of champions. While at the time, many of those fans probably thought the Flyer dynasty
would go on and on, this would actually be end of the championship run.
Clement was traded days later and the slowly but surely members of the teams
were sent elsewhere as the years went by. They would lose in the finals to
Montreal in 1976 and then not make it back to the finals again until 1980.
Thirty years later, they remain Philadelphia's only Stanley Cup Champions.

So, on that bright May afternoon inside JFK Stadium, perhaps it is fitting that the leader of this gritty bunch would be the one with an inkling that
they had reached the top of the mountain.

"When so many people come out to cheer you, you feel like you are on
top of the world," captain Bob Clarke told the *Inquirer*. "Maybe that's as close
to heaven as we'll ever get."

So, in one sense, the celebration of the second Cup was an ending. In
another, though, it was just a beginning. For the members of the championship clubs, there was a lot of life still remaining, both in and out of hockey. As the following pages reveal, while these players would never again be
teammates as a complete group on the ice, they were, in fact, still teammates
in life, walking together forever.

**Once again a huge throng saluted the Cup champs with a memo-
rable parade.**

# Head Coach
# Fred Shero

## *Maybe He Wasn't So Foggy After All*

Scotty Bowman has won more games as an NHL head coach than any other person. In fact, he's won almost 500 more games than any other coach. He's guided teams to a record nine Stanley Cups. It's clear he knows a thing or two about assessing hockey talent, even if it is another head coach. Who better to go to than Bowman when describing the fascinating dichotomy that was Fred Shero.

"Sometimes I don't think he knows Wednesday from Thursday," said Bowman according to Jay Greenberg's *Full Spectrum*. "And then sometimes I think he's a genius who's got us all fooled."

Such was the persona of the man who directed the Flyers to their glorious Stanley Cup run in the 1970s. Right up until his death in 1990, it's doubtful many hockey observers were ever able to figure him out. It's quite possible he wouldn't have had it any other way.

His nickname became "Freddy the Fog" because, in many ways, he was a loner. However, this loner ironically proved adept at bringing the men on his teams closer together. There is a theory that Shero embellished the foggy image. That way he avoided a lot of questions and the people who asked them. But then there are numerous examples that would indicate the "fog" was at least, at times, genuine.

Legend has it that the nickname was spawned by an incident during an exhibition game when Shero went outside the building to smoke a cigarette in between periods. The story goes that he got locked out. When it came time to start the next period, Shero was missing. They had to delay the game until they finally located him!

His players talk about the many times he would walk right past them on the street or in a hotel lobby without the smallest sign of recognition. There

Fred Shero sits alone with his thoughts, or was he in a fog?

were also the frequent occasions when he would seem to appear in a room or a hallway and then just as quickly vanish without a peep. Even some of his coaching strategies mystified them. Some of his coaching drills seemed to lack a purpose. He would allow the players to perform them until somebody questioned the validity of the particular drill. Then he would end the drill and praise that player for being on the ball.

"We always understood that everything he did was aimed at helping us win games," Bobby Clarke says in *Full Spectrum*. "We just didn't understand some of things he did."

One night, as the Flyers prepared to take on the imposing Montreal Canadiens, Shero told the team to skate, skate, and skate the Habs into the ice. Instead of utilizing their normal aggressive approach, Shero called for a finesse game against one of the best skating teams in the NHL.

"He came into the dressing room and told us, 'We are going to kill them,'" recalls Bernie Parent. "He said we were going to out skate them. We were going to play only four defensemen and have everybody else play up front. We all looked at each other like he was crazy. After the first period, the Canadiens had 21 shots on me. The zamboni didn't even have to resurface the other end of the ice! Freddy walked into the dressing room and calmly said, 'I guess it didn't work.' We all laughed!"

Perhaps the signature moment of Shero's air of mystery occurred during the first round of the 1974 playoffs. The Flyers had taken a 3-0 series lead over the Atlanta Flames with a 4-1 win at the Omni the night before. Shero was known for his late walks and occasional stops at local drinking establishments for some alcoholic indulgence. On this particular night, it wasn't a good idea. Details are sketchy. What is known is that Shero wound up with bruises and cuts on his face, a broken thumb and a gash on his arm. He had no idea how it happened, or at least he wasn't willing to divulge that information. Police reports indicated a disturbance around 2 a.m. that morning just outside of the hotel. Shero insinuated he must have been in a scuffle. "From now on, when I'm going for a walk, I'm taking Schultz," he told reporters. Shero was sent home to recuperate. He actually missed the clinching game against Atlanta as assistant coach Mike Nykoluk was behind the bench for Game 4. The perpetuation of the legend of "Freddy the Fog" was well underway.

• • • • •

Now, for his genius.

The same man who told his team to try to out skate the Canadiens that night also directed his club to give the puck as often as possible to the great Bobby Orr in the 1974 Finals. You could excuse the players if they might have raised some eyebrows at this strategy when Shero first brought it up. By the end of the series, though, it was obvious that Shero knew exactly what he was doing.

The Flyers let Orr have the puck and then they proceeded to wear him down over the course of the six-game battle. Sure, Orr could have the puck, but then the idea was to punish him, whether it be with a big body check, a subtle nudge, or even a little crack with the stick. Even the best hockey player in the world is human. His stamina and patience would diminish. Shero's decision was indeed, a stroke of genius.

When the Soviet Red Army team stormed into North America in 1976 and went undefeated until their matchup with the Flyers at the Spectrum, it was no coincidence that it was Shero's outfit that put a decisive end to their roll. Shero had studied Soviet hockey training methods, and in fact had implemented certain elements into his program. However, he knew how to defeat that system, too. The constant weaving and motion of the Soviets had no effect on the Flyers as they simply backed away and dared the Russians to come at them. Mix in some physical play and the result was a convincing win for the Flyers.

"As mysterious as Freddy was," explains one of his pupils, Don Saleski, "he was a leader in that era in terms of coaching. He was the first guy who used to have us watch films. He was one of the first guys who developed a game strategy with specific designs on how we were supposed to attack and how we were supposed to come out of our end. I think he was ahead of other coaches in the league."

Shero's legacy can be witnessed still today in the NHL. He hired Nykoluk as the first full-time assistant coach. Now, teams have two or more of them. Shero was one of the first NHL coaches to utilize a day of game practice skate as well. Those morning skates have become part of the normal routine for all NHL clubs.

Another vital aspect of Shero's expertise was his effectiveness in team building. So much of coaching then and now is involved in this process. Some of the most effective Xs and Os coaches have been abject failures at the helm because they simply did not know how to handle their players. Shero seemed to have the magic touch when it came to getting maximum effort from the Flyers.

"Freddy Shero was the perfect guy for this bunch of characters," reasons his former general manager Keith Allen. "He wasn't one of these guys who told them what they could and couldn't do at every turn. Instead, he let them develop their own personality as a team. As a result, the players developed a great deal of respect for him. He was loved by those guys. You can't say that about too many coaches."

Shero was very careful to make sure his players knew he was on their side. He would never embarrass them in the press. He would defend them when necessary. He even went as far to take their side on those occasions when they were at odds with management. This went a long way in developing the bond that developed between the players and their coach.

"Hockey is a children's game played by men," he would say. "Since it is a children's game, they ought to have fun."

And fun they had, both on the ice and off. His practices sometimes included 12-on-12 games with the winning team getting awarded a small monetary reward. On other days, it would be a one-on-one shootout with the participants representing the other players. Either way, it led to spirited fun.

"I never would have had the opportunity to win a Stanley Cup without Freddy Shero," claims Bob Clarke now. "I'm convinced of that. He brought the discipline and courage to play the game properly to the Flyers. He found a way to narrow you down to be able to focus on the game and your responsibilities. It was all about the team."

Off the ice he stressed team unity and urged the players to become part of the community.

"He always told us our outside responsibilities were our family and the community," Clarke relates. "He always told us to buy a home in the city and become part of the community. The kids will be part of the schools. We took his advice, and I think it was extremely important in developing a close team and a closeness with the fans."

Again, there's that irony. A loner by nature, and yet so effective at bringing other people together.

• • • • •

Another trademark of Shero was his use of quotations as forms of motivation or at the very least thought provocation. The players laughed at some of them. Others they couldn't understand. But many of them hit home, enough so that Dave Schultz kept every one of them. "I loved the guy," says Schultz. "He was such a unique man. I mean he was shy and didn't say much, but he did have all of those sayings. I kept every one of the sheets that he handed to us. I still have all of them."

During the 1972-73 season, Shero wrote a quote dealing with team commitment on a blackboard in the locker room. The team followed with a victory, and whether it was coincidence or not, Shero must have felt the quotation had helped. From then on, he would search for inspirational messages to give to his players before games.

When you look at some of the quotes, you wonder with some of them, just what point Shero was trying to get across. Try this one for instance:

*"When you have bacon and eggs for breakfast, the chicken makes a contribution, but the pig makes a commitment."*

Others would seem to have more relevance to the task that was at hand for the Flyers back then:

*"Success is not the result of spontaneous combustion. You must first set yourself on fire."*

*"Be more concerned with your character than your reputation. For your character is what you really are, while your reputation is merely what others think you are."*

*"There are no heroic tales without heroic tails."*

Then, there's the one that most seemed to sum up Shero's approach to the game and the approach he hoped his players would take:

*"We know that hockey is where we live, where we can best meet and over-come pain and wrong and death. Life is just a place where we spend time between games."*

The one that most people remember and is the basis for this book is the most heralded of all. It has also proven to be dead-on accurate:

*"Win together now and we will walk together forever."*

Through his methods and aided by his quotations, Freddy Shero was looked upon by the players as a father is so often by his children. They didn't always understand him, but they knew he had their best interests at heart. It made for a great relationship.

•   •   •   •   •

The two Stanley Cups and the win over the Russians were the highlights of Fred Shero's coaching career. He spent seven seasons behind the Flyers' bench directing the team to its crowning achievement. Time does march on, however. No matter what the sport is, a coach's influence over a team eventually wanes. The message doesn't seem to get through as clearly. By 1978, that time had arrived for Shero with the Flyers.

Ironically, when that time came, it seems both Shero and the Flyers were aware of it. The Flyers had just been eliminated by the Boston Bruins in the conference semifinals for the second consecutive year. They had failed to win the division title in the regular season for the first time since before winning their Cups. The team seemed to be slipping ever so slightly.

A week after getting eliminated, Shero, despite having one year remaining on his contract, handed in his letter of resignation. To some, this was a stunning development. However, Keith Allen and Ed Snider actually saw the situation as an opportunity. Snider did not trust Shero's agent, Mark Stewart. He thought Stewart might be trying to manipulate Shero's release so that he could coach another team.

The Flyers notified Shero that they would not accept the resignation, and then Snider instructed everyone in the organization to avoid talking about the subject. Eventually, word of Shero's desire to quit leaked to the press, and Shero then held a press conference in which he stated he felt "my effectiveness to motivate the players has been exhausted. The organization needs a change, whether they realize it or not."

It turns out they did. The Flyers agreed with Shero. By then they had information that Shero had been talking with the Rangers. Realizing he was still under contract, they thought they might be able to get some compensation for him should he leave.

A deal was worked out in which the Flyers received the Rangers' first-round draft pick and cash in order to let Shero go. In the end, everybody seemed happy.

"The time had come to make a change anyway," says Snider now. "Everything worked out beautifully for us. We basically suckered the Rangers.

We ended up with a first-round pick for a coach we probably were going to fire anyway."

Shero evidentially got his wish, too. He headed to New York to coach a team he had worked for as a minor league bench boss already. This time, he would be the head coach *and* general manager of the big team. The Shero Era in Philadelphia, a glorious one indeed, had come to an end.

• • • • •

It would not take Shero long to find out that Flyers fans were a little less enthusiastic about how his exit transpired than he or the organization had been. He returned to the Spectrum for an exhibition game as head coach of the Rangers the following September. One look at some of the signs brought by fans told him all he had to know about their reaction.

Signs read: "Win Today and Renegotiate Forever" and "Rangers: Beware He Lies." He was booed loudly upon getting introduced. In retrospect, it was an unfortunate way for the architect of the Flyers' championship teams to be welcomed back. Obviously, at the time, the fans were only thinking about how he left as opposed to what he had accomplished.

As luck would have it, Shero's Rangers would be the second-round play-off opponent of the Flyers later that season. Behind the magnificent goaltending of John Davidson, the Rangers cruised to a five-game series win, outscoring the Flyers 28-8. This was obviously a satisfying moment for Shero. Still, his postgame comments were gracious. He compared this Rangers team to some of his Flyers clubs of the past. His son, Ray, never saw any sign of a feeling of vindication from his dad.

"There was no sense of revenge or anything like that," says Ray now. "My dad was just trying to do the best he could for the Rangers at the time. We all wish the parting with the Flyers could have been handled a little better, but it was in the past. Everybody had agreed it was time to move on."

The elder Shero would take those Rangers all the way to the Stanley Cup Finals, knocking off their fierce rivals, the Islanders, on the way. After winning Game 1 against Montreal in the finals, the Canadiens took over and marched to a five-game series win and the last of four consecutive Stanley Cups. Shero would coach the Rangers for parts of three seasons, never quite able to recapture the magic he had in that first year. In 1979-80, turnabout became fair play when the Flyers eliminated his Rangers in the second round of the playoffs in five games. The next season, the Rangers started 4-13-3 and replaced Shero with Craig Patrick as head coach.

"A whole bunch of key players like Anders Hedberg, Ulf Nilsson, and John Davidson were injured," recalls Ray Shero. "But they had brought Craig in to start the season to be on hand so they didn't hesitate to pull the trigger."

Shero's impressive decade-long run as an NHL head coach was over. More serious problems lay ahead.

**Fred Shero coaches on Broadway.** *Photo courtesy of the New York Rangers*

•  •  •  •  •

Ray Shero noticed some changes in his father during his time in New York.

"I don't think from the second year in New York on he was feeling very well," he explains. "He was the type of guy who would never, ever go see a doctor. But you could tell he wasn't quite right. Something was bothering him a lot. He would even miss a practice or two."

By 1983, Fred Shero was diagnosed with stomach cancer. In typical fashion for him, he handled the news with aplomb. In fact, he harkened back to some advice Ed Snider had given him after his infamous incident in Atlanta back in 1974.

"Mr. Snider told me back then that I had to stop drinking," the old coach recalled. "He told me that the next drink I had on the job would be my last one. I wish now Mr. Snider had told me to stop smoking, too!"

Shero would undergo surgery and recover enough to take part in his new duties as a radio color analyst with the New Jersey Devils. He spent several years in the booth, working with Larry Hirsch and keeping in touch with the game. His son thought the radio job was just what his father needed.

"It was great for my dad," Ray says. "Just being around the game and involved helped him. Max McNab was the general manager at the time, and he did a great job with my dad and helped him out. He would even consult with him. It's always nice when you are at the age my father was to be consulted or talked to about those things. My father really enjoyed that time."

Shero would even get one last taste of coaching as he went overseas to coach a team in Holland in 1987. He wanted to experience what it would be like to coach in Europe. With wife, Mariette at his side, he spent five months overseas leading a team in the elite league in Holland. The Sheros had spent a lot of time traveling when he was taking part in hockey seminars through the years. The time in Holland was a nice reminder of those good times.

• • • • •

On March 22, 1990, Fred Shero was inducted into the Flyers' Hall of Fame. His remarks that day indicated a man whose days in Philadelphia had been the most treasured he had experienced.

"Once a Flyer, always a Flyer," said the old coach. "I knew the day I left here [back in 1978] that I had made a mistake."

His health had been deteriorating in recent years, but he had come home again. The Flyers had hired him as a senior adviser to help allay his medical costs. Ray Shero says the move by the organization was very important to his father.

"That was real exciting for my dad," Ray relates. "He and my mom moved back from New York to Cherry Hill and they were so happy about that. The Flyers gave him a position so that he was under their medical coverage and that was a big help."

By November, though, Shero's health had taken another turn for the worse. The doctors indicated the cancer had spread to various areas of his

**Fred Shero becomes a Flyer again as he enters their Hall of Fame in 1990.** *Photo courtesy of Len Redkoles*

body. On November 24, 1990, the only coach to lead the Flyers to the Stanley Cup passed away. His son feels being reunited with the Philadelphia organization in the months just prior to his death was appropriate.

"When my dad passed away, he was once again a Flyer," the younger Shero explains. "That was the way it should have been. It brought my mom back to Cherry Hill, where she still lives today and is treated like family by the Flyers' organization. Those players who won the Cups meant so much to my father. It was only fitting that he was with the Flyers when he died."

Those very same players carried their former coach's casket at his funeral in Cherry Hill. Bob Clarke put things into perfect perspective in his eulogy when he remembered Shero's famous quote about winning in 1974 and walking together forever.

"Forever didn't stop Saturday [the day Shero died]," Clarke pointed out. "Freddie left a piece of himself with every one of us."

# #1
# Bernie Parent

## *"It's a Beautiful Thing"*

J ust about to a man, when asked what was the key to winning the back-to-back Cups, members of those championship teams answer the play of Bernie Parent. Many hockey observers considered Parent's 1973-74 and 1974-75 seasons to be the best consecutive years a goaltender has ever put together. He helped carry the Flyers to those Cups. One would think the weight of the world would have been on him; all of the pressure that comes with his position and being in the Finals. His response to that pressure is what his former teammates remember.

Take a moment in the final minutes of Game 6 of the 1974 Finals for instance. The Flyers were clinging to a 1-0 lead against the explosive Bruins. They fully realized if they let this lead slip away, the Game 7 prognosis for them wasn't very good. Parent had made some huge saves as the game wore on. But if ever there was a pressure situation for an individual, this was it.

Simon Nolet was getting set for a face off in the Flyers' end with less than ten minutes to go in the third period. Before the puck was dropped, Parent called Nolet over to his crease.

"Simon," the goalie blurted out. "I just got a set of new golf clubs. After we win this thing, we'll go out and play, okay?"

So much for the pressure getting to him. In fact, Parent became known for his quips in the heat of the battle. Bob Kelly remembers one time in a tight game, Parent called him over to tell him he was going to have two pieces of pizza after the game instead of just one. Ed Van Impe recalls Parent getting him over to the crease simply to say, "Some fun, eh?"

And then there was Tinker Bell. That was the name given to Parent's German Shepherd. The players remember Parent going on and on about his beloved dog right before he would take to the ice for a game. He would describe his nap with Tinker Bell. He wouldn't be visualizing the move he would make on a Bobby Hull slap shot that night, he would be chatting about his dog! There was a method to his madness.

"I did my preparation the night before a game," he explains. "I would spend at least 45 minutes visualizing what could happen and how I would react. My philosophy was that by the day of the game, I wouldn't even think about it. I would have my routine. I would watch *The Three Stooges* or whatever. I knew that when the game started, my preparation from the night before would come right back to me. You had to have a way to relax, so I would talk about Tinker Bell or anything but hockey. You have to remember a goalie's world is different. If you are a forward and you make a mistake, there's always a defenseman backing you up. If you are a defenseman and you make a mistake, the goalie can help you. But if you are a goalie and you make a mistake, it is in the net. That's a lot of pressure. I needed to have my release, so I talked about other things."

•   •   •   •   •

The Flyers can thank an oversized pair of skates for having their rock between the pipes during their title years. Parent never would have been a goaltender if it hadn't been for his ill-advised tryout skate as a youngster.

"I am the youngest of seven kids," he relates. "My dad didn't make much money, so we only had one pair of skates for the family. My turn came to use the skates when I was 12. The skates were too big for me, but they were all we had. So I put them on for a tryout with a local team to be a defenseman. With the coach watching, I skated around the outdoor rink one time. The coach grabbed me before I could even start a second lap and he told me I was the team's goaltender!"

Back then the poorest skater a team had was generally the guy who was stuck between the pipes as the club's goalie. Such was the fate for Parent. Having never played the position on skates before, he would allow 21 goals in his first game.

"I told the coach after the game," Parent remembers with his customary cackle, "It could have been 22. I made a heck of a save one of those shots!"

A modest beginning for what became a Hall of Fame career!

•   •   •   •   •

Bernie Parent was the very first Flyer. He was Philadelphia's first selection in the expansion draft (from Boston) as they built their original team. He would have two stints with the club. Of course, most recall his second one, since it included the two Cups. His first stint would last three and a half seasons. He would suffer through the organizational growing pains.

"I remember one night Chicago was blowing us out of our own building [the final would be 12-0]," he recalls. "Doug Favell was the starter and he was giving up some goals. Keith Allen was the coach then and he told me to get out on the ice. I wouldn't budge. He had to literally grab me and force me to get out there! I wanted nothing to do with that game!"

Part of the problem was that Bobby Hull was a member of the Blackhawks. Parent will tell you now that he tried to avoid Hull and his world-renowned slap shot at all costs.

"People always ask me about the toughest shot I ever faced," he explains. "There's no doubt it was Bobby Hull's. It was clocked at 120 miles per hour. He would cross the blue line with that big curved stick of his. And when he would wind up, I would pray, 'God, let him score so he won't hit me!' When he would pass by the net after picking the corner, I would tell him, 'Nice shot, Bobby!'"

Parent realized he had a lot to learn as a goalie in those days. He considered himself a goalie with potential at that point, but still green. Of course, the same could be said about the Flyers teams of the late 1960s and early 1970s. On February 1, 1971, his role would change. The Flyers traded him to Toronto in a three-way deal that brought Rick MacLeish to Philadelphia. Parent cried when Allen told him of the deal.

"I'll never forget the empty feeling I had when I looked over my shoulder at the Spectrum," he admits now. "But I was trying to be a positive person, so I figured the Leafs wanted me more than the Flyers."

His stay in Toronto would prove invaluable to his development as a top-notch goalie. He would spend a year and a half with Hall of Famer Jacques Plante, who would teach him some of the nuances of the game.

"As I look back, it's obvious that it was important that I went to Toronto," he says now. "I went to the Leafs a pretty good goalie with a lot of talent but still very raw. But Plante worked with me on understanding the game, playing the angles, practicing properly and all of those little things that I had been missing. Working with him really turned my career around."

•　•　•　•　•

The refined Parent would see a lot of action in Toronto and then again as a Philadelphia Blazer in the World Hockey Association in 1972-73. The lure of a big contract proved too tempting to turn down so Parent left the Leafs to come back to Philadelphia, only as a Blazer.

The WHA experiment in Philadelphia quickly deteriorated as the fans didn't turn out, and eventually paychecks were missed. Parent would walk out on the team in the playoffs when he did not get his check, a check he jokes now he still hasn't seen and asks Santa Claus for every year.

Still, Parent's year in the WHA was in his eyes, not a total loss. He appeared in 63 games and was able to apply much of what he had learned from Plante as he faced in excess of 50 shots on many nights. He knew the financial situation would eventually lead him back to the NHL. As it turned out, he did not have to leave the city he was in.

The Flyers reacquired Parent in a trade that sent Doug Favell to Toronto. With the team coming off of its first playoff series victory and Parent back in the fold, expectations shot through the roof. For his part, Parent recalls vividly both his first and last games of that memorable 1973-74 season.

"I stepped on the ice for the first exhibition game and got this great standing ovation," he remembers. "The Rangers popped in seven goals on me in a little more than a period. Freddy decided to get me out of there, and as I left the ice, the people started throwing stuff at me. From a standing ovation to that in a couple of hours!"

Parent had gone to training camp in less than tip-top shape. However, by the season opener, he was on his game, shutting out Favell and the Leafs 2-0. From there he just dominated, leading the NHL in games, wins, shutouts, and goals against average. He took the Flyers all the way to the brink of a championship, before one last anxious moment for the goaltender.

"There were only seven or eight seconds left in the game [Game 6 against Boston in the Finals] and the puck was down in the other end," he recalls. "The crowd was so loud I was numb to everything. I started to watch the clock tick down instead of watching the ice. Bobby Orr fired the puck down the ice toward our goal, and because I had glanced at the clock, I lost site of the puck. I spotted it at the last second and it went wide. I said, 'Thank you, Lord!' If that puck had gone in, I would be in a restaurant asking you what you want for dinner!"

Instead, Parent became a legend.

**Bernie Parent's return to Philadelphia brought Stanley Cup glory, although not without some anxious moments.**

• • • • •

This book might very well be about the Flyers' *three-time* Stanley Cup Champions had it not been for a painful neck injury that limited Parent to 11 games played in 1975-76. He would appear in eight playoff games before pulling himself out. Parent was never able to find his groove that season.

Of course, the Flyers made a great run with Wayne Stephenson as the backstop before running into the bourgeoning dynasty that was the Montreal Canadiens in the Stanley Cup Finals. The Canadiens swept the Flyers, but all four games were close, and Flyers fans were left to always ask, "Would Parent have made a difference?"

He was back in form the next two seasons, going 64-20-25 in 1976-77 and 1977-78 combined. He was, at that point, a proven veteran goalie, whose skills were still in tact while his knowledge of the game was at its height. Despite being in his mid-30s, with his style of play, several more productive years seemed to be ahead of him. Then it all came to a sudden end.

On the night of February 17, 1979, Parent and the Flyers were protecting a 1-0 lead over the New York Rangers at the Spectrum. Jimmy Watson and Don Maloney had gotten tangled up in front of the net, and Maloney's stick blade shot up just as Parent was moving from one side of the crease to the other. The blade jammed into the eye slit in Parent's mask.

"As an athlete, you know when you are hurt," Parent relates. "I knew right away this was serious. As soon as I felt the stabbing pain, I skated right off the ice and up the tunnel. They took me right to the hospital."

Parent was taken to Wills Eye Hospital. The preliminary diagnosis at the arena was that it wasn't too serious. It was compared to an injury MacLeish had suffered earlier that season that kept him out of action for only about 10 days. Parent knew it was worse than that.

"When I woke up the next day in the hospital, I was blind in both eyes," he recalls. "I couldn't see a thing. It was the toughest time of my whole life. There was complete darkness for 24 hours. The doctors didn't seem to have any answers. They told me I had to let Mother Nature do her work. When it lasted for two weeks, it was one big question mark. I will never forget it."

Then one morning, he suddenly began to see light in his left eye. Slowly the vision came back in that eye. However his right eye, which had been struck by the stick, was seriously damaged. He says looking through that eye was like looking at something through a smoke-filled room. His depth perception was also affected. Three of Philadelphia's top eye specialists came to an agreement that the stalwart of the Flyer's Stanley Cup teams should retire.

"He can't catch a ball his kids throw him, let alone stop a puck," Flyers team physician Dr. Edward Viner said at the time. "And his eye will forever be more highly vulnerable to future serious injury." At a tearful May 31 press conference, Parent bid adieu to the game he loved.

"It's an awful feeling," he said. "Until I got the official word, I still had my hopes."

**Bernie Parent bids a tearful adieu to his playing career on May 31, 1979.**

Even more than two decades later, Parent can feel the shock that engulfed his life when his playing career came to an end so abruptly.

"There had been no preparation for my future life," he recalls. "I was only 34 years old. With the style I played, I could have played four or five more years. When a doctor tells your career is over, well, my reaction was to go home and pull back from everybody. I had no idea what I was supposed to do. The problem is that you are accustomed to live a certain lifestyle for a lot of years and you're on the top of the hill. Then I looked at myself in the mirror and felt like I was in a huge valley. What was I going to do to provide my family with that same lifestyle? I really had difficulty coming up with an answer."

Some 20 years later, he did receive answers to his vision problems, though. New technology evolved that gave him a chance for a procedure that could restore the vision in his damaged eye.

"They told me beforehand that it would take seven hours and that I ran the risk of losing the eye completely," he explains. "But I figured I couldn't see very well with it anyway, so what did I have to lose? I said let's do it and put everything in the hands of the good Lord."

The operation was performed by Dr. Louis Karp, one of the three doctors who had determined Parent's hockey career over back in 1979. After the surgery, the patch was removed and Parent was asked to read an eye chart.

"I read it perfectly and Dr. Karp thought I had memorized the letters from earlier," Parent recalls. "I told him to find another chart and he brought one out that was for 20/15 vision and I saw it clearly. When I read through it, he was amazed. He had tears in his eyes! The nurse told me that was the first time she had ever seen him cry. He felt like he had just witnessed a miracle."

• • • • •

One morning shortly after his abrupt retirement from hockey, Bernie Parent looked in a mirror and wasn't exactly sure what he saw. "I looked at myself and I said, 'Who the hell are you?'" he recalls. "I saw a simple human being, with all the defects and everything. I knew then that I had to do some research and find out who I was as a man and a human being. I had to in order to move on to the next step."

Parent's trip to self-discovery did not come without its pitfalls. As with so many ex-athletes, making the adjustment from star performer to average citizen proved very difficult.

"People view athletes almost as gods," he reasons. "They almost think of us as never getting sick or growing old, of being without weaknesses, practically not human. Then you retire and the cheers of the 17,000 fans are gone. It really makes you think."

Parent turned to the bottle as his best friend. Alcohol took him away, at least for a short time, from the cold reality. Unfortunately, as so often happens with alcohol, it came to dominate his life. He spent some of his time living in a boarding house. He lost his way.

"One day, I came home around lunchtime," he recalls. "I had taken a cab and had no idea where my car was. The kids started crying when they saw me. These are images you never forget. I went upstairs to lie down, and that is when what I consider a miracle took place. It was like an angel lifted me from the bed. Without any real reason, I walked down the stairs and called Alcoholics Anonymous. I had no idea what they were about, but something made me call them that day."

Divine intervention or not, Parent attended a meeting that night and has continued to battle every day for the last 24 years. He requested help in the nick of time, just as his world was beginning to spin out of control.

"It's like the old story about bringing the horse to the water but not being able to make him drink," he states. "It's the same thing in this situation. You have to hit bottom I guess. I was fortunate enough to be one of those people who got the necessary help and got over it. The program gave me the support because I couldn't have done it alone. It was very difficult. In the end, I found out a lot about myself. Now, it's a beautiful thing!"

•   •   •   •   •

Parent's old team also aided him in his transition into the real world. Linda Panasci worked in community relations for the team and she took a special interest in helping Parent get introduced to the business world.

"She took me by the hand and guided me through so many things," Parent remembers. "She got me into some courses to learn about the world of business. It really helped me to reinstate some confidence that I needed at the time. She was such a big part of my life then. It was incredible. I will never forget her help."

The Flyers also gave Parent a job as an assistant and then goalie coach. Through the 1980s, Parent was called upon to work with the Philadelphia netminders. He found it a rewarding experience.

"I consider myself to be a good teacher," Parent says. "I think what I went through during my career and what I learned from Plante made me so. As a goalie, you don't really arrive, you are constantly developing. You work on a weakness and once you overcome that, something else develops that needs attention. I loved sharing the knowledge with the goalies. Trying to implement techniques to their style was interesting. It's all about finding some consistency."

Parent worked with the likes of Pete Peeters and Ron Hextall during his long tenure as a goaltending coach. Perhaps his most treasured pupil, though, was Pelle Lindbergh, the Swedish goalie who rose to such great heights as a Flyer netminder. He was considered a raw talent who had not been able to reach his potential in the early 1980s as he bounced between the minor leagues and Philadelphia. Parent worked with him though, traveling with him to the minor leagues when necessary. In 1984-85, it all came together. Lindbergh led the NHL with 40 wins and helped carry the Flyers to the Stanley Cup Finals. In June, he was awarded the Vezina Trophy as the NHL's best goaltender and Parent presented him the award. Lindbergh made it quite obvious that Parent had become his mentor.

"The man I really want to thank tonight is the guy standing to the left of me," Lindbergh told the crowd at the NHL Awards Ceremony. "Bernie Parent taught me everything I know about playing hockey in America. Thank you, Bernie!"

The two shook hands and then embraced. If you hadn't known any better, you would have thought they were father and son. When Parent speaks of Lindbergh now, he even sounds like a proud papa.

"The kind of season he had in 1985, you have to earn," he says. "You can't buy that. You have to work hard for it, and Pelle did. I mean I was there to help him, but he did the work. It was a beautiful story."

A beautiful story that turned stunningly tragic just five months later. Lindbergh was killed when he lost control of his Porsche while driving too fast on a road in South Jersey. Potential, just being tapped, and in an instant, not only his career, but his life, was over. Parent delivered the eulogy at a memorial service for the fallen goalie at the Spectrum.

"It was like losing a son," he laments. "His dad told me Pelle liked to call me his dad in the states. That meant a lot to me. But you know, as difficult as it was, you have to remember Pelle got a lot out of life in his 26 years, a lot more than many people do in 60 years. It's nice he left as the top goalie in the league."

And he had been given the opportunity to thank his mentor for helping him get there before his death.

**Pelle Lindbergh stands with his "dad in the States," Bernie Parent.**

•  •  •  •  •

Parent would mentor and tutor Flyer goaltenders well into the 1990s. As he grew older, though, he developed a need to experience life outside of hockey. Perhaps, sinking as low as he once had proved to be the catalyst to what he calls "a maverick approach" to life, the desire to live through as much as humanly possible.

From a business perspective, this translated into getting involved in business outside of the hockey realm. He spent several years as senior vice president of Rosanio, Bailets & Talamo, an advertising, marketing and public relations firm in Cherry Hill, New Jersey. He has since taken charge of Sun Consultants, where he acts as a conduit between manufacturers and sellers of different products and services.

"I came to a point when I wanted to try different things in life," Parent says in explaining his recent approach. "I wanted to see what life had to offer. Hockey was fine, but I wanted more. If whatever I tried didn't work, I could have always gone back to the sport I had been involved with all my life."

He carried this attitude to several aspects of his life. For instance, he's always loved the ocean, so for a four-year period, he actually lived on his boat down at the shore. He says he does some of his best thinking when he's on the water.

"The ocean represents what I have come to respect so much in life, and that's freedom of choice," he explains. "Once I take a boat out of the inlet, there are no red lights. There are no rules. I can go as far as I want and as fast I want. There is so much freedom. It's a beautiful thing. I love the ocean for that. It's such a natural high."

Today, Parent feels that freedom whether at sea or on land. He lives life on his terms. His business allows him to keep his own hours, which he says is essential, given his makeup. He spends ample time with two passions he has had since he was a youth, hunting and fishing. In fact, in recent years, he lived the thrill of bagging a 600-pound deer and catching a 900-pound marlin. Outside of his Stanley Cup rings, you get the feeling these are his most prized possessions.

Life has not always been a cruise for Bernie Parent. There have been setbacks like the bout with alcohol dependency, financial challenges, and the resulting family stress. However, he equates those struggles to his days as a goaltender. Every goalie faces disappointment when he gives up a goal. It's how he responds that matters in the end.

"I believe in life there is a path," he reasons. "I'm where I am today not only because of what I have accomplished, but also through my setbacks. Both have set me on my path. I have no regrets. Why would I? My three kids live in the area. I have four granddaughters and a grandson. I was fortunate enough to win two championships and enjoy all of that excitement and meet so many wonderful people. It has been a beautiful life so far."

As he says so often, it's a beautiful thing!

Bernie Parent, today, says it has been a beautiful life.

# #2
# Ed Van Impe

## *The Warrior*

S ince it is undeniable that members of the Flyers' Stanley Cup teams have
thoroughly enjoyed their time in Philadelphia, it might seem ironic that
some of them were less than thrilled to go to the area when they were
first acquired by the team. Take Ed Van Impe for instance.

In the summer of 1967, Van Impe was a 27-year-old defenseman who
had just completed his first NHL season as a member of the Chicago
Blackhawks. These were the Black Hawks of Bobby Hull, Stan Mikita, and
Glenn Hall. A team that through the 1960s had been considered one of the
glamour clubs in the league. Then the Flyers made Van Impe their first selection among forwards and defensemen in the expansion draft. The runner up
to Bobby Orr for the Calder Trophy the previous season, Van Impe did not
jump for joy upon hearing the news.

"My first thought was one of real disappointment," Van Impe remembers. "I had spent five years in the minors trying to work my way up to
Chicago and finally accomplished that the season before expansion. We had
an outstanding year, finishing in first place during the regular season. When I
was picked by the Flyers, it was like starting all over again. The Stanley Cup
was something I never even thought could happen in Philly. I can't even say I
had mixed feelings. I was very, very disappointed."

His enthusiasm for the move didn't exactly blossom when the Flyers
invited him to attend a Philadelphia Eagles game at old Franklin Field. These
were the dreadful Eagles of the mid-1960s. Van Impe walked into a hornet's
nest.

"I'm walking into the stadium and there were several airplanes hovering
around overhead," he recalls. "One of them had a sign following it that read
'Joe Must Go,' which a fan told me was directed at the head coach Joe

Kuharich. Then as I get in my seat, the player introductions were taking place and every Eagle was getting booed. One defensive back got especially bad treatment, and I found out he had a tough game the week before. I was wondering what kind of town was I in! What the hell was I doing there? It was an eye-opening experience."

Van Impe was impacted enough that he convinced Joe Watson, a fellow disgruntled draft selection, to take part in a joint hold out during training camp. The official reason given was that they wanted compensation for the "disruption to their lives." They reported to training camp but were not signed and refused to negotiate directly with the Flyers. Philadelphia general manager Bud Poile sent both of them home. Eventually, they did sign and were both put right into the lineup when the Flyers opened their first season at the Oakland Coliseum against the California Golden Seals. In fact, head coach Keith Allen played the two as a pair on defense and it didn't go well. They were on ice for three goals against, looking a tad out of shape, in a 5-1 loss.

"We were terrible," Van Impe reflects. "By putting us together even though we had missed the entire camp, it was obvious the Flyers were telling us something. It taught us a lesson in a hurry."

It was a lesson they both apparently learned, as Van Impe and Watson went on to have long and productive careers in Philadelphia.

• • • • •

When you ask one of Van Impe's contemporaries about his style of play, the answer depends on that person's perspective. If he was his teammate, a smile inevitably comes to his face as he refers to Van Impe's toughness and talent using his stick as a "defensive" weapon. If he was an opponent, he grimaces almost as if he is still feeling the pain from one of Van Impe's patented spears in front of his net. If you go to the source, well, he has a way of putting it all into perspective.

"Look, I was limited in terms of skill level," he explains. "I wasn't a very good skater. In fact, a lot of guys felt I was a terrible skater! I wasn't very good with the puck either. And I didn't have much of a shot. If I had an asset, it was that I always liked to claim my little piece of territory on the ice, which I treated as though I owned. Thus, I did most of my work from the corners to the area in front of the net, the areas where goals are scored. I wanted the opposition to know that if they were coming there, I was going to be waiting for them to remind them that it wasn't going to be easy to jab our goaltender or get in his way."

Van Impe's methods of reminding opponents are what everybody remembers. A hack here. A whack there. They were less than subtle reminders, but very effective.

Actually, while Van Impe downplays his skill level, it's obvious others recognized him as a quality hockey player. He was selected to play in the NHL All-Star Game three times during his tenure as a Flyer (1969, 1974, 1975).

During his nine seasons in the orange and black, he had a lot to do with the Flyers establishing an identity as a difficult team to play against.

In short, he was a warrior, using whatever means available to do the job. Playing through pain was part of the job. He took this philosophy to a new level one night at the Spectrum. Van Impe attempted to block a slap shot by an Oakland defenseman and caught the puck square in his mouth. In effect, his mouth had been shattered. Seven teeth were smashed (some knocked out, while others were broken off) and his tongue and lips were badly cut. He went into the locker room, got sutured up, and amazingly, went back out to finish the game with the blood stains all over his jersey as a reminder of the pain he was enduring. After the game, all he had to do was go to the hospital to have what was left of his damaged teeth surgically removed. He played some subsequent games with his mouth wired shut as part of the recovery process. Yet he barely missed any action!

"That was in my younger, macho days," he smirks now. "Every athlete goes through their macho days. Also I was the team captain at that time, so I felt I had to play through it. In the locker room, they told me not to go back out, but I insisted. Was it the smartest thing to do? Absolutely not. Would I do it again? Absolutely! It was a special thing to play for the Flyers and be their captain. I wasn't going to set any trends, but I sure wasn't going to break any, either."

•   •   •   •   •

With stories of his toughness known throughout the hockey world, perhaps it is not a coincidence that Van Impe found himself in the middle of an international incident when the Russians came calling in 1976. There was a huge buildup to the January 11 game at the Spectrum. The NHL's combined record against the two touring Soviet teams was only 1-5-1 to that point. Suddenly the Flyers were being asked to uphold the honor of North American hockey. On to this stage skated Van Impe.

He had just exited the penalty box midway through the first period when he drew a bead on Soviet star Valerie Kharlamov. Van Impe collided with Kharlamov, who immediately went sprawling to the ice as if he had been the victim of a sniper attack. He stayed on the ice for several moments and the Soviet team was aghast that no penalty was called. After a couple of minutes of protest, the Russians made the decision to leave the ice and go back to their locker room as a sign of protest and as a threat to not finish the game.

"The story that I've told people is that he basically ran into my elbow with his head," Van Impe says now with his tongue firmly implanted in his cheek. "I've always said I just couldn't understand how a world-class player would have wanted to do such a thing!

"The true story, though, is that it wasn't anything near what it appeared to be. If you hit a player in the NHL at that time like that, they would basically laugh it off. I think it was more frustration on their part. They just wanted to draw attention to the North American style of play."

**Ed Van Impe's crushing hit (or was it?) became an international incident in 1976.**

Say it ain't so! The hockey hit that was heard 'round the world wasn't really even a real hard hit?! Well, evidently, the Russians got over it. After being reminded that they would not get paid for the game if they didn't return to the ice, they suddenly found a way to deal with the alleged roughhouse tactics and came back to the ice.

They were assessed a two-minute penalty for delay of game for their antics. Reggie Leach would score on the ensuing power play, and the Flyers cruised to a momentous 4-1 victory. Van Impe has practically relished the role he played in that afternoon's drama.

"The way I look at it," he explains now. "It's better to be known for something that really didn't happen the way it is described, than not being known at all. So, I take the recognition and say, 'Thank you!'"

• • • • •

Less than two months after his legendary body check, Van Impe was dealt one of his own. In early March of 1976, the Flyers traded him to Pittsburgh with goalie Bobby Taylor for netminder Gary Inness and cash. After nine seasons of pouring his blood, sweat, and tears into the Flyers' cause, Van Impe was gone.

**Ed Van Impe (far left) poses as a Flyers' broadcaster with (left to right) Bobby Taylor, Gene Hart, and Steve Coates.**

"My time with Alexander & Alexander had maxed out," he reflects. "I didn't have my MBA from Wharton and I wasn't going to move from the Philadelphia area, so it was time to move. I really enjoyed my time at Noyes as a minor equity broker. It was closer to what I had envisioned selling insurance to be."

Once he was a rough-and-tumble defenseman in the NHL whose job was to protect his zone and his goalie. Now, Van Impe protected the interests of his clients. It made for a seamless transition into his post-hockey career.

• • • • •

Life can change drastically in an instant. Ed Van Impe and his family found that out in a tragic way on December 10, 1990. It was on that day that Van Impe lived every parent's most dreaded nightmare.

"There was a knock at our door and I saw a trooper standing there," he recalls as if it was yesterday. "Your mind goes a lot of places, but I just knew something terrible had happened."

The trooper then informed Ed and Diane that their 17-year-old daughter Melanie had been killed in a car accident. She had been driving the family BMW on that rainy day and veered off onto the shoulder of the road. Being a relatively inexperienced driver, she overcorrected and went into a spin. A truck was coming up over a hill in the other direction and smashed into Melanie's car, breaking her neck and killing her instantly.

"We went to the hospital just to identify her," Van Impe explains. "It was just such an empty feeling. I would not wish that kind of pain on my very worst enemy. Until that day, I had always believed that kids that were killed in car accidents happened to other families. That doesn't happen to me. That doesn't happen to my family.

"I remember people, meaning well, in the days after Melanie's accident and at the funeral telling me how sorry they were and how they knew how terrible I had to feel. I used to think, 'How in the hell do you know how I feel?' I never said anything, but so many times I wanted to. It's different than losing a parent. It's just so empty. Even as time goes by, there's a tremendous void."

Life went on for the Van Impes and their two sons, but it would never be the same. In fact, it is the time after Melanie's death that still haunts Ed.

"The family had a very hard time dealing with it," he remembers. "I was of absolutely no help to them. I was self-centered. It was my daughter, my grief."

Van Impe turned to alcohol as his way of dealing with the pain. "I can pretty much tell you that I was drunk for three years," he laments now. "Morning, noon, and night, I was drinking. I simply was not there for my family during the grieving period."

Eventually, Van Impe was directed to get help. His wife contacted Gary Dorshimer, a Flyers team doctor, and he helped get Ed into detoxification and then rehabilitation. Van Impe persevered through those difficult procedures. As a member of Alcoholics Anonymous, he continues that battle to this day. However, it's the guilt that won't go away.

"It's been over 10 years that I dealt with the alcohol problem and don't drink anymore," Van Impe explains. "But a lot of the hurt that I feel for not being there for my family in their time of grief I still carry around with me today. I still look for understanding and forgiveness from my family. It's something that I will probably carry around with me for the rest of my life."

•  •  •  •  •

The events of December 10, 1990, quite obviously forever changed Ed Van Impe's life. Still, his life did go on. During his struggles in dealing with the death of his daughter and subsequent reliance on alcohol, he desperately needed and received the help of those closest to him, including his former teammates.

"I think there are a lot of similarities between life and the type of team we were," he reasons now. "When we were winning Cups, we had so many people making contributions. We faced adversity with injuries. Barry Ashbee even gave his eye in sacrifice for the Cup. Somehow, some way, we stepped up and supported one another. All that did was make us tighter as a group.

"When it came to my situation, I had to deal with the alcohol problem by myself at first. Eventually though, my concerns were what other people were thinking about me. All I can tell you is that the people who cared about me, such as my former teammates, knew, and were so happy for me that I was getting help, that it was truly amazing. My anxieties were for naught."

With the help of this support, Van Impe has resurrected his business career. In fact, he went in a slightly different direction. While still in the insurance business, he decided to run his own company. With the help of his mentor back in his Alexander & Alexander days, Van Impe opened a small, regional brokerage called Dublin Hall Brokers, Inc.

"I was tired of working in the large, international insurance houses," he explains. "So I formed my own business, and the only regret I have is that I didn't do it sooner. The key was to go and get good people to work for me. I was never that strong in terms of the technical end of the business. The people I hired had managed branches in the national houses so all I do is open the door at the beginning of the day and close it at the end of the day. In that way, I suppose I'm sort of like a good hockey coach. I just have good players and let them do their jobs!"

Through the twists and turns of his life, Van Impe never forgets the impact his teammates have had on his life from his playing days through his challenges in retirement from the game. He says Fred Shero's quote about the Cup winners "walking together forever" was dead-on accurate.

"The people closest to me not only stuck by me, but they actively supported me during my struggles," he explains. "That's just the way our team was. We hung together and we stayed together."

**Ed Van Impe is now happy running his own small brokerage firm.**

# #3
# Tom Bladon

## *The Young Guy*

Tom Bladon was all of 19 years old when he arrived at his first NHL training camp with the Flyers in 1972. Little was expected of the second-round draft pick that season. While his talent was obvious, the Flyers had several established defensemen already in tow, and Bladon went into camp just hoping to use it as a learning experience.

"A series of events took place that gave me a shot at a job with the big club," Bladon recalls. "First of all, one defenseman [Rick Foley] reported to camp overweight. Then there were a bunch of injuries, including Ed Van Impe's broken jaw and all of a sudden, they gave me a shot. I was fortunate enough to get quite a few points in my first two or three exhibition games, and I made the club."

As it turned out, the fresh-faced rookie became a symbol of the Flyers in that eventful 1972-73 season. He grew into his role and emerged as a key defenseman for the team just as the Flyers were developing their identity and making the rest of the NHL take notice that season.

"I saw the team developing that first season," says Bladon, who also was growing more comfortable as evidenced by his 11 goals and 42 points that led the Philadelphia defense corps. "We were learning how to win. I think one of the turning points came in a game at Chicago [on January 13, 1973]. To that point, we were good at home, but only average on the road. Chicago back then was a hotbed, a very difficult place to get a win. We played real well that night and grinded it out to get the win [3-2]. All of the sudden, we started believing that we could win anywhere."

The Stanley Cup confidence was beginning to emerge, and Bladon had gone from a rookie pegged for the minors to the team's leading offensive defenseman. His confidence had grown with the team's confidence.

"I went back home to Edmonton after my first season," Bladon recalls. "I sat down with a couple of buddies having a couple of beers and told them, 'Bet on us to win the Stanley Cup next year.' They all looked at me like I had had more than one too many! But I told them we were at that point where we can take the next step. I told them they could get some good odds on us. We were a good bet."

History says that if Bladon's friends listened to him, they had a profitable 1974!

•　•　•　•　•

Through the Cup years, Bladon continued to be an offensive force on the blue line for the Flyers. His greatest memory from those seasons is that same moment that is stamped indelibly in the memories of so many Flyers' fans. It was the countdown of the final seconds to the first Cup in 1974.

However, Bladon also admits to nearly as big a thrill in 1976 when the Flyers took on the Russians. It wasn't the Stanley Cup, but it was special.

"I think it meant a lot to everybody," he explains. "I don't mean to blow it out of proportion, but the Russians tried to use everything, including hockey to prove their system was better than the capitalists. When they started playing the anthems, you could just feel yourself getting pumped. We had just come off a long road trip and could have been physically tired, but once we heard the anthems and the crowd, we were ready. Without a doubt, it was a big deal to us, and to the prestige of the NHL, since we were the defending Cup champs."

The Flyers won convincingly and thoroughly frustrated the vaunted Russians.

"Barry Ashbee had scouted them, and Freddy was aware of their system," Bladon reasons. "Barry said, 'Guys, if we go and chase them all over the ice, we are going to get killed. We can't skate with them.' Everybody talks about the trap now. Well, we played it all day in that game, and it worked. They didn't know what was going on. They kept going back in their own end and circling and circling. We didn't chase them. They had to come to us."

The satisfaction in Bladon's voice when he describes that victory speaks volumes. It was clearly a career highlight.

•　•　•　•　•

Tom Bladon spent six years in a Flyers uniform. In addition to the two Stanley Cup rings, he played in two NHL All-Star Games (1977, 1978), and he left the team as its all-time leading point-getter among defensemen. He reached double figures in goals in five of his six seasons in the orange and black.

Yet to say he was a crowd favorite all of the time would be a stretch to say the least. Despite all of his accomplishments, Bladon did find himself the target of the infamous Philadelphia boo-birds from time to time. Mind you, this does not put Bladon in exclusive company. Many athletes, some of them among the best in their sport, have met the same fate. Bladon doesn't seem to have taken the catcalls to heart.

"Well, it didn't necessarily help me," he reasons. "However, the way I always looked at that was that people paid their money so they were entitled to their opinion!"

There certainly was no booing directed at Bladon on the night of December 11, 1977. It was on that evening that Bladon had his night of all nights. It seemed everything he touched led to a Flyers' score.

He potted the first goal of the game and then assisted on a pair of tallies just 25 seconds apart. When he scored two more times in the second period, he already had a monster evening of three goals and two points.

Bob Clarke did his duty and fetched the hat trick puck for Bladon. However, when Clarke presented it to him, Bladon said he didn't want it. Clarke responded jokingly, "What? Do you think you are going to get more?"

As it turned out, he did. Bladon would score his fourth goal of the game early in the third period and then get the helper on a Rick MacLeish tally. With his seventh point of the game, Bladon had tied Bobby Orr's record for points in a game by a defenseman.

"Unless your name is Gretzky or Orr, you just don't experience nights like that very often," Bladon explains. "Everything seemed to slow down for me for some reason. I could see everything I was doing."

**Tom Bladon found himself in "the zone" on December 11, 1977.**

They call it being in the zone. Well, Bladon's zone continued along. His point shot was deflected into the net by Bill Barber later in the third period, giving him the NHL record. It's a record that has been tied once since (by Paul Coffey), but not broken. For one night at least, it was all cheers at the Spectrum for Tom Bladon.

·  ·  ·  ·  ·

Ironically, just six months after his spectacular, record-setting night, Bladon found himself an ex-Flyer. Now, throughout this book, circumstances under which the Cup winners were traded will be recounted. In most of them, there was a certain degree of surprise that accompanied news of their departure. None compared with Bladon's situation.

"I was in a charity golf tournament," he recalls. "My wife [Diane] was four or five days overdue with our second child, so I was on notice, of course. When I got word that I needed to call home because there was an emergency, you can figure out what I was thinking. It was time for the baby."

Not quite. Instead came word that he had been dealt with Ross Lonsberry and Orest Kindrachuk to the Pittsburgh Penguins in exchange for the Pens' first-round draft choice (used later to select defenseman Behn Wilson). Instead of an addition to his family, Bladon now had to think about moving that family.

"You go from pretty high to pretty low, pretty quickly," he understates. "I was very happy with the Flyers, but I guess they decided they needed to go in a new direction. A lot of the guys from the Cup teams had already been traded, so at that point, our era, in effect, was over. I was only 25 years old, though. I didn't think I had gone that far downhill, but I guess some people, obviously, felt that way."

Adding to Bladon's disappointment was his destination. The Penguins were in the same geographic state as the Flyers, and that was about the only similarity between the two organizations at that time.

"I have to be honest with you," Bladon asserts. "I had gone from one of the best organizations in hockey to an organization that was basically in disarray, pretty much in every way."

The Penguins were run back then by general manager Baz Bastien and head coach Johnny Wilson, who had been involved in professional hockey a long time, including NHL coaching stops in Los Angeles, Detroit, and Colorado.

"Johnny Wilson was a very nice man," Bladon explains. "However, the coaching part of it had really passed him by. He tried to get by simply by being a nice guy. My first year there we went through training camp and the day before the season started, he finally called a meeting of ten of us.

"He walks into the meeting and tells us that this group will basically be the power-play and penalty-killing units. Well, we figured that was what this meeting was about, although it seemed pretty late to be having it. Then he says, 'Most of you guys have been around a fair amount, so you guys figure out what you want to do.' And he turned around and left the meeting. I sat there scratching my head wondering what in the hell was going on!"

The team would win only one of its first 11 games. However, led by Greg Malone, Peter Lee, and the three ex-Flyers, the Pens did gradually improve. Eventually, they made the playoffs and eliminated the Buffalo Sabres in a preliminary-round series. The Bruins swept them in the second round, however.

The next season the Penguins slipped back below .500 and lost in the first round. Bladon appeared in only 57 games during the regular season and just one in the playoffs. His contract was up at the end of the year, and so was his largely disappointing stay in the Steel City.

• • • • •

Edmonton native Tom Bladon was probably feeling very positive about the prospects for his next NHL location. The Oilers had acquired his rights from Pittsburgh, so he was going home to play NHL hockey, which at the time was an appealing proposition. And yet it all went wrong so quickly.

Bladon got into a contract dispute with Edmonton general manager Glen Sather that got things started on the wrong foot, and things never got better. Bladon claims Sather had known what Bladon was looking for in his contract before he acquired his rights and then had a change of heart once the negotiations started.

"He had the reputation that if you didn't do it Glen Sather's way, you didn't do it any way," Bladon says. "By the time training camp started, I wasn't too pleased with him, and who knows, maybe he wasn't too pleased with me. I was assured I would have a legitimate shot at making the team. However, going along in training camp, I became the first player I have ever seen benched in camp. I suspect they wanted it to look like I couldn't play any more so as to reduce the compensation owed the Penguins."

Bladon would appear in exactly one regular-season game with the Oilers, and even that was as an emergency replacement due to an injury to another defensemen. This despite the fact that Bladon had one of his best camps in several years.

"In the end, I asked for my outright release," Bladon remembers. "Even that was difficult, because Sather was looking for compensation for me. I ended up sitting for about six weeks before I finally was let go."

His homecoming ruined, Bladon moved on to Winnipeg and Detroit that season. The Jets were in the midst of one of the worst seasons in NHL history. The Red Wings weren't much better. General manager Ted Lindsay signed Bladon and then was promptly fired. The new regime wasn't as interested in Bladon's services. He appeared in only 12 NHL games that season.

"It was a very difficult year," he admits. "At first, I stayed in great shape with the hope things could be worked out. But then as you can't see any light at the end of the tunnel, you get disheartened and are not as committed as you could and should be."

His season ended in the American Hockey League, his first taste of minor league action, where he helped the Adirondack Red Wings to a Calder Cup. Still, it had to be small consolation to a player who just eight years earlier had burst upon the NHL scene as an impressive rookie with the up-and-coming Flyers.

His 1980-81 odyssey was enough to cause Bladon, just 28 years old at the time, to walk away from professional hockey.

"My daughter was at the age where she was going to school," he reasons. "I just was not going to subject her to bouncing around like I did that year. It left a bad taste in my mouth."

• • • • •

Tom Bladon was the youngest Flyer on the first Stanley Cup team. He was also the youngest of them to retire from hockey on his own. Just 28, he was moving on. More than 20 years later, he isn't haunted by the fact that he left the game at such a young age.

"At the time, I still thought I could play," he explains. "But that was my decision, and I try not to look back."

Bladon does admit though to a difficult time making the transition to the "real world." When retirement hit, he wasn't ready for the mental and financial changes it would bring.

"I think everybody has trouble with that transition," he says. "To go from the lifestyle that we had into the real world is difficult, especially the first year or so. When we played, there was instant gratification. You knew if you played well and worked hard, you would see results and get a win. In business, it's different. You can work hard for years and not necessarily see any rewards right away."

The father of four daughters, he had no choice but to bear down. Eventually, he became a corporate sales manager for a national moving company in Canada. Based in Edmonton, he won awards for his work, becoming one of the few sales reps not located in the Toronto or Montreal to do so.

Later, he moved to Victoria, British Columbia, and ran a trophy and award shop there. He spent a decade in B.C. running that store and by that time, had come to terms with his lifestyle, one without the fame and fortune of his playing days.

"Well, I can't say as I disliked being recognized back when I was a player," Bladon states. "However, it certainly wasn't anything that drove me, either."

He recently moved to Calgary as he remains in Western Canada, one of only a handful of former Flyers Cup champs to not come back to the Philadelphia area.

"When I finished playing, my home area in Alberta was just thriving," Bladon explains of the area then enjoying the oil boom. "It was just going crazy around here, so I figured the opportunities for me were better out here. As it turned out, three months after I got back here, the prime minister put in the National Energy Program, which in effect turned off the drilling and everything else in Alberta, which had, of course, an energy-based economy. You've never seen a drought until you've seen one like that. In spite of it, though, I've done well.

"Don't get me wrong. There have been times when I've thought it would be nice to be back in Philadelphia. I enjoyed that area and the people. I had a lot of good friends there. But overall, I don't have any misgivings about where I ended up."

Bladon is a firm believer in the bond that exists with his former team-mates, even though he is more than half a continent away from most of them.

"I think the number-one reason why we won was because we were a team in every sense of the word," he maintains. "I don't think that can be stressed enough. If one person was in some trouble, either on or off the ice, then we were all in it. There's no question Freddy was accurate with his state-ment about walking together forever. I have friends on that team that I still can rely on. I'll have fond memories of all of them until the day that I die."

**Tom Bladon chose Western Canada as his destination after his career without regret.**

# #4
# Barry Ashbee

## *His Legacy Is Secure*

So seldom is one's story so tragic and yet so inspiring. Barry Ashbee came to Philadelphia a journeyman defenseman with a grand total of 14 NHL games played during 10 years of professional hockey. He is now, and forever, a Philadelphia Flyer legend. His journey to that status was filled with pain and heartbreak, but his name is now attached to accomplishment and success.

Keith Allen's second trade as general manager of the Flyers sent Darryl Edestrand and Larry McKillop to the American Hockey League's Hershey Bears for a 30-year-old blue liner whom few knew much about. It turned out to be one of Allen's first brilliant deals. Ashbee had spent the previous eight seasons almost exclusively in the minors in Hershey. His one shot at the NHL came in 1965-66 with the Boston Bruins when he appeared in 14 games. Other than that he played his usual, steady, solid and tough brand of defense with the Bears, his highlight being part of a Calder Cup championship team in 1969. His best chance to get back to the NHL appeared to be in 1967 when the NHL expanded from six to 12 teams. However, a cruel twist of fate, something that became an unfortunate trend for Ashbee, interceded. Ashbee was forced to undergo back surgery in September of 1966 and missed the entire 1966-67 season. Thus, teams were unwilling to take a chance on him in the expansion draft. It would be easy to understand how Ashbee might have become depressed, spending such a long period of time in the minors with only the proverbial cup of coffee with the Bruins to show for a decade worth of bumps and bruises. His wife Donna, though, says quite the contrary, Barry did not complain.

"There was some disappointment when he didn't get picked in 1967," says the lady who was Barry's high school sweetheart and with him every step of the way during his hockey career. "However, especially after the back surgery, he was just determined to play again. Just to be able to come back, do well, and win the Calder Cup gave him a great deal of satisfaction. He came to the conclusion that he still wanted to play hockey, and if it was going to be the minors, we were in a good spot because Hershey was a great place to be."

A year after Ashbee won the Calder Cup, Allen gave him his long-awaited and much deserved chance by trading for his rights. It's a short trip to go from Hershey to Philadelphia. For Barry Ashbee, it was, in essence, a 10-year pro hockey journey. But his time had finally come.

•   •   •   •   •

Ashbee arrived on the Flyers scene before the team was considered a contender. For those who followed the team, it was obvious he brought grit and consistency on the back line that had sorely been needed. It would not take long for those around him to understand how tough this veteran defenseman was. Tough, not necessarily as a brawler, but tough mentally.

"He was a leader, a quiet leader," remembers Joe Watson. "He just went out on the ice and did his job. He played through some tough injuries and just pushed ahead."

"He was the strongest guy mentally that I've ever seen," says Bob Clarke.

"I have always said that he taught the younger players on our team about what it took to win," asserts Allen. "He played through so much pain. I remember one time his knee was in such bad shape that I didn't think he should play that night. The coaches told me there was no way I could keep him out of the lineup. Sure enough, there he was gutting it out. He was the toughest, and as it turned out, bravest man I ever have seen."

During the 1972-73 season, Ashbee played on, despite partially torn knee ligaments. The next season a chipped vertebra in his neck caused shooting pain from his shoulder to his hand. He would wear the horse collar brace during games, and then when need be tape his arm close to his body with the stick jammed in his glove and find a way to perform at a quality level.

"I sat next to him in the room," recalls Tom Bladon. "I would pat him on the back as we got ready for a game or a period, forgetting about his cracked vertebrae, and he would collapse to the floor on his knees in pain. The next period, he would be out there knocking people around into the boards. He was something."

Complaining was not part of Ashbee's repertoire. For all he went through, one would have allowed him to feel sorry for himself from time to time. He would have none of it. In fact, he would tell any player who started to complain about anything to go elsewhere.

Ashbee's determination paid off. He watched as the Flyers got better and better through the early1970s. By 1973-74, they were ready to climb to the top of the mountain. His work was rewarded with his selection to the NHL's second-team All-Stars. A Stanley Cup was all that was needed to make his remarkable journey complete.

**His teammates knew Barry Ashbee played through all kinds of pain.**

• • • • •

Ashbee was playing in the most important games of his career in the spring of 1974. After having spent a decade toiling in the minor leagues and another four seasons experiencing the growing pains of a developing expansion team in Philadelphia, he appeared to be making it all worthwhile. The Flyers were just six wins from the ultimate goal of a Stanley Cup when fate once again frowned on him.

New York Ranger defenseman Dale Rolfe wound up to take a slap shot and Ashbee was positioned in front of him. The puck took off and rose quickly, too quickly for Ashbee to be able to raise his arms up or even turn away. It smashed into his face just above the right eye. Ashbee slumped to the ice with blood spurting out and Madison Square Garden went silent. "It was like a softball was stuck in my eye and then there was just a big red ball of fire," Ashbee told the *Philadelphia Inquirer.* He was taken immediately to the hospital and then eventually transferred to Wills Eye Hospital in Philadelphia. Both eyes were patched up and the doctors waited for some of the blood to drain in order to determine the amount of retinal damage. He would not play again in the playoffs.

So as the Flyers churned closer to Stanley Cup glory, Ashbee was forced to observe from the sidelines. He attended the final couple of home games in the Stanley Cup Finals, wearing dark glasses and being careful not be jostled so as to disturb his recovery. What bittersweet emotions he must have felt as he watched his teammates celebrate the ultimate hockey victory. He was there at the parade, too.

"He never said anything to me about any disappointment," recalls Donna. "We had many family members in from out of town and we all seemed to feel Barry was just happy to have his name on the Stanley Cup."

Just two weeks after the Cup had been won, Ashbee announced his retirement from hockey at a press conference. Doctors had determined that while he would get back substantial vision in the right eye, his depth perception would never again be very good, making performing on the ice a risky proposition at best. Ashbee's remarks at that press conference reveal his mental strength.

"These things happen and you just have to accept them," he stated. "The one good thing I've found out from this is that this old world isn't such a bad place after all. I can't begin to count the number of letters I've had from people offering to give me one of their eyes. I'm just happy that I was able to get my name on the Stanley Cup once. I look at it this way. I'm only 35. I've got a long time to live."

• • • • •

Ashbee remained a Flyer after his retirement as a player. The organization quickly offered him a position as an assistant coach. At first, he hesitated, feeling the offer was simply made out of pity. But he thought about it and eventually decided to accept the job.

"I'm not sure if he had even given any thought to what he was going to do after he was done playing," Donna admits. "So he needed to think about

**Flanked by Ed Snider and Keith Allen, Barry Ashbee announces his retirement.**

it. But once he took the position, he grew to really enjoy it. He came to like the teaching aspect of the job, being able to answer questions the guys had and working with them. Another major plus was the fact that he was still around the guys on a daily basis, going to the rink every day."

In his three years as an assistant coach, he was in charge mainly of the defensemen. He worked with the younger guys like Tom Bladon, Jimmy Watson, and Andre Dupont, trying to mold them into better players.

"Barry was a huge part of any success I had," Dupont asserts. "He helped me to control my temper better. He helped me know when to join the rush and when to stay back. That makes a big difference for a younger player, especially when you just start in this game."

Ashbee was clearly making an impact as a coach. So much so that just prior to the 1976-77 season, he actually intimated to Donna that maybe he could be a head coach some day. He realized it probably wouldn't happen in Philadelphia with Fred Shero being entrenched there, but maybe he could look elsewhere. He planned on looking into it the next summer. He never got a chance to conduct that search.

**Barry Ashbee, the assistant coach, helped in the development of many Flyers.**

• • • • •

The Flyers were involved in a first-round playoff series with the Toronto Maple Leafs in April 1977. The Leafs had won Game 1 the night before. A group of team members were discussing the loss in the players' lounge when Ashbee entered the room and showed them some bruises on his arms and hands. The players all assumed he had fallen or otherwise acquired the bruises, but Ashbee had a hunch it was more serious.

He went to see team physician Dr. Viner, who immediately called for blood tests. His worst fears were realized when the results confirmed that Ashbee had acute leukemia.

"I remember seeing one big bruise on his leg," Donna recalls. "He just told me that Moose had bumped into him at practice. Barry just blew it off. He didn't let on to me that he was any more concerned than that. Looking back now, though, I had a family member who had multiple myeloma and I found out later Barry had been asking people a lot about her symptoms, so perhaps he had an idea something was wrong earlier than we thought. He never told me."

Dr. Viner informed Barry and Donna that it was the most virulent form of leukemia and a rigorous chemotherapy was necessary. The news hit like a bolt of lightning.

"It was a total shock. Everything was a blur," Donna recalls.

Ashbee met the players on April 12. He made his feelings quite clear.

"The last thing I want is sympathy," he stated. "I'll beat it. I'll win."

He went right to Hahnemann Hospital and gave the doctors instructions to give him as potent a dose of chemotherapy as was needed. Donna recalls Barry telling the doctors to "shoot me as hard and as with as much of it as you can." She said he wasn't worried about the pain. Dr. Isadore Brodsky, one of the best in the field, was treating Ashbee and he told Donna they gave Barry enough medication for a horse. The hope was that he would go into remission and then a bone marrow transplant could be attempted.

Ashbee even called a press conference in his hospital room. "I don't want everybody in town to think I'm lying up here dying," he declared in *Full Spectrum*. "The doctors are optimistic. They think they caught it in time. I told my family the three weeks of chemotherapy is no different than any other long road trip. They say the chemotherapy makes you nauseous. I'm not worried about that. I've had hangovers that made me feel that way.

"I don't want this to be written up as a 'Win One for the Gipper' story. The players know I'm sick and I'm going to get better, that's all. They have their battle to win in Toronto, and I have mine right here."

Early on in his treatment, Ashbee continued his coaching duties. He would watch the games on television or on a video recorder the players had gotten him and then report to Joe Watson what he thought could be better.

"He would critique us just as he had been doing as coach," recalls Watson. "We came back to beat Toronto in the first series and he was happy with that. When we got into the Boston series though [in the second round],

I started to notice a change in him. He was having trouble remembering conversations we had, and he was starting to slur his words."

The massive doses of chemotherapy were taking their toll. Eventually, his kidneys failed and Ashbee was put on dialysis. The Flyers were eliminated in four games by the Bruins in the second round. When they returned home, they were shocked at how his condition had deteriorated.

"Jimmy and I visited him and he didn't realize who we were or even that we were there for about 45 minutes," Joe Watson remembers. "He finally did acknowledge us and told us to stop fighting even though we weren't. A doctor came in and gave him a shot and told us it was probably the last time we would see him alive. Sometimes, I wish I hadn't seen him like that."

"He didn't want the kids to see him the last little while," recalls Donna. "He didn't like for them to see him getting sick. Right up until the final day, he said he was going to lick it. And he did mention more than once, how happy he was to have won a Stanley Cup."

Barry Ashbee passed away on May 12, 1977, one month to the day after having been admitted to the hospital. He was only 37 years old. Donna remembers that month as being the quickest and at the same time, slowest moving month of her life. The funeral took place four days later in his native Weston, Ontario, just outside of Toronto.

"It took an incurable blood disorder to quell a spirit that the loss of sight in one eye, a spinal fusion, torn knee ligaments in his knee and a pinched nerve in his neck could not dampen," Bob Clarke said in his eulogy. "Barry never gave in to the luxury of exhaustion or pain. He always played the hand he was dealt. He may be gone from us physically, but he will never be forgotten because he left a little bit of himself with all of us."

•  •  •  •  •

Bob Clarke was so correct. There are so many reminders of Barry Ashbee quite evident almost three decades after his death. Most prominent of course is his family. His wife, Donna, has remained in the Philadelphia area and continues to be part of the Flyers family. His two children, Heather and Danny, are in the area as well. Ashbee's No. 4 also hangs from the rafters at the Wachovia Center. He was the first Flyers player to have his number retired back in 1975. Currently, Ashbee joins only Bernie Parent, Bob Clarke, and Bill Barber as Flyers having their numbers retired. Not bad for a guy some thought was going to remain in the minor leagues his entire career. Furthermore, each year the Flyers hand out the Barry Ashbee Trophy to their top defenseman for that season. Appropriately enough, his son, Danny, presents the trophy. His grandson Kyle (Heather's son) is reportedly making requests to join in on those proceedings soon!

Finally, there is the annual fund raising event known as the Flyers' Wives Fight for Lives Carnival. Barry and Donna attended the first ever Carnival on February 1, 1977. Ed Snider had wanted to create some kind of vehicle in which the Flyers could give back to the fans and help charities at the same time.

When Ashbee died just three months later, the Carnival developed a truly heartfelt purpose. It has become the model charity event for professional sports teams. In its first 27 years, the Carnival raised more than $18 million for various area charities. The primary benefactor has often been the Barry Ashbee Research Laboratories at Hahnemann University. Yes, an entire laboratory wing was built in memory of the former Flyers defenseman.

"It's so impressive to see the equipment and technology in that wing that is there thanks to the money raised through the Carnivals," beams Donna. "Barry would be absolutely amazed."

Yes, one gets the feeling Barry Ashbee is somewhere right now looking down in shock over the impact he has had. Always one to downplay his own significance, Ashbee is now a prominent symbol of the glory days of the Flyers franchise as signified by his No. 4 hanging from the ceiling, defensive excellence as represented by the Barry Ashbee Trophy, and hope for those afflicted with blood diseases getting treatment in a wing not possible without donations made largely in his memory.

Ashbee's often-tragic life has now become an inspiration for so many after his death. His legacy is secure.

**Barry Ashbee attends the very first Wives' Carnival with his wife, Donna. Just over three months later, he was gone and the Carnival took on a truly heartfelt purpose in his memory.**

# #6
# Andre Dupont

## So Much for First Impressions

Some people truly believe that your first impression is quite often your most accurate one. Thankfully, in the case of defenseman Andre Dupont, that was not the case.

Dupont was acquired by the Flyers from the St. Louis Blues on December 14, 1972, along with a third-round draft choice in exchange for Brent Hughes and Pierre Plante. Dupont had played for Fred Shero back in his minor league days in Omaha and Shero knew what the rugged defender could bring to his team. However, Dupont was greeted by what he considered a lukewarm reception from his new teammates when he arrived in Philadelphia. He figures a large part of the reason for this was simply his style of play.

By the time he became a Flyer, Andre Dupont had long been known to the hockey world as "Moose" Dupont. It was, by his account, a well-earned nickname, and it helps explain the reaction from his new teammates. "The nickname started when I played junior hockey in Montreal," he explains. "I used to charge players in the middle of the ice and give out big hits. Some of the writers and fans said that a moose when really mad used to charge like that, too. They started calling me Moose and it stuck!"

For parts of three seasons (with the New York Rangers and the Blues), Dupont had been making those charges and dropping the gloves with some of those same players he was sharing a locker room with after the trade in 1972. He figures they weren't entirely happy to see him there, especially since the departed Hughes and Plante must have been liked.

"When you lose a few friends that get traded from your team, it's quite harsh," he reasons. "It's not always easy. Apparently Hughes and Plante were really well liked in the dressing room. Then, here I come after having fought with some of these guys as an opponent. Everybody seemed a little mad."

Of course, all it took to change those prevailing opinions was for Dupont to strut his stuff on the ice. Once his new teammates saw his "do anything for the team" approach, Dupont quickly worked his way into their good graces.

"After a couple of weeks, I had played a few games with them," he recalls. "After I got involved in a few fights and played my game, they got to know me a little better and eventually there was no question that I was part of the team. As time went on, I really began to appreciate the team we had. We were so close. You could sense that something good was about to happen."

•  •  •  •  •

Flyers Hall of Fame broadcaster Gene Hart loved to tell the story about Andre Dupont's response to a reporter's question just after a brawl-filled game in Vancouver that had followed the delay of a court hearing regarding a nasty brawl on their previous visit. The Flyers had won the game 10-5.

"Great trip for us," Hart quoted Dupont as saying. "We don't go to jail. We beat up dere chicken forwards. We score 10 goal. We win. Now, de Mooze drink beer!"

Such was the developing attitude of the Flyers back then and the spawning of the aura of the "Broad Street Bullies." During Dupont's first year with the team, the image of the Flyers took hold. Teams weren't going to push them around anymore. Not with the likes of Schultz, Kelly, and Dupont on board.

Moose was a major part of the toughness quotient of those clubs. He was willing to sacrifice his body for the good of the team. Opponents viewed him as somewhat of a loose cannon on the blue line. One never knew when the "Moose" was going to charge!

•  •  •  •  •

Andre Dupont was a Flyer for parts of eight seasons. He used his 6', 200-pound frame to punish opponents through 529 games in the orange and black. Make no mistake about it, he is remembered for the warrior that he was, not necessarily for his offensive game.

Ironically, though, Moose was involved in two of the most important goals during the Flyers' run to their first Cup. In Game 2 of the Stanley Cup Finals he beat Gilles Gilbert with a slap shot with just 52 seconds remaining to tie the game at two. Dupont went into his patented "Moose Shuffle" in what turned out to be his greatest memory from the Cup years. "I didn't score much, so that one was easy to remember," he says now.

Without his goal, Bobby Clarke would not have had the chance to be the hero with his memorable overtime marker that evened the series at a game apiece and gave the Flyers their first win in Boston in more than six years.

**Andre Dupont performs the patented "Moose Shuffle."**

Then, in Game 6, it was Dupont who fired the puck toward the Boston net that was deflected by Rick MacLeish past Gilbert giving the Flyers the only goal they would need in the Cup-clinching 1-0 victory. There was the shuffle once more, even though it was an assist in the scorebook rather than a goal.

There would be plenty of shuffling and scuffling over the eight seasons in Philadelphia. After the Cups, he was involved in the momentous win over the Russians in 1976, one that he called "satisfying, especially for Freddy."

Later that year, Dupont would experience one of the most bitter disappointments of his career, losing in the Stanley Cup Finals to the Montreal Canadiens. Being a native of Quebec, and having played for the Montreal Junior Canadiens, Dupont had a special craving to beat the Habs.

"It was a heartbreaker for me," he laments even now. "I wanted to beat the Canadiens so bad. As a kid in Quebec, if you don't grow up to play on the Canadiens, you grow up and want to beat them. But Bernie Parent was injured and we had others out, too, and we couldn't quite pull it off. It was devastating to me."

Four years later, Dupont would experience a similar contrast of ecstasy and disappointment. The Flyers' 1979-80 team went on an incredible run of 35 consecutive games without a loss. By then Dupont was one of the veteran leaders of an overachieving defense corps that included unheralded names like Bathe, Busniuk, and Barnes. "Pete Peeters was unbelievable during that streak," Dupont recalls. "We had a lot of younger players and the older guys that were still there were working their butts off. We knew with these young guys, that we had a real shot at another Cup."

Unfortunately, the Cup glory did not materialize as the Flyers lost in six games to the New York Islanders in the 1980 Finals. That was the series remembered for two officials' calls, one debatable on a goal off of a high stick and one flat-out awful miss of an offside call by linesman Leon Stickle leading directly to a NY Islanders goal. Those calls swung Game 6 the Isles' way. Most everyone is convinced that if the series had gone back to Philadelphia for Game 7, the Flyers would have prevailed.

"I thought we were really in control of the game until those calls," Dupont reasons. "Then we sort of panicked for a little while and the Islanders got right back in the game. In that sense, the bad call cost us the Cup because we would have won Game 7. It probably hurt me more than anything else in my career to lose that series. I realized being 30, that my time with the Flyers was getting closer to the end. They were getting younger. I knew that. Losing like we did was very tough for me."

•   •   •   •   •

Dupont's analysis of the situation proved accurate. Game 6 against the Islanders was his final game as a Flyer. He was traded by Philadelphia to the Quebec Nordiques before the next season was to begin for a seventh-round draft choice and cash. Even though he had somewhat expected a trade, the pain was still intense.

"You are always going to be upset to leave an organization as good as the Flyers," Dupont explains. "They were the best. They were really good to me. Mr. Snider was so good to all of his players. When you leave what I considered the great family that we had with the Flyers, it is going to bother you. The players who won the Cups together were closer than any family you can imagine. When you have been there as long as I was, it's always hard to leave."

Dupont says the Flyers took care of him right through his last day with the organization. They gave him a three-year contract just before the deal. They even offered him his choice of two or three teams to go to. In the end, he picked Quebec because he figured "it would be good to play at home for a change."

The treatment he got from the Flyers organization will never be forgotten.

"The Flyers were always number one in my book, and I guess they will remain that way."

• • • • •

The final three seasons of Andre Dupont's NHL playing career were spent as a veteran leader on a young Quebec Nordiques club that had joined the league from the World Hockey Association in 1979. It would not take long for Moose to realize he was no longer with the perennially strong Flyers. The Nordiques won just once in their first 15 games in 1980-81.

However, one look at the rosters from those early 1980's Nordique teams, and one finds plenty of talent. Peter, Marian, and Anton Statsny piled up points up front with other offensive contributions coming from the likes of Michel Goulet, Real Cloutier, Jacques Richard, and Wilf Paiment. A young Dale Hunter was around to spice things up. Dan Bouchard was a capable netminder.

On defense, Dupont was a veteran influence on younger blue liners like Mario Marois, Normand Rochefort, and Dave Pichette. The experience brought him back to his early days as a Flyer.

"I ended up being like Barry Ashbee, Joe Watson, and Ed Van Impe were to me when I was first with the Flyers," he remembers. "They were like my coaches on the ice. I did some of that for the younger guys in Quebec. You try to tell them when to go on the rush and when not to. Things like that can make a big difference to a young player."

It all came together for the Nordiques in 1981-82. Despite finishing in fourth place in their division, Quebec went on an impressive playoff run, making it all the way to the conference finals before losing to the dynastic New York Islanders. On the way they gave Dupont another big thrill by defeating the Canadiens in an intense Battle of Quebec playoff series. The Islanders ended the Nordiques' run on their way to their third consecutive Stanley Cup. The Nordiques fell in the first round the following season and Dupont's contract, signed before his trade, had run its course. He was offered a deal by another team (the Hartford Whalers), but decided it was time to hang up the skates.

The Moose was no longer on the loose, at least as an NHL player.

**Andre Dupont went back to his native Quebec to finish his NHL career.** *Photo courtesy of the Quebec Nordiques*

•   •   •   •   •

Dupont remained close to the game he loved though as his first two and a half years after his playing career he spent behind the bench as head coach of Trois-Rivieres Draveurs of the Quebec Major Junior Hockey League. "I had learned so much from Freddy and some of the other coaches I had, that I wanted to see if I could teach that to the kids," Dupont explains. "The process of building from one season to another that Freddy had been so good at was coming along fine."

Dupont took over a team that was in need of a lot of work. He counted only six players returning to the club from the previous season. The rest were rookies to the QMJHL.

"When the first season started, we couldn't even get the puck out of our zone," he says now with a laugh. "For a while, I wasn't sure we were going to win a single game. That's how bad we were."

Eventually, they did improve. His clubs, in fact, won 55 times during his first two seasons at the helm. Future NHLers Claude Lemiuex and Donald Dufresne passed through Trois-Rivieres. Dupont was happy with the progress his club was making when an off-ice issue interceded.

"We were really starting to play well in the third year when I had an argument with the owner of the team," Dupont recalls. "He wanted to have a coach that was more or less a puppet behind the bench and that wasn't my style. I offered to buy the team from him so I could stay, but he refused, so I told him to find another coach."

And so ended Moose Dupont's coaching career.

•   •   •   •   •

It's quite possible the unfortunate end to his junior coaching stint led Dupont to explore areas outside of the sport of hockey. He opened a sporting goods store in Trois-Rivieres called Pro Sports that he ran for close to five years. For the first time in his adult life, he was not at the rink, getting ready for practice or a game.

"It was different," Dupont points out. "I learned so much. I found out about all of the things you have to do to run a store. Originally, I figured it was just about showing up. But it was a lot of work, and you had to put a lot of time into it. If an employee couldn't make it, I was the one who had to do the work. All aspects of the job were learning experiences for me."

For the first time, he was living the nine-to-five life. He was able to spend time with his wife and two children. He says he enjoyed it, and yet something wasn't quite right. Call it the pull of the game of hockey.

"The game is always part of you," he reasons. "Any player that has been in the game, even if he has been away from it for a while, it's always there. You give a pair of skates and a stick to anybody who has played the game and tell them there is a game, he will show up."

•   •   •   •   •

Dupont received his call to arms so to speak from former Flyers' team-mate Mel Bridgman in 1992. Bridgman had been named the first general manager in the history of the Ottawa Senators and he needed a scout for the Quebec Major Junior Hockey League. He called Dupont and Andre figured it was worth a try. So much for the nine-to-five life!

Dupont found himself trying to help build a team from scratch. The early years of the Senators were lean on the ice, but fruitful off it. Players that are now starring for the Sens or who were used in trades to gather talent for the perennially contending Ottawa teams, were accumulated back then.

"When you work as a scout, it's always a team thing," Dupont explains. "I'm proud today as I see that team having so much success. We saw it coming along way back then, but of course it takes a while for these players to mature."

Dupont worked under Bridgman, Randy Sexton, and John Ferguson in Ottawa. As luck would have it, Pierre Gauthier came in and basically cleaned house in 1996 and Dupont would never get to witness the blossoming of players like Daniel Alfredsson and Radek Bonk as the franchise turned the corner.

"Gauthier brought in most of his own men to do the job," Dupont remembers. "It's just part of the game. I wasn't mad at him or anything. The guy felt comfortable working with his own group."

Moose would not be idle for long, though. One of his acquaintances from his days in Ottawa was an agent who wanted Dupont to observe his prospects and impart some of his knowledge on them. Before long, Dupont had a career in doing just that. Since, 1997, he has become a "personal trainer" of sorts for young hockey prospects. "I am expected to make sure the kids' games are all right," he explains. "I talk with them to help them keep improving. We try to mix my knowledge of the game with the type of game these kids have. There is a lot of traveling associated with it, but I really enjoy the scouting part of the game."

He is, in a sense, both a scout and a coach to these young hockey hopefuls. As a member of Group Paraphe, he tours Canada trying to help develop these kids so that they can get drafted and have a chance to realize their NHL dream.

• • • • •

Today, Andre Dupont is much the same as he was back in his days as a Flyer. He is enjoying life. He still likes his scouting consultation work. He gets more than his share of actual game action in (by his count, as many as 30 games or so a year) by playing in the Hockey Legends Series up in Canada with players such as Guy Lafluer and Gilbert Perreault. He and his wife,

Ginette, have been married for well over 30 years. Their two kids are grown with kids themselves. Andre is now "Grandpa Moose" as he likes to say. His son Danny was actually drafted by the Ottawa Senators but gave up the game when he was used mainly as a fighter. He is now an assistant coach in the junior ranks. As for Grandpa Moose, he is one of only a handful of the former Flyer Cup winners who did not settle in the Delaware Valley. Yet he feels the bond that exists among them even given the actual distance between them.

"Whenever I get back to Philadelphia and get around the guys, the teasing starts right

**Now, Andre Dupont is a content "Grandpa Moose."**

back up," he says. "It's like we never left. That's how close everybody is in that regard. We had a gathering for an all-star game back in the early 1990s, and the locker room was exactly as it had been back in the 1970s.

"You could never be able to erase those great years we had, especially the closeness we had. When I talk about family, I mean it. Those guys were closer to me than any brother could ever be."

Not bad from a guy who initially felt out of place with those same Flyer teammates.

# #7
# Bill Barber

## *The Loyal Soldier*

It is so easy to get caught up in the numbers and accolades. There were the 420 goals, 51 tallies more than any other player to wear the orange and black of the Flyers. Or the 883 points, second only to Bobby Clarke as a Flyer. Five times he reached 40 or more goals in a season, once hitting the hallowed 50-goal mark. He was a seven-time NHL All-Star. He played in four Stanley Cup Finals, winning twice. He participated with the best in the world in the Canada Cup. Most important, he was inducted into the Hockey Hall of Fame in 1990 and had his Flyers' jersey No. 7 retired shortly thereafter.

Yes, the resume of Bill Barber is mighty impressive. However, what gets lost in the numbers is what made Barber more than just a statistically superior player.

"He was the guy who gave you great effort every night," Barber's one-time general manager Keith Allen recalls. "And he could do it all. He was effective as a point man on the power play or as a penalty killer. He also had a great shot. He was a very good player in a lot of ways."

When Bill Barber hears those words, a smile is sure to come across his face. That's because it is the consistency and versatility that Allen alludes to that was his mission as a player.

"I wanted to be the type of player that a coach would come down the bench and give me a tap no matter what the game situation," Barber explains. "Whether we were ahead in the game or behind in the game, up a man or down a man, I wanted to be trusted to be able to go out and perform. I tried to be as responsible in the defensive end as I was at the offensive end. Also, I wanted to play different positions so I could help out if the team was injured."

Given Allen's description, it is a good guess to say Barber succeeded in his career objectives. "I attempted to play the same game very night," he reasons. "I wanted people to watch me play and say, 'There he is again, the same tonight as he was last night.' Whether I was ill or slightly injured, I still wanted to be that same guy out there."

His other source of pride from his playing career was his longevity with one organization. He was drafted in the first round, seventh overall, by Allen in June 1973. He was part of the final wave of additions to the Flyers' team that brought it over the championship hump in 1973-74. It began a 30-year run with the Flyers from player to scout, to minor league coach and eventually head coach.

"Let's face it," he points out rather emphatically. "There aren't many guys who have hung around with one team as long as I did. Talk to people in hockey. How many of them can say, 'Hey, I was with my team for 30 years?' I'll tell you they are few and far between."

Indeed, he has a point. Thus, it is important to remember Barber's career with a broader brush. It wasn't all about the impressive statistics. No, it was about much more than that.

• • • • •

Leach-Clarke-Barber. The mere mention of the names brings back memories of excellence for Flyers' fans and thoughts of terror for many of the NHL's goalies from the 1970s. The LCB line was as dynamic as any of its era, or any era for that matter.

In particular, the threesome was phenomenal during the 1975-76 season. Reggie Leach scored 61 goals. Barber notched 50. Bobby Clarke potted 30. Doing the math, that's 141 goals for one line in one season! They totaled an incredible 322 points among them as they victimized goalies across the NHL.

The trio was obviously very talented. But its success was based on more than just that. There was an obvious chemistry that the three shared as their individual strengths seemed to accentuate the positives of their line-mates.

"You had three different type of players on the line," Barber reflects. "Clarkie was a tenacious fore checker with tremendous anticipation. He was so good at getting in on the puck and extremely unselfish. He made things happen by getting the puck to both Reggie and I. Reggie was the gunner. I mean he could rifle the puck home with the best of them. His nickname [The Rifle] was perfect.

"I was a guy who could score some too. But then again, I always felt I needed to complement the other guys' abilities. I had responsibilities back in the defensive zone, making sure I was one of the guys on the back check. All of our abilities complemented the others."

Barber admits that being unselfish wasn't always a part of the trio's keys to success.

"Reggie and I had a deal that whenever we were in on a two on one, unless the defenseman committed entirely to the puck carrier, we shot the

**The LCB line collected a lot of hardware in its day.**

puck," he reveals. "Very seldom did we ever pass to one another on a two on one. Gun, and then go to the net for the rebound. It worked.

"That year [1975-76] was really something special. The numbers were incredible. Quite frankly, we were pretty tough to stop. Believe me, we faced specific players put out to check us in every arena. It was our challenge to overcome that. I think we did a pretty good job on most nights."

Among Barber's many attributes also apparently is his ability to master the art of the understatement!

•   •   •   •   •

Whether he was scoring big goals or drawing penalties, Barber's Philadelphia career spawned all of the glory the Flyers' franchise achieved in its early years. He came aboard just as the team learned how to win in the playoffs, became an integral part of the two championship teams, participated in the victory over the Russians in 1976 and then took part in the remarkable 35-game unbeaten streak in 1980.

The controversial ending to the 1980 Stanley Cup Finals became an inglorious moment for the organization and quite frankly, for the National Hockey League itself. The two blown calls had a direct impact on the eventual victory by the Islanders. For Barber, the fact that he already had two Cup rings already did not lessen the impact of not finishing the job in 1980.

"I would have loved to have the opportunity for us to play that game all over again," he says wistfully now. "I would love for that outcome to be different and to have three rings [as a player] instead of two. It still enters my mind when the subject is brought up. Having the other rings doesn't soften the blow at all. You always like to win."

• • • • •

The end of Barber's playing career was as bizarre as it was unfortunate. Early in the 1982-83 season he tore the medial collateral ligament in his right knee and missed a month of action. He came back to play that season and still posted 60 points in 66 games. However, his knee would never be the same. He knew he would have to give it special attention for the remainder of his career.

Despite the discomfort and swelling that would occasionally hamper him, Barber put together a decent first five months to the 1983-84 season. The Flyers were now a team built upon youth but still heavily reliant upon a veteran nucleus that included Barber. The head coach and general manager at the time was Bob McCammon. He came up with the idea to rest some of the veterans down the stretch and send them on mini-vacations, if you will, so as to have them fresh for the playoffs. Bob Clarke was the first to reluctantly go on a sabbatical as he went to Florida. The plan was for Barber, Darryl Sittler and Moroslav Dvorak to follow. Upon Clarke's return, Barber's turn was next.

At the time, Barber was, as always, the good soldier, saying the right things.

"I want this team to do well in the playoffs," as quoted in Jay Greenberg's in *Full Spectrum*. "If this is going to help, then I'm all for it."

However, just as Clarke had reservations about taking the time off, so did Barber, as he admits in retrospect.

"I was wishing I didn't have to go," he says now. "I had some difficulty with my knee that season, missing some time, but I was just starting to get back to where I felt good again. In fact, I remember telling Jen [his wife] that while it had been a tough year, I had a good feeling that things were starting to turn for the better."

Still, Barber made his required sojourn to the Poconos for some rest, relaxation, and participation in an exercise program that had been provided by the coaching staff. That program included some modified squat thrusts that Barber was wary of. As he exercised with a friend, he heard the dreaded pop in his right leg.

"My friend asked me what that was," he recalls. "I said it isn't a good sound, I'll tell you that. I knew right then I was in big trouble."

He went to the hospital and learned that his knee had come right out of joint and his femur was broken. Doctors told him it looked like a hand grenade had gone off inside of his knee. Reconstructive surgery was necessary.

Doctors told him that he would eventually have a decent knee for everyday life, but that playing hockey again was extremely doubtful.

That, of course, did not stop the determined Barber. He rehabbed for an entire year trying to get the knee to cooperate. "I worked hard through the next spring," he laments. "I eventually got back on skates, and had hopes of even coming back to play on defense. I started as a junior on defense and I thought I could get back to that, of course, still playing the point on the power play. Maybe I could have played three or four years back there and helped the younger guys. I think I would have cherished those years as much as I did the prime seasons. But the pothole in my knee just would not allow me to.

"That was definitely the biggest professional disappointment I've had. I would just as soon have had an off year and been faded out than go out the way I went."

A Hall of Fame playing career came to an end not with an injury suffered with some heroic effort on the ice, but in an exercise room in the Poconos. Sometimes, you wonder just how cruel the hockey gods can be.

• • • • •

It was Barber's desire to advise younger players that kept him from leaving the game of hockey upon the conclusion of his playing career. His first duty was to finish out the 1984-85 season as the head coach of the Hershey Bears. While the team was not that talented and met with no postseason glory, Barber became convinced he was going to stay in the game. He wasn't ready to become a full-time coach yet because he wanted to spend more time with his wife and two children.

The Flyers made him an assistant coach in 1985, although his duties had more to do with searching for prospective new talent at the major junior level. Eventually, he became the Flyers' director of pro scouting, with duties that included keeping an eye on three different leagues (other National Hockey League players as well as those in the American Hockey League and the International Hockey League). The Flyers were one of the first NHL teams to go this route. It was a lot of work that entailed an arduous travel schedule. One might wonder why Barber would choose such a challenging task.

"I loved the game," he bluntly responds. "I loved that when you were asked about a player, there was a challenge to be accurate. If you made a bad trade based upon a poor evaluation, it could really set you back. I took a lot of pride in what I did." He must have. Barber stayed in his scouting capacity with the team for well over a decade.

• • • • •

Some coaching careers are planned and thought out. A player thinks about a potential job in the coaching ranks while his playing career is ongoing. Then he takes all of the logical steps toward assuming those responsibilities, usually including a stint as an assistant and then the necessary lobbying to take over eventually as a head coach. In Bill Barber's case, a coaching career happened practically by coincidence.

"I was driving to Hershey with Clarkie to go to a Bears game and he was going to relieve Jay Leach of his duties," he recollects. "Bob had already talked with Tommy McVie [a longtime head coach in both the NHL and in the minors] about taking over the team. We stopped at one of those roadside areas and Bob called Tommy to check in, and low and behold, he found out that McVie was backing out and couldn't take the job. I figured I would help out and told Bob that I wouldn't have a problem taking over for the rest of the year. Believe it or not, that is how it all started."

The day after Christmas 1995, Barber took over as the Bears' head coach. The following season the team was moved to Philadelphia and renamed the Phantoms, and who better to have as the head coach than a Philadelphia hockey legend named Bill Barber.

"That was an era that will stay with me forever," he beams as he remembers. "Being able to handle a newborn team, win as much as we did, and put up some unbelievable numbers was a great experience."

The Phantoms' first year resulted in a regular-season championship before a disappointing, yet thrilling, seven-game semifinal series setback to the Hershey team that had replaced them. In 1997-98, there was no stopping the Phantoms. Led by veterans like Peter White (the AHL scoring champion), captain John Stevens, Jamie Heward (voted the AHL's best defenseman), and goaltenders Neil Little and Brian Boucher, the Phantoms steamrolled to another regular-season title and then to Calder Cup glory in the playoffs.

"It's not easy to win at the minor league level," he explains. "In addition to all of the elements that make it difficult to begin with, you have the instability caused by recalls. I will say, though, that the Flyers gave us every opportunity to win. We had a good veteran nucleus, and after the disappointment of the previous playoff year, they were on a mission. As it turned out, I don't think there is a single award that team didn't claim in 1997-98. They have something like six trophies as proof.

"I really pounded away at them that year. I told them that we basically had to do it that year because there were quite a few veterans on that team. Due to the Eric Lindros trade, the organization wasn't loaded with young prospects at that time. The time was now. We had to have the commitment and we did."

It culminated in a glorious night at the Spectrum. On June 10, 1998, there was a spirit of deja vu sifting through the old building. The Phantoms cruised to a big lead in Game 6 of the Calder Cup Finals with the Saint John Flames. For the final six or seven minutes of their 6-1 series-clinching win, the sellout crowd stood and roared. For the Phantoms' players it was euphoric. For their head coach, it brought memories of other glorious days and nights in that building flooding back.

"In my opinion, many of those same people cheering on the Phantoms, had been rooting on the Flyers to their Cups in the 1970s," he states. "I told that to the team. I urged them to go grab that trophy and give these people

**Bill Barber's legacy as a Calder Cup Champion coach was "a memory, not just a moment."**

the same feeling they had back in the day. It was great! It was unbelievable. It is a memory to me not just a moment."

• • • •

By 2000 Barber was back in the NHL as an assistant coach to Craig Ramsay with the Flyers. The year before, Roger Neilson's cancer diagnosis and treatment had forced him to leave the team. Ramsay had taken over and guided the team to the brink of the Stanley Cup Finals before losing in seven games to the New Jersey Devils in the Eastern Conference Finals.

The interim tag was removed from Ramsay's title for the beginning of the 2000-01 season. However, the team never re-established any kind of rhythm in the first half of that season. They opened 1-5-2 before rebounding to climb three games above .500 by late November. But then they slipped again, losing five of their next seven games while showing very little passion.

General manager Bob Clarke chose this time to pull the trigger and make his old linemate the Flyers' new bench boss.

"I didn't expect that," Barber recalls. "Things materialized so quickly. I was kind of in shock when word came that I was going to be the head coach. I had planned on gaining a year or two of experience as an assistant at that level and then going after a head coaching job somewhere. It happened so soon. I felt bad for Rammer, and yet it was a dream come true. There were a lot of mixed feelings."

The team responded. A more aggressive approach brought out the passion that seemed to have been lacking. Barber took over a 12-12-4-0 team and guided them to a 31-13-7-3 finish from December 10 through April. The winning touch he had at the minor league level carried over to the National Hockey League. He won the Adams Trophy as the NHL's top coach in his first kick at the can.

"I approached it as a potentially perfect way to cap off my hockey career," he reflects. "I had already been part of championships as a player in the NHL and in the minors as a coach. Now, I wanted to take a stab at this. Let's coach a team at the NHL level and see if we can win ourselves a championship here. Then I would have conquered every challenge, to say the least."

• • • • •

In the spring of 2001, first-year head coach Bill Barber took his Flyers into the first round of the playoffs against the Buffalo Sabres. The fact that the team was upset by Dominik Hasek and the Sabres in six games, including a dreary 8-0 loss in the deciding game, would be disheartening enough for a

**Bill Barber's dream come true was coaching the Flyers.**

competitive guy like Barber. However, the setback on the ice ranks a distant second to other events of those weeks. It was about this time that Bill's wife, Jenny, was diagnosed with lung cancer. Jenny had always been such a pillar of strength for the Flyers' wives and the entire organization with her tireless efforts. She was always there to lend a helping hand whether it be as a hockey wife to Bill, as a loving mother to her son, Brooks, and daughter, Kerri, or for support for family members of the Flyers. The news that she had a sizable tumor near the lymph nodes in her lung shook her family as well as anyone connected with the Flyers.

"I knew we were in trouble with the initial diagnosis," he reflects. "We had to prepare our family. It was obvious there wasn't a lot of longevity with this type of cancer. Doctors talked about a year, but we didn't even get that. It was a very, very difficult time for our family. People often tell me they don't know how I did it, meaning supporting her through the illness while coaching an NHL team. Well, when you are put in that position, you have to find a way. I couldn't be weak. I couldn't fold. I had two kids who were adults, but very young adults. If I showed weakness there, everything would have been destroyed."

Jenny continued to show her incredible emotional strength through her illness. I can remember seeing her at a Flyers' Alumni picnic in August of 2001, and you would never have been able to tell the pain she was going through. She was as full of life as ever. One month later, Bill's second season as head coach of the Flyers began with training camp. The stark contrast is unavoidable. Here was a guy living his dream professionally, coaching the one and only NHL team he had ever been associated with, while at the same time dealing with the nightmare of watching his lifelong partner battle a fatal illness.

"We made the best of it," he recalls. "It was a tough thing to go through, and I don't wish it upon anybody. We got her home for stretches of time, and the kids were remarkable preparing for the inevitable and yet cherishing their time with her. They spent time with her, which allowed me to continue on with the team. I didn't make every trip with the team, but I showed up. I was there."

The Flyers won more than they lost in the early months of that season. However, everyone associated with the team understood what Barber was dealing with. In late November, Jenny's condition deteriorated and just after noon on December 8, she quietly passed away at the Barber home surrounded by her family. She was only 48 years old. Later that day, Bill was behind the bench as the Flyers defeated the Minnesota Wild 5-1.

"Jen battled cancer here for a while," Bill said, choking back tears at the post-game news conference. "She lost the battle. I just want you to know why I am here today. It is very important that I express this. For my family's standpoint, Jen and my kids thought I should be here. It's been a tough time over the past few months. We lost a great lady. A true wife, mother and a lot of other qualities. We, as a family, will go along with things as she would want them.

"Everybody says that maybe I should have taken the time off," he says now. "I'm not going to buy that. It would simply have been an excuse."

At the time, Bill dove right back into coaching the Flyers. In fact, just after Jen's death, the team rallied, winning 17 of their next 21 games to again climb into contention among the NHL's elite. However, a couple of years removed from his wife's passing, Barber is fully aware of the loss.

"Where I find it hard now is in terms of the goals I had set for when I'm done with hockey," he admits. "We had some great plans to spend some time in Florida and going back to our cottage up north. We were going to do some of the things that she had always wanted to do, but because of hockey, we never had time for. And some of the things I wanted to do, too. We, as a couple, in fact. Now, it's not there. Where do I go from here?

"We, as a family, are still adjusting. I have a grandson now and that has really helped. So we are finally moving ahead here."

· · · · ·

The storybook ending to the 2001-02 season would have been for the Flyers team to win the long sought after Stanley Cup in Jenny's memory. It just wasn't meant to be. After winning eight games in a row, the Flyers were sitting pretty at 29-12-5-1 in mid-January. From there, the team slowly but surely unraveled. The team would finish 13-14-5-2 for the remainder of the regular season, including 2-6-1 in its final nine games.

There was hope they could recover in time for the playoffs, but it didn't happen. The Flyers were defeated in five games by the Ottawa Senators, scoring only two goals in the process. Furthermore, as the series went along, some of the players began to criticize what they saw as a lack of a system. The day after the season ended, goaltender Brian Boucher initially, and then several other players, including team captain Keith Primeau, pinned the club's failures on a lack of structure.

Given the uproar, Bob Clarke was more or less forced into a spot where he had to fire his former teammate. Barber was relieved of his duties and to this day has continued to take the high road when it comes to discussing the events that led to his dismissal.

"I knew what was going on," Barber states today. "I knew if we didn't get past Ottawa, where the supposed axe was going to fall. I told both of my assistants [Mike Stothers and E. J. McGuire] as well as my two kids what was about to happen. I told them somebody was going to take the fall here, and it sure as hell wasn't going to be anybody else but me. Fair or not fair.

"I've got my opinion on it. But I told my kids that day there were two ways we could go with it. We can stand tall and take the bullet. Or we could go the cowardly way of defending or asking how they could do this to us, or telling people this is really what happened. We, as a family, know what happened. Good hockey people know what really happened. We took the right road and I will stay with that road.

"I had responsibilities as a coach that when things don't get done, you have to face the fact that you probably won't be around any longer. I accepted that responsibility. I just wish everybody took the responsibility I had on my shoulders and took it to heart. I don't think that was the case. In fact, I know it wasn't.

"When it counted [in the playoffs], we didn't get it done. I was criticized by some players for being too hard on them. They don't know what hard is. Hard is finding ways to win.

"I'll be honest with you. I was disappointed the way the players handled the situation at the end of the year. When I walked out the day I was fired, my thought was that if that was going to be the attitude, I didn't want to have any part of it anyway. I was glad to be on my way."

Thus, the loyal soldier who had served more than 30 years in this particular unit said goodbye. He went home to his kids, and a family in dire need of some time together, found it. "We went out to some restaurants," he remembers. "Believe it or not, we actually had some chuckles and laughs about the situation. We talked about what Jen would have been saying through all this. We, as a family, got through it."

The two constants in Bill Barber's life for the past three decades, Jen and the Flyers, were gone. He had to find a way to move on.

•  •  •  •  •

Today, Bill Barber is the director of player personnel for the Tampa Bay Lightning. He is still often seen at Flyers games, but now he's scouting for the enemy. He continues to reside in the Delaware Valley and in many ways, he is still seen as a Flyer even though he is no longer officially with the organization.

However, after some time of reflection following his dismissal by the Flyers, he did eventually take the Lightning up on their offer to join them in the scouting department. He is happy to be part of the club's management team. "I am very pleased to be where I am right now," he says. "I have a great opportunity with the Lightning. Jay [Feaster, Tampa Bay general manager] leans on me heavily on issues that go on internally with our hockey team to make our organization better."

Thirty years after being part of championship teams in Philadelphia, Barber was part of building one in Tampa as the Lightning lifted Lord Stanley's Cup in 2004.

If ever there was going to be a situation in which the Flyers' bond could be broken, or at least damaged, one would think it would be in Barber's case. After 30 years of loyal service, he was let go under trying circumstances within five months of the death of his wife. Grounds for bitterness? Not according to Barber.

"I am not bitter in the least," he states emphatically. "I was involved with a great thing for 30 years. I gave everything I had. I bled orange and black through my entire time as part of the organization. Why in the world would I be bitter? They saw something in me as a junior player and brought me here and I got the chance to win the Stanley Cup. I got to play for an unbelievable owner [Snider], an unbelievable manager [Allen], and an unbelievable coach [Shero]. You talk about your cards falling right! I got to play with some great hockey players. Then I was able to scout, coach in the minors, and then coach in the NHL all with that same organization. Why would my heart change? It's not going to change. I was so lucky to have that opportunity!"

**Bill Barber is still seen often at the Wachovia Center, only now he's working for the Tampa Bay Lightning.**

# #8
# Dave Schultz

## *He'll Always Be "The Hammer"*

I t was a late November 2003 game at the Wachovia Center in Philadelphia between the Flyers and the Minnesota Wild. What made it a night to remember wasn't the fact that the Flyers remained unbeaten for the season on their home ice with a 3-1 win. No, most of the fans in the building that night will recall a beauty of a scrap between Philadelphia rookie defenseman Jim Vandermeer and veteran blue liner Brad Brown of the Wild.

The two combatants went at it in what has become a rarity in today's NHL, a long-lasting fight to the finish. By some accounts it lasted a minute and 20 seconds as both players got their licks in before Vandermeer eventually wore Brown down. Throughout it all, the crowd roared as only a Philadelphia throng can during a hockey fight. There is a true sense of appreciation that develops in the building when a good fight is taking place.

A couple of nights later, Vandermeer was the guest of Flyers' broadcaster Steve Coates on an in-between period segment of the local telecast. The segment was played on the jumbotron during the second intermission, and the crowd was thoroughly enjoying Vandermeer's account of his tussle with Brown.

Suddenly, though, I noticed a stir in the crowd. What had been only a murmur was becoming a dull roar. I wasn't really watching the segment as I was busy preparing for the start of the third period. However, it was impossible not to notice the stir in the crowd. I wondered what was causing it.

Then I looked up to the scoreboard and saw Dave Schultz making an appearance with Vandermeer and Coates. The premise of the skit was for Coates to proclaim Vandermeer's fight the best he had ever seen. Then Schultz busts on the set to dispute it as only he could. It was a great idea and it went over quite well, but what I noticed most was the immediate and obvious reaction the fans had to Schultz's appearance on the set.

It is so obvious that Dave Schultz is still a type of folk hero in Philadelphia. Thirty years after he was the enforcer on the Stanley Cup-winning teams, he is clearly anything but forgotten. The fans still see Schultz and they remember "The Hammer" pummeling foes back in the day. They remember Schultz as the undeniable symbol of the aggression that produced such an aura around those Flyer clubs.

What is forgotten is that Schultz's stay in Philadelphia was actually rather brief. One would think for a guy to be as revered as he is, he would have been a stalwart for many, many years with the team. In Schultz's case, however, his tenure with the Flyers lasted a grand total of four seasons.

"People come up to me all the time and ask me how many years I played with the Flyers," Schultz says now. "Most think it was at least nine or 10 years. When I tell them four seasons, they are shocked!"

Schultz was officially a Flyer for one game during the 1971-72 season and then full time from 1972-73 through 1975-76. He was traded to Los Angeles just prior to the 1976-77 campaign, and despite many rumors during the ensuing years of a return to Philadelphia, he never did appear again in an NHL game in the orange and black.

"I would have loved to have stayed here for at least a few more years," he laments. "But change is part of the game and eventually everybody moves on. Still I always saw myself as a Flyer."

And so, obviously, did the fans. They still do. That's because he made his four full seasons count. He was a huge force and an important part of the championship fiber of those Cup teams. The fans will never forget that. The persona of "The Hammer" lives on.

• • • • •

Before there was "The Hammer" there was "Sergeant Schultz." In actuality, before there was even a "Sergeant Schultz" there was a junior hockey player not known for his fistic abilities at all. Let me explain.

Schultz spent two years in Canadian Junior Hockey before his pro career got underway. In those two years, he built a reputation as a physical and tough player for sure. However, by his account, he had a grand total of one major penalty as a junior.

"I scored 35 goals in my first year of junior in Swift Current," he points out. "I was sort of a scrappy player, but I wasn't a brawler by any means. I was in the 100- to 150-penalty-minute range for the season. The next year, I scored 50 goals in 80 games when you count regular season and the Memorial Cup playoffs together."

Dave Schultz, the goal scorer? Yes, indeed, at least as a junior. That all changed when he turned pro. Well he still scored, but there was a decided change to his overall game after he was drafted by the Flyers and sent to Salem of the Eastern Hockey League in 1969.

"I got in a fight in my first game in Salem against a smaller French Canadian kid that I knew from junior," he recalls. "I did fairly well. Then I got in a fight the next game and then the game after that. Before long, the fans had nicknamed me 'Sergeant Schultz,' and it just took off. It wasn't a conscious decision by me to suddenly become a fighter. In junior I used to punch people with my gloves on and then get my ass out of there. Once I turned pro the gloves came off! And once everybody expected it, I just had to keep doing it."

In the minors Dave was known as "Sergeant Schultz."

Schultz still found time to score 32 goals for Salem that year. He also spent 356 minutes in the penalty box to lead the league. From that point on, he would forever be known for his ability with his fists more than any other aspect of his game.

•   •   •   •   •

Take a look at any clip of Dave Schultz engaging in fisticuffs and it would appear he is actually enjoying himself immensely. There was a fierce anger, of course. A rage, in fact. But when the fight was over, and more often than not Schultz was the victor, his body language and facial expressions would indicate a man taking some type of pleasure in what he was doing.

In actuality, the role of being an enforcer was anything but pleasurable. The nightly demand of sacrificing your body could wear on even the most energetic of pugilists.

"I loved the rewards, big time," Schultz admits now. "The accolades from your teammates, the attention from the media, and the fans loving it. That part I liked. But overall it was not a lot of fun. The toughest part was preparing, knowing that I had to be ready every single game. If we were playing Boston, there was a good chance I was going to have to fight Terry O'Reilly. With another team there was always another guy. That can wear on anyone.

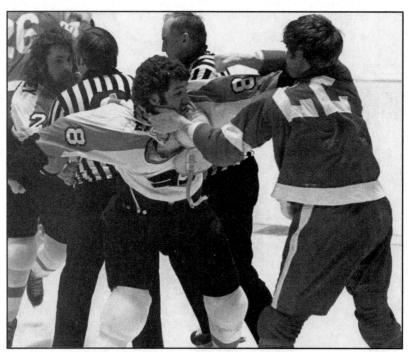

**Dave Schultz lays down the "Hammer."**

"The situation fed upon itself, too. Once we became the Broad Street Bullies, it was expected of us to drop the gloves. We would go into another team's building, and the pressure from the fans for the other team to stand up to us was always there. I would go into the corner with a guy and he would feel as though he just about had to challenge me. I always had to be ready."

Whether it was his first big NHL fight (with Chicago's Keith Magnuson), or his much publicized pummeling of Rangers defenseman Dale Rolfe, or any of his numerous clashes with O'Reilly, Schultz's scraps usually stood out. Not only was he punishing, but he also fought with a flair. In fact, many times, when the linesmen cut in on the fight, Schultz still seemed to have something left. He always wanted to get in another lick. This the fans loved.

Through it all, though, it was hard work. So much so that despite appearances, Schultz wasn't necessarily as thrilled about partaking as many people might have imagined.

•　•　•　•　•

The rewards that Schultz mentions came in different forms. One odd reward, if you can call it that, was the release of his single entitled "The Penalty Box" during the 1975 playoff run to the second Cup.

"Love is like an ice hockey game," went the lyrics. "Sometimes it can be rough. You get me checking and holding and hooking and then you blow your whistle on me. I'm not defending my style. It's just that every once in a while, you've got to leave the rules behind."

While the release of his song might have caused hoots of laughter and derision from his teammates in the locker room, it soared to the top of the play lists at local radio stations, another indication of the popularity of Schultz and the team. Not that Schultz needed any reminders.

He was in high demand during the Cup years. He would speak to local high schools, attend local hockey camps, and even model clothing, all for a pretty penny. He even agreed to take his musical prowess on stage one night in a Cherry Hill, New Jersey club. Needless to say, it was not the beginning of a new career for "The Hammer." He was much more comfortable plying his trade on the ice in front of 17,000 people than he was singing in front of a couple hundred on stage.

•　•　•　•　•

After the Flyers were defeated by the Canadiens in the 1976 Finals, the winds of change were in the air. It's doubtful Flyers fans had any idea that those changes would involve their beloved "Hammer."

However, in September 1976, Keith Allen sent Schultz to the Los Angeles Kings for a pair of draft choices. There has always been a hint of mystery around the actual reasons for Schultz's departure. Purely from a roster standpoint, youngsters like Jack McIlhargey and Mel Bridgman were deemed ready to take on larger roles with the club, making Schultz expendable.

However, there was also talk that Schultz had tired of his role as the resident policeman. Among the believers of this theory was the team's general manager.

"With those type of guys, I think there comes a point where they get sick of it," Keith Allen explains. "That's the point I thought Schultz had gotten with us. He had lost a couple of fights to O'Reilly earlier the year before, and I just sensed the fighting part of it was becoming distasteful to him."

Schultz didn't feel as though he was mellowing, however. He thinks that he perhaps had started to get a little too caught up in being "The Hammer" for his or the team's good.

"At the time, I certainly never tried to be bigger than the team," he relates now. "But maybe I did become a little arrogant. Maybe I became that element where I was getting too much individual publicity. Throw in the fact that I was a marked man by the officials by that point and took some penalties that the team didn't like, and the young guys coming up, and I suppose it all added up."

The trade, although long-rumored, still stung Schultz. It came as no surprise that, as with seemingly everything regarding "The Hammer," his exit would not be a quiet one. That's because the NHL schedule-maker played a cruel trick and had Schultz and his new team in Philadelphia for the third game of the 1976-77 season.

With wounds caused by the trade still fresh, it got ugly. After a rousing ovation from the fans upon his introduction in the pregame warmups, Schultz got involved physically with members of his former team. He slashed Andre Dupont. He even taunted the Flyers from the Kings' bench. Eventually, Dupont led a bench-clearing charge toward Los Angeles forward Dave Hutchinson after he had high-sticked Bridgman. Schultz sought out Flyers rookie Paul Holmgren and baited him into taking off his visor (which was protection from recent eye surgery) and fighting. Dupont had to be held back from going after his former teammate. Schultz was among six players ejected.

"I know nobody's supposed to hit the Flyers in their own building," Schultz offered after the game according to Jay Greenberg's *Full Spectrum*. "About four guys jumped Hutchinson. That's the way the Flyers have always done things, even when I was here. I don't want to be part of that."

So much for a long goodbye. They were the words of a man still hurt by his exit from Philadelphia. That night made Schultz's departure from the Flyers official. Almost 30 years later "The Hammer" has more perspective on his trade.

"It stung because I always saw myself as a Flyer," he states. "Why couldn't I have been a Flyer for at least a couple of more years? You know you hear that theory that change is good for a player from time to time. Well, change at that time was not good for me."

• • • • •

It would not be the only change for Schultz. After leaving Philadelphia, he would spend parts of two seasons each with the Kings, the Pittsburgh Penguins, and the Buffalo Sabres. There would always be rumors of his imminent return to the Flyers, but it never happened.

Schultz appeared anything but disinterested in fighting during the 1977-78 season. In a year split between Los Angeles and Pittsburgh, he totaled 405 penalty minutes to once again lead the NHL. He clearly was still very much "The Hammer," but just in different uniforms. Still though, he thought it never was quite the same as in Philadelphia.

"Some of the attitudes on those other clubs were difficult to take," he remembers. "I mean it was like, 'Win a few games, lose a few games, who gives a care?' It was tough for me to accept that after playing in Philly where we expected to win each and every night."

Detroit's Dennis Polonich drew him into a couple of penalties in a December game as a Penguin and that precipitated a trade to Buffalo which Schultz called "a blessing." The Sabres were a talented bunch poised for a run at the Stanley Cup in 1979. It was Schultz's last run at a title. It ended suddenly and surprisingly in a preliminary series loss to, of all teams, the Penguins.

The next season, Scotty Bowman took charge of the Sabres, and Schultz realized there was little room for him. He would play in 13 games before being dispatched to Rochester of the American Hockey League. It was there that The Hammer finished his playing days.

"I went to John Muckler [the Buffalo general manager] and asked for a trade," he recalls. "All they wanted to do, though, was buy me out. I should have stayed with it and not agreed, but eventually I let them do it."

At the tender age of 30, Dave Schultz was finished as an NHL player.

• • • • •

Having been traded three times in four years and eventually winding up in the minors for the conclusion of his playing career, one can understand why Dave Schultz might have felt some bitterness back in 1980. It was at that time that he was approached about writing a book detailing his career.

"I thought it would be something different," he reflects now. "Maybe it could lead to something down the road. I really didn't think about any of the possible negatives. In answering the questions posed by the writer, I did have to really think about some of the reasons I had done what I did as a player. From that standpoint, it was good."

The book was titled *The Hammer: Confessions of a Hockey Enforcer* and it was co-written by well-known hockey author and broadcaster Stan Fischler. *The New York Post* reviewed the book by saying it probed the "ugly side of hockey…very revealing."

Dave Schultz' NHL career wound through Los Angeles, Pittsburgh
and finally Buffalo. *Photo courtesy of the Buffalo Sabres*

It's true that the book does provide a lot of insight into what goes on in the life of a hockey player, especially one expected to drop the gloves as frequently as Schultz did. However, in talking with Schultz, you get the feeling that if he had it to do all over again, he would have foregone this literary effort.

"It became a frustrating experience," he says now. "I used to argue with the writer and the publisher all the time about the way things were worded. I would say that I wasn't like that. But then after arguing, I would give in and tell them to print the damn thing. Sometimes, you take one sentence out of a paragraph and it changes the whole meaning of what was said. Other times, I might have said something with a smile on my face, but that doesn't make it into print. Despite all that, though, I did have to take responsibility for it because it had my name on it."

The chapter that garnered all of the attention in the book and causes the most regret for Schultz now is the one on Bobby Clarke. In it, Schultz describes the roles he and Clarke filled on the Flyers' Cup teams.

> "It is an indisputable fact that Clarke rarely backed up his stick work with his fists. Too often, I was called upon to do the fighting for him and now, I have to admit, I did not appreciate backing Clarkie when he 'sticked' one of his enemies and then was challenged by the victim. I felt that if he was going to start something he should have been able to finish it. When he didn't, I lost respect for him."

Schultz said the first thing he did after the book was published was go to lunch with Clarke.

"He told me he hadn't even read it," Schultz recalls. "He seemed cool about it. I just didn't like the way it read once it came out. Looking back, when I was having disputes over the wording, I should have just bagged the whole idea. At one point, after seven chapters were written, I picked up the manuscript and threw it out and said we needed to start over. I only wish I had stopped the whole thing then and there. I realize now I shouldn't have done it. It became a true learning experience.

"If you want to look at it from a positive standpoint, the whole reaction to the book made me take a real hard look at myself. I realized I had to be more sensitive about what I said about others. I saw that I had to make some changes in me. I knew that I had to just go to work and keep my mouth shut. I looked at Clarkie and I saw him so successful and it's all about just doing your job.

"I was ostracized by the Flyers organization to some degree. I knew it was going to take some time to fix that."

He had always seen himself as a Flyer. There was work to do in order to restore that label.

• • • • •

Schultz returned to the Philadelphia area to live just as his book was being released. Not the best timing. After seeing the reaction to it, he realized he had to "go underground, so to speak, just go to work."

Schultz wound up getting involved in several different types of businesses. There was his brother's cable installation business in Paulsboro, New Jersey. Then there was a short-lived job with Tropicana World Casino in Atlantic City where he entertained high rollers. He began a limousine service in South Jersey. He also managed a public ice rink in Havertown.

Through his many endeavors, though, he never lost sight of the game of hockey. Four times Schultz ventured into coaching. They became experiences he wouldn't soon forget.

His first crack at it came in 1985, when he was named the general manager and coach of the New York Slapshots of the Atlantic Coast Hockey League. The team played out of Bricktown, New Jersey, with promises of a new arena eventually going up in Staten Island. That rink never was built, and the team ended up in Roanoke, Virginia, before the season was out. It all made for an adventurous year for the coach-GM.

"I was actually the GM, coach, and bus driver," he explains. "I bought a bus for the team, had a few bunk beds put in it, and we would travel from Bricktown to Erie, Pennsylvania, play a game, and then head south to Roanoke, Virginia. I would do most of the driving. I would have some of the guys, including my goaltender, fill in for an hour or two. Mostly it was me doing the driving, though!'

Schultz also spent part of that season painting the old Ironbound Arena in Newark, New Jersey, trying to get it into game shape as a temporary home for the Slapshots. Despite his best efforts, though, the team eventually moved to Virginia without its GM. Schultz stayed in New Jersey and continued to handle some of the paperwork duties, but he put an end to his days of traveling with them.

I suppose it was no big surprise that it took Schultz about 10 years to give minor league coaching another whirl. After coaching the Philadelphia Bulldogs of Roller Hockey International, one of his players, Kent Hawley, helped him secure the head coaching job with the Madison, Wisconsin entry in the Colonial Hockey League.

He was happy to learn he no longer had to drive the bus! His team even had some success as they amassed over 100 points during the regular season before losing in the first round of the playoffs. Still, fan support was a problem, and when Schultz got an opportunity to move up a level to the East Coast Hockey League, he jumped at it.

Off to Baton Rouge, Louisiana, he went. This time, the team did not produce the same kind of results. The team was up and down and finally down late in the year, and general manager Ron Hansis took over the coaching duties from Schultz.

"I really enjoyed coaching," Schultz reflects. "I was tough on my players, but they respected me. My biggest problem was getting a handle on the Xs and Os. I had been out of the game for 15 years and it was hard to get caught up on all the changes."

He had one more fling at it. The following winter he found himself back in the Colonial League (by that time renamed the United League) in Utica, New York. This just happens to be my hometown. I remember saying to Schultz just before he left to coach there, that after a winter in Utica, he would never be the same. His response was that "Utica would never be the same after a winter with The Hammer!"

I suppose we were both right. It became a season of roster flux with more than 60 players filtering in and out of Utica. The team never got on a roll and had financial problems. Schultz grew tired of moving from city to city from year to year that came with minor league coaching. He felt it was time to get back to the Philadelphia area. The team, on the other hand, ceased operations shortly after the season ended and lost minor league hockey for the time being. So you see, neither Schultz nor the city were ever the same after a year with each other.

• • • • •

For the better part of two decades, Schultz followed his mission. He simply went to work. There were many different jobs and locales, including the various coaching stints, but in general he just did his job and tried not to make any more waves. Slowly but surely he began to get back involved with the Flyers' organization.

"I just tried to be a nice guy in the community for them," he relates. "When they asked me to do something, I made sure to do it. I just hoped I could get back in good with them."

When he returned from his coaching forays, plenty of time had passed. Any wounds that had existed had pretty much healed. Opportunity then knocked for him.

"Timmy Kerr had been the president of the Flyers' Alumni but felt he didn't have enough time to devote to it anymore," Schultz reflects. "I thought taking over as the head of the alumni was perfect for me. I volunteered to become the new president. When I got voted in, I said to myself, 'I'm finally back!'"

His long road back into the Flyers' good graces complete, his duties with the alumni led him into the sports memorabilia business. He had developed some products in conjunction with the 25th anniversary of the Cup years and took a liking to it. The result is Hammer Enterprises that he operates out of Allentown, Pennsylvania.

In recent years, Schultz says he is making more frequent public appearances and promotions. He looks forward to increased work with charities and in the corporate sector. He has reestablished his niche in the Philadelphia area, where fans still think of him as the Hammer.

**Dave Schultz became president of the Flyers' Alumni and is involved in sports memorabilia.**

"I've learned to just play the game," Schultz admits now. "People come to me and describe and even embellish certain fights I was in, and I don't even remember some of them, although I don't tell anybody that. But I still play the role. Sometimes when I'm in the crowd at a Flyers game, I will pretend to be mad and put on the old game face with some fans and they absolutely love it. In some of our alumni games, I have to play that part again as well. People seem to still know me pretty well. I'm just trying to have some fun with it. I certainly don't mean any harm by it."

And it's doubtful any harm comes from it. Dave Schultz spent four action-packed years as a Flyer, and in that relatively brief period of time established himself as a Philadelphia sports icon. Through the ups and downs of his relationship with the Flyers organization, the fans have always seen him as the one and only Hammer!

"It's amazing how the fans here have remembered us," he beams. "I appreciate it so much. Hopefully I give back by trying to help others while having some fun at the same time. It's been a great ride. I've loved it. Who the hell wouldn't have?"

# #9
# Bob Kelly

## *What You See Is What You Get*

In covering sports, it is quite common to observe athletes on the ice, field, or court, and be amazed at how completely opposite that player is in personality away from his particular sport. The obvious example of this phenomenon is the hockey tough guy. So many times those hockey pugilists are also the most gentle and docile guys away from the ice. They are completely opposite of their on-ice persona.

Well, in the case of one Bob "The Hound" Kelly, you can throw this theory right out the window. On the ice, he was a pugnacious, high-energy performer, always ready to stand up for a teammate and never able to stay in one place very long. Off the ice he is exactly the same. Always has been, and one gets the feeling, always will be.

"The Hound is great for a lot of laughs," says his longtime teammate Joe Watson. "However, let me tell you, if I was going to war, I would want him leading the charge. That's the type of athlete he was and person he still is. We were all team-oriented, but the Hound led the way in that regard."

If one word comes to mind when you think of Kelly, it is energy. He brought it to the equation every time he hit the ice. He brings it to the table every day of his life. "Basically, I was very thankful to be part of the Philadelphia Flyers organization as a player for 10 years," he relates today. "Now every time I look in the mirror, I know I am working as hard as I can and I'm still thankful for everything that I have. I'm comfortable with where I'm at and don't feel the need to impress anyone. I just want to have a good time with life."

In short, with Bob Kelly, what you see is what you get!

• • • • •

He arrived on the Flyers' scene in 1970-71 as part of the bulking up of the club. Dave Schultz and Don Saleski would arrive two years later as the Flyers reacted to getting manhandled in the playoffs by the St. Louis Blues in 1968 and 1969. Thus, Kelly was one of the first tangible pieces of evidence of the Flyers new direction.

"I always liked to get in a game early," Kelly states today. "I wanted to get a hit, or be hit so I was at least into the game. Even if it was hitting a referee! I had to hit something!"

**Bob Kelly had a way of getting "involved."**

With that kind of mentality, it's no wonder the Flyers began to take on the image of a difficult team to play against. Kelly was there to see all of the pieces come together, and by 1973-74 they were on their way to Stanley Cup glory. Kelly did not actually play in the Stanley Cup clincher that year since he was injured earlier in the finals. However, he claims he still played a role in the team wrapping things up in Game 6.

"I limped into the locker room with my crutches and cast," Kelly remembers. "I told the guys that if they didn't take care of business that day, I was coming back for Game 7. With that thought, they made sure to get it over in Game 6!"

In reality, the second Cup meant more to Kelly than the first one. Not being able to actually dress for the clinching game left him with somewhat of a bittersweet recollection of the first championship.

"If you don't go the distance, you don't feel like you got the job done," Kelly explains. "I still paid my price and did my due, but since I got knocked out, I didn't go the distance."

In 1975, Kelly not only went the distance, he scored what turned out to be the Cup-clinching goal. His wrap-around goal on the first shift of the third period of Game 6 against Buffalo was the only tally the Flyers would need in wrapping up their second Cup.

It's no surprise that the second Cup felt "sweeter" to Kelly.

•  •  •  •  •

There was another role that Kelly served quite well. He was one of those players who kept everybody loose with his wit, both intentionally and unintentionally. The stories that still float around to this day involving Kelly bring a chuckle.

There was the incident shortly after the Flyers had won their second Cup in the crowded and cramped Memorial Auditorium locker room. Kelly was chatting with reporters, explaining how sweet it felt to score the big goal and to be a part of the championship celebration. When he finished, he looked over at his stall and told a guy sitting on his bench to get the hell out of there. That guy just happened to be Pennsylvania governor Milton Shapp who apologized and walked away!

There was the "snipe hunt," a charade used on rookies as a way of indoctrinating them into the NHL way of life. According to most accounts, Kelly was the perfect subject. The plan was to go hunting at night for grouse using flashlights. It was set up so that when Kelly took a shot, it was followed by an agonizing scream of pain from teammate Earl Heiskala. With some artificial blood, it was made to look like Heiskala had been wounded and thus, he was taken away in an ambulance. Kelly was taken by authorities to court where he was charged with illegal hunting, carrying firearms without a permit, attempted murder, being an alien without proper paperwork, and on and on. Kelly was in a near panic, thinking he was going to need thousands of dollars for bail and fearing what his future now held. Of course, in an adjoining room off of the court, his teammates were observing the proceedings and Kelly's reaction with a combination of satisfaction and amusement!

There is the story about how a group of teammates had Kelly convinced that he could get a great deal on snow tires for his vehicle on one particular road trip. Now, given some of the locales the team visited during the course of the NHL season, that might not seem so strange. However, this particular road trip had the team in Southern California and the so-called deal that Kelly was excited about was said to be on Catalina Island! Snow tires in Southern California? Not quite.

And then there is the almost legendary story about teammate Wayne Hillman's car windows. Kelly and Hillman lived in the same apartment complex and one day, Kelly arrived during a rainstorm to notice Hillman's windows down in his car. He promptly knocked on Hillman's door and razzed him about being so stupid to leave his windows down during a storm. Hillman thanked him for rolling the windows up. Kelly said he couldn't because the doors were locked!

Of course today Kelly claims many of these stories have been embellished over the years. In fact, he maintains the real problem with Hillman's windows was that they were power windows. Still, he understood that being the victim of practical jokes, as well as perpetrating some himself, had become his role.

"It was all part of it," he reasons today. "One time we were telling Wayne Stephenson that it was time to get a new pair of cowboy boots. He had this old, brokendown pair. When he didn't get new boots, we took the old ones and glued them to the ceiling of the locker room. When you travel and live with one another for the length of time that we did, you've got to get creative and keep things loose. We were pretty wild in those terms. I suppose we all got what we deserved at some point."

•   •   •   •   •

Kelly saw so much in his career as a Flyer. He spent 10 full seasons in the orange and black. It is so rare in these days of free agency and such for a player to be with one organization for a full decade. Kelly was there to watch the championships team build, to take part in the Cup years, for the triumph over the Russians in 1976, and then for the remarkable 1979-80 season that included the 35-game unbeaten streak and the heartbreaking defeat in the Finals at the hands of the Islanders.

"That team had a lot of the same qualities as the 1974 and 1975 teams," Kelly maintains. "We had plenty of skill, surrounded by the toughness of guys like Paul Holmgren and Behn Wilson. But most important was that locker-room drive. We knew no other word but win."

And win they did, or at least tie, for a professional sports-record 35 consecutive games. They did not taste defeat for nearly three months! Yet the season ended on a bitter note. The two erroneous calls that led directly to two

New York Islander goals in Game 6 of the Stanley Cup Finals propelled the Isles to an overtime win that gave them their first championship.

"They were brutal calls," Kelly remembers. "It was a shame. It would have been so nice to pull that off together, especially in the same year that we had the streak. It was a tough way to have it end."

In typical Kelly fashion though, he would not sulk over the disappointment.

"Sure, you go through your sorrow time," he admits. "But it didn't demoralize me or flatten me out in the long run. Eventually, it's time to recover and go on."

• • • • •

Kelly would go on but not as a Flyer. The controversial season-ending game at Nassau Coliseum was his last in the orange and black. In August 1980, the Flyers traded Kelly to the Washington Capitals for a third-round draft choice. His decade as a Flyer was over. Yet, unlike some of his former Cup teammates, he really was anything but bitter about getting traded.

"I saw the younger guys like Kenny Linseman, Behn Wilson, and Brian Propp coming in," Kelly reflects. "I knew my number was coming. Given my role with the team, I was just thankful to have the opportunity to play ten years with such a great organization and to have the chance to win two Cups. The fans had been super to me and my family. It had been a great run. Whatever the future was going to be, it was what I was going to make of it. I just had to go down to Washington and apply myself the best way possible."

The numbers would indicate he did exactly that. In his first season with the Caps, Kelly set career highs with 26 goals, 36 assists, and 62 points (his Flyers best had been 22 goals in 1976-77). He received increased ice time and took full advantage of it. However, it all went south in a hurry after his first season.

Head coach Gary Green and general manager Max McNab were gone, and in their place came Bryan Murray and Roger Crozier. "We gave it everything we had the first year down there," he recalls. "Then they brought in the henchmen. That's what they did. They stabbed everyone in the back. They didn't seem to have any use for me. It seemed like we were barely part of the team."

Kelly appeared in only 16 games during October and November of 1980. As the Christmas holiday approached, he left the team to gather his thoughts. His decision was that he had had enough. He negotiated a buyout of his contract, and his days as a Washington Capital were over just like that. He then tried to persuade the Flyers to allow him to come back with them but there wasn't really a spot. Same thing in Chicago.

"It's ironic," he says now. "I scored the goal on Roger Crozier in the Finals back in 1975, and then he helps to end my career six years later!"

**Bob Kelly plays as a Cap. He had his best statistical year in Washington in 1980-81.** *Photo courtesy of the Washington Capitals*

Kelly was so aggravated by the way things had transpired in Washington that he sat down and penned a five-page letter to Capitals owner Abe Pollin. It was time to vent.

"For me to write a five-page letter gives you some idea how upset I was," Kelly explains. "[Pollin] obviously didn't have the guts to respond one way or another. I can tell you that if I had written a letter like that to Ed Snider, you can bet he would have responded. After coming from an organization that had such respect for its players from the owner on down in Philadelphia, it was difficult to understand the lack of respect from the owner, general manager, and coach in Washington."

The only time you sense bitterness of any kind from "The Hound" is when he discusses how his career ended in Washington.

•  •  •  •  •

You cannot keep Bob Kelly down for long. He reacted to the end of his playing career the same way he did to receiving a body check. He got right back up and got into the swing of things. His first of many business ventures was a liquor store called Hound's Booze Shop that opened in 1982 in

Deptford, New Jersey. It was a successful store for nearly eight years before his business partner left him high and dry to the tune of a million-dollar loss. It was a "live and learn" experience in Kelly's words.

Since then he has moved from working in construction to running an athletic apparel store in a New Jersey mall, to being vice president of marketing and sales for the Philadelphia Bulldogs roller hockey team, to helping to build the roller rink at the Coliseum in Voorhees and a fun place with a roller rink in Glasgow, Delaware, to helping to build Blue Diamond Park in Wilmington, Delaware.

You get the picture. The Hound has stayed on the move in retirement just as he did as a player on the ice. "I would say that is fairly accurate," Kelly says when the comparison to his on-ice and off-ice approaches is made. "I like to make things happen. I like to be on the move. That's me."

• • • • •

Today Bob Kelly has come full circle in one respect. After several stops along the business path, he officially went back to the Flyers' organization in 2003 when he was hired as the team's point man for community relations. The official title is Team Ambassador.

**Bob Kelly returned to the Flyers as the Team Ambassador in 2003. He is often seen mingling with fans.**

"In my mind, I represent the Flyers and Comcast-Spectacor," he explains. "It's certainly not a job where I shuffle papers. I am expected to be out and about. I'm getting a chance to do things with kids, go to hospitals, to do clinics, whether it be roller hockey or street hockey, or I can do meet and greets. I'm thankful to have a job with this organization and just want to do my best for them."

He has remarried after his first marriage broke up in 1998. He and his wife, Stacey, are the parents of a beautiful young girl named Lindsay. Kelly says he has calmed down since his younger days, although one senses there's still plenty of spark in the guy who showed so much of one as a player. "I have absolutely no regrets with my life," he asserts. "Life takes its turns and you have to deal with them. It's not always easy, but when I think back to where I could have ended up, I probably would have been an auto mechanic because college wasn't even a possibility for me. Hockey provided me the opportunity to make a difference and to be part of something. How could I have any regrets about that?"

# #10
# Bill Clement

## *From Hero to Zero and Back*

W hen hockey fans of the Delaware Valley think of Bill Clement, one of two images come to mind. There's the fresh-faced young- ster who helped the Flyers to their two Stanley Cups back in the mid-1970s. Or there's the polished, color analyst seen so often on national tel- evision today. Either way he would seem to represent the epitome of success. His story, though, is more complex than most people realize.

It's easy to remember Clement as one of the young additions to the Flyer championship teams. He served a role as a defensive forward on those clubs. He wasn't one of the Flyers who got involved with the fisticuffs all that often, as in his words he "picked up a lot of gloves" in his day. However, he did con- tribute. In fact, he scored the goal that put away the second Cup in Game 6 in Buffalo.

It's equally simple to envision him in his current broadcasting role on ESPN. He's recognized as one of the best in the business with good reason. His quick wit and excellent analysis make watching his telecasts very enjoy- able. He is totally in command of his craft.

However, to summarize Clement's life as the definition of triumph and accomplishment, does him a disservice. His success came after some serious struggles. In the end, it makes his achievements that much more impressive.

• • • • •

A good microcosm of Clement's experience occurred just as his career as a Flyer came to an end. Consider this. When Clement scored the Cup-clinch- ing goal against Buffalo, he had already been traded. General manager Keith Allen had shaken hands on a deal with Washington general manager Milt

Schmidt during the 1975 Finals to send Clement, defenseman Don MacLean and the Flyers' upcoming first-round pick to the Capitals in exchange for the first overall selection that year (later used to pick Mel Bridgman).

Thus, just as Clement was experiencing one of the penultimate moments of his hockey life, things were being set in motion that would lead him to one of his lowest ebbs. He would not find out about the trade until a week or so after the season ended. He was on his way back to Canada for the summer, staying with family in Syracuse, New York, when his wife told him Allen was on the phone.

"It was morning and I was lying down when my wife came in and told me I had a phone call from Keith Allen," Clement recalls. "I said, 'Uh-oh.' I knew exactly what was coming. There had been rumors that one of five of us was going to be traded. I guess I should thank Keith for letting me sober up from the Cup celebration before he told me!"

While he wasn't surprised about getting dealt, Clement still had a difficult time accepting the fact that he was no longer a Flyer.

"I felt an overwhelming sense of rejection," he relates now. "There was also fear of moving forward to reacclimate my life. As close as our team was, I felt like some of my vital organs had been ripped out. It was really traumatic for me. People who haven't won a championship could never understand how close the bond was for us. Today players are more used to moving with free agency and multiple trades and such. Back then getting traded was like part of my family had been taken away from me. It was extremely difficult."

**Bill Clement had already been traded in principle as he celebrated the second Flyers' Cup in Buffalo.** *Bruce Bennett Studios/Getty Images*

Clement had spent only three and a half seasons as a Flyer. However, two of those ended with the team hoisting Lord Stanley's Cup, so his depression upon news of the trade is understandable. Making matters worse, Clement was going from the defending Stanley Cup Champions to a club that had managed a grand total of seven wins in 1974-75, the Capitals' first season.

"I went from the best team, the most exciting team, and the toughest team to the worst team and the team with the least toughness."

And the move was already made while he was scoring perhaps the biggest goal of his career.

•  •  •  •  •

Bill Clement would spend seven more seasons in the NHL after leaving Philadelphia. He would have some tremendous highs such as his two appearances in the All-Star game (1976 and 1978). On the flipside, he would also experience some of the consequences of becoming an ex-Flyer.

"It wasn't until I had moved on in my career that I realized that the players that got moved out of Philadelphia instantly became targets," Clement explains. "I didn't realize that other players were out to get me. Phil Russell told me that all of us were absolutely targets. He said that as each one us got cut out of the pack, we became like prey. They wanted to destroy us! I really was oblivious to it. I just tried to do what I needed to in order to compete. It's a good thing I wasn't aware of it. I don't know what the hell I would have done if I had known the whole league was out to get me. I was like the dog that had been separated from the pound pack!"

Clement survived although he also had to suffer through some inglorious moments off of the ice. His trade right after the All-Star game in 1976 from Washington to Atlanta has to rank up there.

"Max McNab was the Washington GM then," he recalls. "He sits down with me and takes a big bite of this hamburger and mumbles, 'We had to make a trade. It's a good one for you. Cliff Fletcher [Atlanta's general manager] wants to talk to you.' And he handed me the telephone. That was all he said. I always remembered Keith Allen being very respectful and a gentleman when he traded me. I also remember that Max McNab mumbled through a mouthful of hamburger when he dealt me. And you know what? As I talked to Fletcher, Max finished that hamburger!"

While he learned of his deal to Atlanta in rather ignominious fashion, Clement admits the trade was good for him. He would play his final six and a half seasons with the Flames, the final two in Calgary after the team had moved there. In 1981, he would take part in what he calls the second biggest thrill to winning the Cups. Ironically, it was defeating the Flyers in the second round of the playoffs.

The Flames jumped to a 3-1 series lead, only to lose Game 5 in Philadelphia and then Game 6 in Calgary. It seemed like a forgone conclusion that going back to the Spectrum for Game 7 would result in a Flyers victory.

In fact, there were reports of partying on the Flyers team plane as they returned home after their Game 6 triumph.

However, the Flames shocked the hockey world by dominating the Flyers in the deciding game. The final score read 4-1.

"The 48 hours leading up to Game 7 were so quiet for our club," recalls Clement. "Before the game, little was said. We just said, 'Let's go out and just play.' By the beginning of the third period, we were dominating. I remember the look on Ken Linseman's face and other players too. It was a look of disori-

**Bill Clement was with the Flames in Atlanta and Calgary, and his time there included a satisfying playoff win over the Flyers.**

entation, a look of confusion. It was like they felt they were trapped in a vortex and there was no way out. It was a satisfying look for me to see. We came prepared and they really weren't. The feeling I had after that game was just about as good as it gets!"

Unfortunately, Clement's feelings for his head coach did not match the euphoria of beating his old team. Al MacNeil replaced Fred Creighton behind the Flames bench in 1979, and immediately Clement saw his ice time diminish. An all-star the season before, he did not understand nor respect MacNeil's use of him.

"Al MacNeil was the single greatest joke as a head coach I had ever encountered," Clement maintains. "I remember Henri Richard saying publicly when MacNeil coached the Canadiens that he thought they had a midget coach. I thought that was pretty harsh until I got a chance to play for him. MacNeil was a zero on a scale of one to 10 in terms of organization, motivation, and communication. He was an embarrassment."

Clement says he talked with Fletcher years later and asked him if he knew he had made a mistake in hiring MacNeil and signing him to a five year contract. Clement says Fletcher admitted he had. However, MacNeil still lasted three seasons behind the Flames bench, not coincidentally, they became the last three seasons of Bill Clement's NHL career.

• • • • •

In the summer of 1982 Bill Clement finally was energized again. The Flames had finally dismissed MacNeil. Badger Bob Johnson had been hired as the replacement and Clement was looking forward to playing for the well-regarded coach. He was hoping to rekindle his zeal for the game under a new bench boss.

"I was so excited because Bob Johnson was coming in and Al was finally gone," Clement recalls. "I called Cliff and asked to sit down and discuss my situation. The meeting didn't happen until August. I sat down and to break the ice jokingly asked Cliff, 'Well, am I still part of the organization?' He replied simply, 'No, you aren't. You are being fazed out.' I was caught by surprise."

Clement says Fletcher told him Johnson had indicated he didn't want the veteran center around. Clement claims he later asked both Johnson and his assistant coach Bob Murdoch and they said it was Fletcher who made the decision. Either way, it was not the way Clement envisioned his stay with the Flames ending. Even so, he did receive interest from two struggling franchises, the Hartford Whalers and the New Jersey Devils, to play one more season or so. He decided against it.

"My confidence level was so low after those last three years," he remembers. "I wasn't nearly capable of the things I had been two or three seasons earlier. And let's face it, I had lost my taste for the game. The Whalers and Devils showed interest, but probably with one-year offers. I figured, 'Why leave for just one year?' So, I took a one-third buyout and headed out into yonder as they say. The question was what was I going to do?"

．　．　．　．　．

Bill Clement considers himself an overachiever. Normally, one would think that label would have a positive connotation. Certainly, any athlete tabbed an overachiever is thought of in positive terms. However, Clement will tell you there are inherent pressures and negatives that come along with being an overachiever. "No matter what you do, it's never enough," he explains. "The super achievers just beat themselves up all the time. It is sometimes very difficult to come to terms with."

Given this state of mind, it is then not surprising why Clement had so much trouble dealing with developments in his life the year after his retirement from hockey. His mission was to gain the rights to a restaurant franchise called Grandma Lee's Bakery and Deli, develop a pilot store in Atlanta, and then open other stores, perhaps in Tennessee and Alabama.

"Nobody told me that Atlanta had more food and beverage establishments per capita than any city in North America," he relates. "But that wouldn't have stopped me. I thought I could overcome any disadvantages. Because there were so many restaurants, there weren't really any prime locations available, but instead of waiting for one to open up, I settled for a disadvantaged spot. Again, I figured I could overcome it, even though deep down inside I knew it was all about a good location. That's when the wheels really started to fall off."

The pilot shop in Atlanta never took off. No matter how good the product was, his below-par location doomed the endeavor. Slowly but surely, Clement came to the conclusion that for the first time in his life he was about to fail.

"On more than one day, I would get up early in the morning and get into the shower," he recalls. "Without even thinking of anything in particular, I would start to cry. I would get out of the shower and walk straight back to the bed without even getting a towel and get underneath the covers soak and wet. I would cover my head and get into complete darkness and be back asleep in no more than 30 seconds. Sleep was my escape from depression."

He would eventually get up and go into the restaurant. But many times, before noon even arrived, he would find himself in a bar having a couple of drinks. It felt like the world was crashing down on him.

"I faced quite a dilemma," he explains. "I basically had no job. I had no career. I had no training in anything. I had no college education. My second marriage had fallen apart as a result of the problems. I had overhead. I had filed bankruptcy and still had to eat. I had $4,000 to my name. I had 40 $100 bills stashed in a steel box in my apartment. That was it!"

At 34 years of age, the overachiever found himself in very unfamiliar territory. It was the advice of a friend that rescued him at his lowest point. One of the investors in his restaurant, John Quattrocchi, was concerned with

Clement's condition. He presented Clement a book entitled *Think and Grow Rich* written by Napolean Hill back in the 1920s.

"It's not necessarily about financial riches," Clement asserts. "Hill studied some of the most successful people in the world and developed a correlation among them. He found 16 similarities among all of them. It really opened the door to me about the whole notion of human development. That's when I first embraced the idea of change and growth. Then again, I had no choice."

• • • • •

The first step in starting over was a rather basic one. Clement needed to earn a paycheck or two. He had dabbled in acting after his playing days had ended. He figured the time was now to give acting a shot.

"I wanted to find something that wasn't time consuming, that may be financially rewarding and that I may have had an aptitude for," he reasons. "I had always wanted to try television commercials and some kind of acting. So while I was still trying to find a location for the restaurant, I actually got a couple of auditions and appeared in one supermarket commercial. But once the restaurant went under, I figured it was time to fish or cut bait when it came to acting."

He enrolled in the Alliance Theatre School in Atlanta and set about becoming the best full-time actor he could be. He worked extremely hard at. After about a year, Clement says he was pretty much at the top of his category for Caucasian, male actors between 31 and 38 years old.

"It was the only thing I've done my entire life that actually has spoken back to me and said, 'You've got to do this.' That's how much it meant to me."

It marked the beginning of his life reconstruction. He met his current wife, Cissy, through an audition for a Blue Cross, Blue Shield commercial. He took part in commercials like the one for Deep Woods Off, which would run for six years on national television. You may remember that one. He gets into a mesh tent wearing only a pair of shorts and some hiking boots with some 15,000 mosquitoes. Of course, he was also wearing Deep Woods Off, so no harm could be done. Then again, it took 37 takes to complete! (He even shot a remake of that ad in 2004.)

Clement survived it though, and to this day still has a craving for the acting profession.

"I am so much better now," he claims. "I've gotten to the point where I know you have to take chances to be a good actor. I've learned to do that."

• • • • •

His love of acting alone was not enough in the long run, though. There were always those bills to pay, of course.

"At some point the notion of auditioning for commercials every week to buy lunch and pay rent grew thin," he says now.

In 1985, those days came to an end. Clement got a call from ESPN inquiring about his interest in auditioning for the analyst position on their National Hockey League package. He had done a couple of games for the New Jersey Devils on a freelance basis so he had some idea what he was getting into. He was surprised to find out though that his audition would consist of live, on the air work for a game in Chicago.

Four others were also auditioned. Clement got the job and the rest, as they say, is history. He has become regarded as one of the top analysts in his field. He has worked the Stanley Cup Finals on national television for close to two decades running now. He's been honored with the Ace Award as the top color analyst in cable television over such heavyweights as Dick Vitale and Peter Gammons. As with everything in his life, he attacks his job with high energy.

"We try to create the illusion that we just cruise up into the booth, crack open a six pack, and just schmooze while we watch the game," Clement explains. "In actuality, we spend hours on our preparation. I tell people it's like anything else in life. You get out of it what you put into it.

"When I first started, I asked myself, 'Who am I as a broadcaster? What am I supposed to be doing?' I realized that I was part journalist, because you obviously have to do journalistic things. I was part expert because I was supposed to know the game. I was part tour guide because I had to take people inside the sport to let them know what it's like to get hit with a shot or to explain how difficult a certain move is. The fourth aspect was the toughest for me to figure out. But of course, I had to be a fan. I was the conduit for the fans. People watching the telecast want to latch on to the broadcasters, to feel the excitement of the game. As a player, I never understood that. As a broadcaster, I had to work at getting that emotion as part of the equation."

It all came together for him, quite obviously. When SportsChannel gained the rights from ESPN, Clement went back to the Flyers as their analyst along side Mike Emrick. He remembers those years as quite challenging.

"The unfortunate part of the timing was that when I came back, the team promptly entered one of the few down periods in its history," he points out. "After my first year, they didn't make the playoffs. It was kind of difficult. It's so much different broadcasting for a local team than it is nationally. If a team gets beat 9-1 and you are working the game nationally, you could care less. But when you are working for the team and care about the team, you have put the proper spin on it. Mike and I had to make chicken salad out of chicken poop on a lot of nights."

In 1993, he went back to the national arena with ESPN, where he has become a fixture. According to many fans, he's the best analyst in the game. His days of worrying about lunch and rent money are well in his past.

•　•　•　•　•

In the late 1980s Clement more or less stumbled upon another form of income and satisfaction. He had settled in Morrisville, Pennsylvania, and was

**Bill Clement made his way back to Philadelphia as a Flyers' broadcaster. He is pictured here with his partner, Mike Emrick (left).**

just beginning to enjoy his broadcasting career when a friend asked him to speak to the local Chamber of Commerce breakfast gathering of about 250 people to relate the story of his comeback from financial difficulty.

"First of all, I didn't really know if I had made it all the way back from my difficulties at that point," he says now. "This was only three years after my bankruptcy filing, so I wasn't quite sure I had indeed made it back. I wasn't exactly examining my timeline at that point. To me, it felt like was I was on the treadmill of life, just trying to keep up.

"I finally did agree to do the speech. It lasted 20 minutes and I titled it 'From Hero to Zero and Back.' It was the first time I had spoken publicly from the heart. It was the first time I wasn't the former pro athlete up after a dinner trying to make people laugh, which I was always uncomfortable doing anyway. As I spoke, you could have heard a pin drop in the room. I spoke genuinely about my financial ruin and some of the steps I had taken to get out of it. I was honest. It was one of the most powerful experiences of my life because of the faces looking back at me and the energy going back and forth between me and the audience."

Clement immediately set a goal to become nationally recognized as a motivational speaker during the 1990s, a mission that he did accomplish. He now calls himself a human development speaker. He figures the people who come to see him speak are already motivated, so that title no longer fit. I witnessed one of his presentations at an NHL Broadcasting Meeting, and let me vouch for his effectiveness in providing the impetus for personal change and improvement. It was powerful indeed.

He is registered with 15 of the top speaking bureaus in the United States. He has spoken everywhere from Hawaii to Bermuda, to Florida, to Seattle. It is obvious people can relate to his story and the way he presents it.

•　•　•　•　•

"I tell people honestly, that if I ever complain about my life now, a bolt of lightning should strike me."

The words of a man who 20 years earlier had just $4,000 dollars to his name and was sleeping to avoid depression. Yes, Bill Clement has come a long way.

Today, he's as energized as ever. In addition to his broadcasting and speaking duties, he has found time to coach a soccer team and take it from Division IV to Division I, begin writing a book, and formalize ideas on making some CDs on human development. Through it all, he has tried to set aside time for his family, which now includes two children (Chase and Savanna) with his third wife and his daughter Christa from an earlier marriage along with Cissy's daughter Regan. His plate is full and he seems to relish it.

**Bill Clement works with his partner on national NHL broadcasts, Gary Thorne (left).**

Clement still sees another mountain he will want to climb, although he isn't completely sure what it is yet. He says teaching broadcasting could be part of it. One thing is for sure, as his life journey continues, his days as a champion with the Flyers will always be part of him.

"You can never really describe the feeling of love, the closeness and the bond among men that are part of winning a championship like that," he relates. "I tell people it's like being in a competition of lawyers or accountants or whatever and adding the physical sacrifice element to it. Going through the battle with people you care about and then being victorious at the end. It is one of the most difficult things to put into words. It is the greatest feeling of fulfillment I've ever had.

"Winning the two Stanley Cups and being with the players on those nights and the days afterward. Every time we saw one another, we kept hugging each other. It was an emotional overload of the senses. It was second to none. I wouldn't trade those two moments, because of the love, for anything else that happened in my entire life."

Given the life he's had and what he has achieved, that statement in and of itself says a lot about the chemistry of those Cup teams.

# #11
# Don Saleski

## *Lessons of Success*

W hen the term "Broad Street Bullies" is mentioned in conjunction with the Flyers' Cup teams, certain individual names automatically come to mind. There was, of course, Dave Schultz, the perceived leader of the ruffians. Often the second name that pops up is that of Don Saleski. This is probably because Saleski was a good-sized player at the time (6'3", 205lbs), performed on the same line with the Hammer, and often found himself in the middle of a scrap that had been an offshoot of Schultz's fights.

In reality, Saleski totaled only modest penalty-minute numbers during the Cup years (131 in 1973-74 and 107 in 1974-75). His reputation as one of the Flyers who "plundered the opposition" or was "a menace to the NHL" was basically fostered through guilt by association as much as anything else.

"I was kind of an instigator," Saleski recalls. "And I happened to play on a line with a guy who finished them all off. I think the reputation was more of a perceived team toughness, though. I mean behind Schultz we had guys like Andre Dupont, who was one tough guy. Bob Kelly was as tough as they come. Ed Van Impe was a mean, nasty guy to play against. The Watsons were tough. Barry Ashbee was a tough guy. I could go on and on. You look at those teams and they were full of hard-nosed players. When we smelled blood in the water, we were like piranas, or sharks. When we could sense fear in a team, then we knew they were done. When teams came into the Spectrum, there was a whole lot of fear!"

Thus the legend grew. It fed upon itself. Guys like Don Saleski, not necessarily a brawler by nature, got involved in a couple and became one of this aggressive gang that other players in the NHL truly hated to play against.

**Not necessarily a brawler by nature, Don Saleski still found himself in plenty of scraps.**

Saleski on another team would not have had that same aura about him. As a Flyer, he was thought of as one of the "Bullies."

• • • • •

There were occasions when even the former Flyers felt the perpetuation of the roughhouse image might have gone too far. One incident in Oakland on October 25, 1974, was a clear case in point. A fight had carried into the Oakland penalty box where the Seals' Mike Christie found himself outnumbered by several Flyers. After taking several punches and realizing his desperate plight, Christie backed up against the glass and in disgust said, "All right, go ahead and hit me with all you got!"

Saleski obliged him and pounded his face with a blow that caught him flush.

"His face basically exploded," Saleski remembers with regret. "You can hit someone a lot of times and nothing like that would happen, but it just so happened that I caught him in a way that gashed him under the eye and broke his cheekbone. There was blood all over the place. As soon as I hit him, I felt awful. I was thinking, 'What did I do to this guy?' They had to carry him off the ice."

Years later, Saleski would have to face his remorse in a more direct way. As a member of the Colorado Rockies, who would end up as his teammate but the same Mike Christie.

"I would sit there in the locker room and see that scar under his eye and feel terrible," Saleski explains. "Making matters worse, I found out that Mike Christie was one of the nicest guys you would ever want to meet. Finally, one day I went up to him and apologized. I said, 'Mike, I just want to tell you how sorry I am about what I did to you. It's the worst thing I have ever done in my life.' It still bothered me that many years later."

This lesson of humility would continue later that season. Once many of the former Flyer Cup winners got moved to other teams, they became targets of opponents looking to beat up on them for their past transgressions. Nowhere was this payback more acute than in Boston where the Bruins just loved to get back at the old Flyers.

"One night in Boston, some of the Bruins really came after me," Saleski recollects. "They had me outnumbered. Who do you think was the first guy to come help me to even up the situation? Of course, it was Mike Christie. That tells you something about the character that guy had."

Saleski obviously learned quite a lesson through the Christie incident. However, it's a lesson that didn't manifest itself until after his Flyers days were done.

"At the time, I realized that particular situation went a little overboard," he reasons. "But did it influence what I did on the ice with the Flyers? No, I don't think so."

He was a Broad Street Bully after all.

•  •  •  •  •

Another well-known trait of those Flyers teams was their penchant for playing as hard off the ice as they did on the ice. Now many of the stories have grown into legend. Some have basis in truth, while many have been embellished through the years.

Saleski jokingly told me he had no idea what I was referring to when I brought up the wild off-ice reputation. He did recall one story that stood out in his memory, though.

"Those Saturday afternoon games with no game the next day were always trouble for us," he smirks. "Those were really dangerous for us afterwards. I can remember one time we had been at one place drinking for quite a while and it closed up. We all staggered out, ready to get into our cars and go on to another bar. All of the sudden, some cops pulled up and asked us where we were going. Everybody recognized us in those days in the city. The policemen knew who we were. Before we knew it, they had rounded up a paddy wagon and loaded us up. They took us all to another bar! There we were, going in a paddy wagon to another bar. In fact, they told us to call them when we were ready to go home rather than drive home."

Talk about an official designated driver! But that story reflects a couple of facets of life for the Flyers back then. First of all, the community was willing to help them in any way possible. Secondly, they did know how to have fun.

"We enjoyed ourselves," explains Saleski. "We worked real hard on the ice, and we played real hard off the ice. That was part of what brought us together."

• • • • •

Saleski's tenure in the orange and black was a lengthy one. He would spend the bulk of the decade of the 1970s in Philadelphia. In 476 games with the Flyers, he found time to score 118 goals and register 235 points, while spending 602 minutes in the penalty box. By the 1978-79 season, though, he had become a part-time player. Frustrated by his increasing time in the press box, he made it known to management that we would prefer a trade to a team where he might see more ice time. Keith Allen, as he did with so many of the former Cup winners, found a spot for him. Saleski was traded to Colorado on March 3, 1979.

"I suppose it was a case of be careful, you might get what you ask for," Saleski says now. "I knew I didn't have much time left in my career and as much as I was sitting, I felt my skills were deteriorating that much more quickly. It was tough to leave here, but I couldn't have any hard feelings because I asked for it. But because of all of the memories and the relationships with people in and around the team, it was difficult to say goodbye."

His stay in Denver would not be a lengthy one. The adjustment in going from a team that perennially won 50 games to one that won 15 was not easy. However, more than that, Saleski ran into trouble dealing with his new coach, Don Cherry.

"In all fairness to 'Grapes,' it was a tough adjustment for him going from coaching in Boston with a successful, veteran team to Colorado where we had a young club with a lot less talent," Saleski reasons. "He couldn't deal with it. It was very difficult for him to accept. He lost control behind the bench on more than one occasion. It was not a good situation."

That became very obvious when things got heated between the player and the coach during a game in 1979-80. It was the beginning of the end of Saleski's NHL playing career.

"He was pretty aggressive in going after some of the guys," Saleski recalls. "He never figured out that no matter how much he yelled, it wasn't going to make the players any better. One night he was all over one of our guys and I turned around and said, 'Don, why don't you just shut up for a while?' He said, 'What did you say?' I said, 'Why don't you just shut the hell up?!' He went nuts. He came at me. Some guys got between us and I just sat there for the rest of the period."

**Don Saleski's stay in Denver wasn't long, but it was eventful.** *Bruce Bennett Studios/Getty Images*

In between periods, the situation only intensified in the locker room. Cherry approached Saleski and took a swing at him. Saleski blocked it with his arm and was ready to swing back when some of the players jumped in again and broke the scuffle up. Days later, Saleski was sent to the minors. He would never play in the NHL again.

"Don Cherry is an idiot," Saleski snaps. "He's doing what he can do now, shooting off his mouth on television [as a nationally known commentator on CBC in Canada] and saying whatever he wants. It doesn't seem like he is held accountable for anything he says. I am not a big fan of Don Cherry."

•   •   •   •   •

Two-time Stanley Cup Champion Don Saleski wound up his pro hockey career with the Fort Worth Texans of the Central Hockey League. He was 30 years old when the Rockies sent him down. For many players, it would have been time to pout. Saleski chose to make the best of a bad situation.

"Once I went down, I figured I might as well make the best if it," Saleski remembers. "They made me captain and I scored a lot. It turned out to be a good experience. We got on a run and went to the league finals before losing in seven games. There was a bunch of young guys down there. We had a great time."

It was his swansong in pro hockey. Saleski felt the time was right to get away from the game.

"I suppose I could have gone back to Colorado because Cherry had gotten fired and I did have a year left on my contract," Saleski reasons. "But I thought at some point I needed to make a transition from hockey and that seemed like the right time. So I retired."

Hockey had been good to Saleski. He was the owner of two Stanley Cup rings after his seven-year run with the Flyers. He met his wife through the sport. Marianne was Ed Snider's secretary when Saleski asked her where he could go to shop for groceries. Less than a year later they were married. However, Saleski had thought often about life after hockey. In fact, at least to some degree, he had prepared for it. In the summer of 1980, that life began.

•   •   •   •   •

Retirement did not sneak up on Don Saleski. When he had played junior hockey out west he had taken university courses. Then again as a Flyer, he took some courses at Villanova. During the summers of his hockey career he ran a hockey school and worked in sales at various times. In short, he had begun his preparation for life after hockey many years before that day came.

The Saleski family headed back to Philadelphia where Don knew his name would help open some doors for him. He interviewed with Aramark (known then as ARA Services, Inc.) and was immediately placed in a training session.

"I started my training in sales," he recalls. "It was quite a reality check. Part of my duties early on was to stock vending machines. On more than one occasion I remember people recognizing me and saying, 'Hey, isn't that Don Saleski of the Flyers?' as I was stocking a machine. It was a different feeling."

He paid his dues, though, and it wasn't that long before Saleski was climbing the Aramark corporate ladder from sales into management. He would eventually spend the better part of 18 years with the company, rising all the way to vice president of sales before going over into operations and management. It was obvious Saleski thrived in the business world.

He left Aramark in 1998 for SMG, a facilities management business as a senior vice president. In 2001, Jay Snider approached Saleski about becoming president of a software company called Club Systems Group that he ran for another three years. Then, seeking yet another challenge, Saleski moved back into the concession business by heading up the facilities management business for a company called Center Plate.

Two and half decades or so after leaving hockey, Saleski is now an accomplished businessperson. His family lives in a huge house in Media, Pennsylvania, and life seems good.

•   •   •   •   •

The sports landscape is littered with examples of athletes who struggle with the transition from the playing surface to the real world. Saleski is the antithesis. He feels the first few years after his playing career ended were crucial in his eventual post-career success.

"It's that transition period," he states. "I went from playing hockey to working for Aramark that next September. I got a real reality check stuffing vending machines and then receiving a paycheck that looked like what I used to get as meal money. That quickly put to rest any 'pie in the sky' aspirations of making a million dollars that I might have had. I had to worry more about finding a way to feed my family. That experience helped bring me back to reality in a hurry. It helped me refocus on what I had to do.

"I think other ex-athletes sometimes wait too long adjusting to that and have more difficulty as time goes along. It's hard for some people to adjust to not getting that recognition that you get when you are an athlete. You know, we get put up on this pedestal and treated special wherever we go for so long. Those first few years are the key."

Saleski also feels he took many principles from his hockey days and applied them to his business career. He sees some definite parallels.

"I took some basic principles that I learned from my parents and from Freddy and applied those kind of disciplines to life after hockey and my work at Aramark," he maintains. "I don't like losing. I may not have been the most skilled player or the most skilled executive, but I'm very competitive. That makes me resourceful. When I played hockey, I figured out a way to be successful. In business, I'm also fairly resourceful and I figure it out as I go. I'm always thinking about what I need to do to be successful."

Saleski takes this approach down to each day of his life as an executive. He equates it to his attitude as a player when wins and losses are so definable on a day-to-day basis.

"Whether it's sales or management, you have to have goals, be it for the year or for the day," he asserts. "You have to understand your market place just like you have to understand your competition or opponent in sports. Then you initiate your market strategy or game plan just like a coach would do. You break it all the way down to what you have to do each day, just like in hockey. At the end of the day, you have to assess if you accomplished your goals and it was a win or a loss.

"Those disciplines, having that self-discipline, I gained from hockey, especially from Freddy. Some of the things Freddy taught us were so profound in terms of discipline and what you had to do to be successful."

These were lessons learned and applied by one Don Saleski.

**Don Saleski, here in his home office, applied many lessons that he learned as a player to help him become a success in the business world.**

•   •   •   •   •

"I still have a long way to go," Saleski says as he assesses his future. "I feel like I have acquired a lot of knowledge and wisdom. At some point, I think I would be good stuff to transfer. The next phase of my life I have to work on taking everything that I have accomplished and transferring to others to help them be more successful."

Perhaps there is a future in seminars or even classes with Saleski in the front of the room. He's come a long way from his days instigating some of those famous brawls along with his teammates in the 1970s. Yet he makes no bones about the fact those days shaped him in many ways, and memories of the championship years remain with him to this day.

"There's a bond among us guys even though we don't always see one another very often," Saleski relates. "When we do get together, there's immediately that rapport like we've never been apart, that good feeling for each other. So there is a bond. There's no question."

A lot has gone right in the life of Don Saleski. He is well aware of that.

"I tell everybody I'm a lucky guy," he admits. "I've been so fortunate. I have been blessed with good health and a healthy family. A lot of things have gone right for me in my life away from hockey. I'm fortunate because a lot of people haven't had the same circumstances."

# #12
# Gary Dornhoefer

## *A Competitor on the Ice and in Life*

Call it coincidence or call it an omen. There has to have been some meaning behind the fact that in the Philadelphia Flyers' very first period of NHL action in their very first game back on October 11, 1967, in the Oakland Coliseum, Gary Dornhoefer was hit with a shot and suffered a deep bruise to his left instep. He became the first Flyer to officially get injured. There is meaning behind it because as the years went by, Dornhoefer would suffer injury after injury, playing through many of them, in his quest for Stanley Cup glory. To look at a list of his many wounds through his 14 NHL seasons, you have to wonder how he managed to see action in 787 games.

He tore cartilage and ligaments in both knees. He fractured an ankle. He broke his wrist. He underwent surgery on a shoulder. He fractured his cheek-bone. There were operations on both of his elbows. In addition, he had his "bell rung" on numerous occasions. Back in his day, that wasn't a big deal. Today, it's called a concussion and players miss extensive time when they are diagnosed with one. Dornhoefer was a warrior in every sense of the word. After spending four seasons bouncing from the minors to the NHL in the Boston Bruins organization, he was rescued by the Flyers when they selected him in the expansion draft. As an original Flyer, he took part in the rapid growth the franchise undertook as it was transformed into a Stanley Cup Champion.

His role was to do the dirty work, to get the puck on the forecheck and then cause trouble in and around the net. Few players of his era had a more distinct reputation for getting in the goaltender's way. Pucks would deflect off of various body parts and into the net, and he wouldn't mind because in the box score it would look like a blistering slap shot.

Of course, such a style of play is accompanied by a stiff price. Thus, all of his many aches and pains. Dornhoefer wouldn't let them stop him, however.

"When we got injured, it was still difficult to get us out of the lineup," he reflects. "If it wasn't broken, we played. There was no such thing as taking time off. If you had a sore groin, you taped it up and went out there and played. It was as simple as that. If the trainers and doctors could figure out a way to get you through a game, you played. You didn't think about how you were going to feel the next day or even ten years down the road."

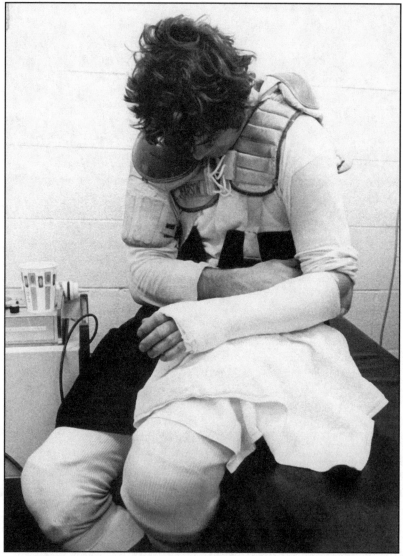

**Gary Dornhoefer found himself in the trainer's room often.**

In another cruel irony, Dornhoefer was injured during the 1974 Finals and did not participate in the clinching game. A Don Marcotte check in Game 3 had separated his shoulder and finished him for the series.

"I sat in the press box during the clincher, all drugged up from the painkillers, so it was always a little fuzzy in my memory," he says about the Cup clincher. "It was great, but I didn't get the true emotion, the real feeling of accomplishment because I wasn't on the ice. The Flyers won, but I didn't feel like the rest of the guys. As an athlete, you have to be there. You can't be sitting in the stands."

He was there the next season when the Flyers won their second Cup.

"Then I knew what it felt like," he beams even today. "All the work you do during training camp and the regular season, it all comes together. And once you win, when people tell you you weren't this or you weren't that as a player, you can always mention being the part of a Cup winner. That's always the ace in the hole that you have to shove in somebody's face!"

And if ever an athlete paid the physical price, it was the guy they call "Dorny."

•   •   •   •   •

Dornhoefer is remembered for his ability to overcome injury. He's remembered for his serious approach. Sometimes his actual contributions as a hockey player in the truest sense are overlooked. After all, he did play in a couple of NHL All-Star games in a career that netted him 214 goals and 542 points.

He also just happened to score some of the most important goals in Flyers history. In 1973, it was his spectacular goal against Minnesota that propelled the club to their first ever playoff series victory. This goal was so significant that a bronze statue was erected just outside the Spectrum of Dornhoefer's outstretched arms as he was lunging through the air just after the puck went into the net. Of course, the humble Dornhoefer does not see being immortalized in a sculpture as an individual honor.

"I think it was more the significance of the goal in finally winning a playoff series more than any personal honor," he explains. "Besides, I've always said you know what pigeons do to those statues! You can't get too caught up in that."

In actuality as is his custom, Dornhoefer rarely gets caught up in anything individual in nature regarding the game of hockey. That goal, so cherished by Flyers fans, was never seen by the goal scorer until years after it had happened.

"I never did see the replay of that goal until I was inducted into the Flyers' Hall of Fame after I retired," he admits today. "When I saw it, I wondered who jumped into my body to make that move!"

That goal was crucial in the development of the Flyers into legitimate Stanley Cup contenders. If they had lost that game against Minnesota, they would have gone back on the road down 3-2 facing elimination. Instead they

**The goal that announced the Flyers as legitimate contenders was immortalized in statue outside the Spectrum.**

wrapped up the series in Bloomington and captured their first post-season series victory. They learned important lessons about what it took to win at crunch time, lessons that came in handy the next season on the way to their ultimate triumph.

Not coincidentally, Dornhoefer came up with vital goals in each of the championship seasons as well. He notched the game-winner in Game 7 against the Rangers in the semifinals in 1974. Then, in 1975, he set the tone for a Game 7 semifinal win over the New York Islanders with a slapshot past Glenn "Chico" Resch seconds into the first period.

His clutch goal scoring should always be considered when his career is remembered.

• • • • •

Dornhoefer was 32 years old when the Flyers won their second Cup. He was clearly one of the veteran elements on the club. Yet he was still a very productive member of the team in the two years after the championships. In fact, his 28 goals and 63 points in 1975-76 represented career highs. The next season, he totaled 25 goals and 59 points and earned a spot in the NHL All-Star Game.

It was in 1977-78 that the injuries began to take their toll. He appeared in just 47 games. The aches and pains of 15 years of professional hockey were more than evident. There is a theory that the athlete is the last person to truly realize when the time has come to leave the game. That was clearly not the case with Dornhoefer.

"I think when you begin to notice that you aren't getting the scoring chances and even the shots, the handwriting is on the wall," he reasons now. "The last two years that I played my knees were giving me a lot of trouble. They always had fluid in them. You can only get them drained so many times and get shot up with cortisone. I probably had too much of that when I played. So I felt I had had enough and it was time to retire."

He approached Allen and revealed his desire to leave the game. However, the general manager wasn't so sure Dornhoefer was finished. He tried to persuade him to play one more year.

"I asked him what games had he been watching," Dornhoefer chuckles now. "When I'm in their end, the puck is in our end. When I finally get to our end, the puck is already in their end! I couldn't keep up anymore.

"I also didn't play a lot that last year [1977-78]. I was in the press box for some games. It's not the way you like to go out. Every athlete has to eventually face the reality that he can't do the job anymore."

The fact that Dornhoefer came to that realization did not make leaving the game an easy process. His final game, ironically, took place in Boston where his career had begun.

"I just wept," he recalls. "The tears were flowing down my cheeks. It was hard to believe that I wouldn't be doing it anymore. I had really enjoyed the camaraderie and competition. I knew all I would have from then on would be the memories."

Thus, with nearly 800 NHL games under his belt and as a proud owner of a couple of Stanley Cup rings, he hung up his skates and limped away from the game that had done his body so much harm but had brought him so much joy and satisfaction.

• • • • •

As with so many of his former teammates, Dornhoefer found a way to stay connected to hockey after his playing days were over. The Flyers signed him as an on-ice analyst for their local broadcasts in 1978-79. His performance was impressive enough that he was approached by network television in Canada, namely *Hockey Night in Canada*, about being an analyst on their telecasts.

"I really did not want to leave this area," says Dornhoefer now. "However, I really didn't have much of a choice. It was a perfect situation for me and my family."

Gary Dornhoefer's broadcasting career began with PRISM in 1978; here he is getting set to interview Phillies shortstop Larry Bowa (left).

So Gary, his wife, Cheryl, and their two children, Stephanie and Steven, moved to Cambridge, Ontario, and a new chapter of his life began. He found himself broadcasting games in Montreal and Toronto in his first few years with HNIC. Hall of Fame broadcasters such as Brian McFarlane, Danny Gallivan, Dick Irvin, and Bob Cole helped to make his transition a smooth one.

"It was a rewarding experience," he recollects. "Having the opportunity to work the Stanley Cup Finals was almost as thrilling as a broadcaster as it had been as a player. I remember in my first year covering the Flyers and the Islanders in the finals and the excitement I felt."

When a couple of blown calls helped the Islanders to a six-game triumph, one had to wonder if Dornhoefer was bleeding a little orange and black even though as a national commentator, he was required to stay neutral.

Later on in his time with HNIC, his duties entailed covering the western package that included the great matchups between the Edmonton Oilers and Calgary Flames. It also afforded Dornhoefer the chance to watch an immensely talented youngster grow to dominate the sport.

"I had been fortunate enough to see Clarkie when he entered the league," Dornhoefer reflects. "Now all of the sudden, here comes Wayne Gretzky. I wondered how this skinny kid could do what he was doing. It looked like the puck was stuck to his stick. He did things on the ice that I've never seen players do before. To see him come to Edmonton as a kid and develop into the type of player he became and eventually win Stanley Cups was very exciting."

There were challenges to his position in the booth, though. To this day, he feels it is important to be fair to the players on the ice.

"It's so easy in our world to cut up and criticize," he points out. "You have to remember that every sport is a game of mistakes. We have to pick those out, yes. But we have to pick out the good plays too. Because I played, I try to bring out some of the things that the players go through that fans may not be aware of."

As a current broadcast partner of his, I feel qualified, if not a little biased, in claiming that he is quite successful in getting those points across.

• • • • •

One of the other challenges to his role with HNIC was the extensive travel it entailed. After 15 years as a player, the assumption was he would be on the road less once he retired. That wasn't the case. It would take its toll on the Dornhoefer family.

"I actually think I spent more time with my family when I played," Dornhoefer admits now. "With *Hockey Night*, I was on the go three to four weeks out of the month. From that standpoint, it was tough."

Dornhoefer understood the strain it was putting on his marriage and family. In 1985, a mutual agreement led to him parting ways with HNIC. By then, he had found a new revenue stream through selling insurance in Ontario. He worked with two different companies during a five-year span, hoping the reduced travel would help repair any damage that had been done to his family.

"Then one day my wife told me she had to get away," he recalls. "She didn't want to be married anymore. I hadn't been home much and she had needed me. Sometimes, people just grow apart and that's probably what happened with Cheryl and me. Going through the divorce was the most difficult thing that had ever happened to me."

He had a hard time dealing with it. While successful as a broadcaster and in the insurance business, he had not been able to keep his family together. He admits now to having thoughts of driving his car into a wall.

"I figured what was the use," he relates. "The divorce really got the better of me."

He needed to get away and so he did, all the way to Australia on a trip with Steven for a month.

"When you talk about getting away so nobody can get in touch with you, that's really getting away," Dornhoefer admits today. "My son was down there for about two weeks and we had a really good time."

It was a brief respite from the problems that would still be there when he returned home. Problems that wouldn't be solved until his old team came to the rescue.

• • • • •

Dornhoefer considered his life to be at its low point. It should be no surprise that his lifeline came from none other than the Flyers. He had not been part of their organization in more than a decade. However, in 1992, he was called to fill in for a month for Flyers television analyst Bill Clement, who had another commitment. He enjoyed it so much he wrote Ed Snider a letter asking him to consider him for any position he might have within the Flyers organization. As it turned out, Clement and Mike Emrick were moving on and an opening as the permanent television analyst existed.

"The timing could not have been better," he relates. "I just had to get out of Canada. Getting back to Philly probably saved me from total destruction. It really was like a new lease on life. It didn't take me more than three seconds to say yes."

Thus Dornhoefer was in effect a Flyer again. He would join the legendary Gene Hart on the television broadcasts as the Eric Lindros era was beginning in South Philadelphia. Everything seemed right in the world once again.

To see Gary Dornhoefer now, one would have no idea of his personal turmoil of the late 1980s and early 1990s. He has settled in as the television analyst, even putting up with breaking in a raw rookie play-by-play guy back in 1995. Hockey fans around the Delaware Valley have grown accustomed to his concise analysis with help from the telestrator and his bellowing voice for the tape operators to "Stop it right there!" when he needs to freeze the footage to make a point.

His passion for hockey is satisfied by his job. However, he has other passions in his life, too. Through a blind date he met Jacqueline Snow and they were married in 1995 and the two have developed a love for animals. Perhaps one might call it an obsession.

"I have Turk Evers [Flyers equipment manager] to thank for that," Dornhoefer maintains. "He did a great sales job, pumping up parrots to Jackie and me. Eventually we went and purchased one. We found we really enjoyed the bird so we got another one and then another. Before you know it, people started to give us birds because they found them to be too much work. At one point, we ended up with 15 different birds!"

But it didn't stop there.

"We each had one dog when we got married," he explains. "Prior to meeting me, Jackie had had a greyhound and we decided to get one of those. Well, wouldn't you know, we got involved with the National Greyhound

**Gary Dornhoefer, working the telestrator, has been back with the Flyers as their television analyst for over a decade.**

Association [NGAP] and before you know it we had three of those plus two Italian greyhounds."

Doing the math, that's seven dogs to go along with all of those birds, a couple of stray cats in the garage, several guinea hens, and two chickens that call the Dornhoefer homestead their home. Yes, I would call that an obsession!

Another of his passions is the game of golf. To watch him amble up to a golf tee, showing the wears of three knee replacements brought on by his hockey battles, you wonder how he will be able to swing the golf club. Then, once he addresses the ball, it's like poetry, to the tune of a two or three handicap.

You have to witness the transformation of Gary Dornhoefer as he arrives at a golf course to understand how much he loves the game. It is almost as if he takes a happy pill. This is one guy who seems to be at total peace when he is on the links. "It goes back to my hockey days and the competition," he reasons. "In hockey, I competed, and it's the same in golf. I love to compete."

• • • • •

A competitor. That is Gary Dornhoefer in a nutshell. Obviously, he was a competitor as a player. He has also been forced to show that same steely resolve when facing life. Even as his life came back together in Philadelphia, the twists and turns that life presents challenged him.

His daughter Stephanie was diagnosed with cancer in the late 1990s. Only in her mid-30s, the mother of a toddler daughter battled the disease for two years. Then, in January 2002, while the Flyers were on the road in Toronto, Gary received a call that Stephanie wasn't faring too well. He left the team to spend time with his daughter.

"I was thankful that the Flyers let me miss some broadcasts and spend a couple of weeks with Stephanie," he reflects. "I learned a lot from my daughter and her faith. In spending two weeks with her, there were times when my emotions got the best of me and tears would start rolling down my cheeks. I didn't want to show that weakness, but I couldn't help it. I can remember her putting her hand on my shoulder and saying, 'Don't worry, dad, I'm going to be in heaven and there's nothing for you to worry about.' That had such a calming effect on me. I was able to get through it because of her faith."

Stephanie passed away in late January 2002. As was the case during his long career, Gary Dornhoefer had been dealt a cruel blow. Back then they were physical wounds. This time it was an emotional one. Now, as then, the competitor battled through it.

I'm often asked what it's like to work with Gary Dornhoefer. My answer always is that if I found myself in a war trench, I would want him right next to me. That sums up the type of individual he has been through his many trials and travails, the quintessential competitor.

# #14
# Joe Watson

## "What the Hell Is Philadelphia?"

Life was good for 24-year-old Joe Watson in the summer of 1967. He had just completed his first full NHL season as a member of the Boston Bruins, a team clearly on the rise now that Bobby Orr, a close friend of Watson's, was on the scene. Watson was spending his summer working in construction in his tiny hometown of Smithers, British Columbia. He was looking forward to continuing his career beside Orr in Beantown in the fall.

Then suddenly his life changed. It was, in retrospect, a change for the better, although Joe hardly saw it that way at the time.

"Talk about depression," recalls the original Flyer. "A guy told me I just got drafted [in the expansion draft] by the Philadelphia Flyers and I said, 'Who? What are you talking about? What the hell is Philadelphia?' I knew nothing about it."

He was so distraught that he took a leave of absence from his job with the Public Works Department and went off and "got inebriated and felt sorry for myself. I was in shock."

Things didn't necessarily get any better when Joe reluctantly made his way to Philadelphia for his first season as a Flyer. In fact, his first impressions of the City of Brotherly Love remains dreadfully clear to this day.

"My first introduction to Philadelphia was when I came over the old Penrose Avenue Bridge," he recalls as though it was yesterday. "I looked over to the right and saw this big machine crushing cars. I asked the driver about it and he told me that the mafia ran the machine and that people were still in the cars as they were being crushed. I said to myself, what in the world I am doing in a city like this?"

A month later, after the team had played a couple of road games, they returned to an official "Welcome to Philadelphia" parade to City Hall. If this was the predecessor to the famous parades that would take place seven and eight years later, you would not have been able to tell by appearances.

"There were more people in the parade than there were watching it!" Watson laughs now. "People were giving us the finger and telling us we would be in Washington in six months. Others didn't know whether we were an ice hockey team or a field hockey team. When we got to City Hall, the mayor didn't even show up to welcome us. That's how well regarded we were."

Here was this disillusioned young hockey player, taken away from what he saw as a perfect situation in Boston, and now this. Given this beginning, it is almost impossible to fathom that Joe Watson and Philadelphia could co-exist. Well, co-exist they have. In fact, one could say they have thrived together because Watson has spent three and a half decades in the city he claims "he couldn't stand" when he first arrived.

"It's obvious it grew on me," he admits in retrospect. "I never thought in a million years I would spend 30-plus years here, but you know, after my first year and a half, I realized how beautiful this area really is. I got to know a lot of people and settle down. It turned out be a great experience."

•　•　•　•　•

The first 11 years of Watson's Philadelphia story were as a player, of course. He was the quintessential defensive defenseman. Every quality team has to have that reliable blue liner that simply takes care of business.

Watson filled that role from 1967 through 1978 for the Flyers. He appeared in 746 games in the orange and black, more than any other defenseman in team history. Twice he was selected to play in the NHL All-Star Game (1974, 1977). Always he was there to secure his own zone.

"He was a great competitor," remembers Watson's former coach and general manager Keith Allen. "Joe was fierce and he took his hard knocks. But he didn't mind giving the other guys on the team a piece of his mind when he felt they weren't pulling their weight, either."

Ah, yes. Watson's famed auditory abilities. They earned him the nickname "Thundermouth." Even he admits it was well earned.

"I was born and raised in Smithers, B.C. where there are more animals than there are people," he justifies. "So I grew up having to holler and scream to get anybody's attention!"

The result was one of the loudest and most talkative players on the bench and in the locker room. To this day, when you walk into a room and Joe Watson is in that room, you know instantly where he is. His voice stands out over all the others put together.

•　•　•　•　•

But even a strong personality like Watson needed some help at times. Early in his career that help, quite often, came from fellow defenseman Ed Van Impe.

"Eddie was kind of a mentor for me in those days," Watson says now. "He was a few years older than me so he helped me through the trials and tribulations of my early career. He practically saved my career in 1971."

That was the year that Joe almost gave up his hockey dream. During the playoffs the season before, Watson had been used sparingly by then-head coach Vic Stasiuk. He was disgruntled and depressed. He gave serious consideration to retirement altogether. That's when Van Impe stepped in.

"Eddie approached Bobby Orr and got him on the telephone," recalls Watson. "The two of them spent time talking with me and giving me some good advice. I changed my mind and kept playing. In that sense, Eddie did save my career."

• • • • •

Watson went on to enjoy the two Stanley Cups and the glory that went along with them. He also experienced glory in 1976 when the Flyers met the Russian Central Red Army team at the Spectrum. The touring Soviet team had gone without a loss on its tour through the NHL. Thus, it was up to the Flyers to defend the honor of North American hockey.

The game has received a lot of attention because the Russians left the ice surface to dispute what they perceived as the Flyers' roughhouse tactics. They did return, however, and suffered perhaps even more embarrassment for what transpired later in the game. Namely, they allowed Joe Watson to score a goal.

In fact, Watson did slice down the middle, take a feed from Don Saleski and score with a backhander in a shorthanded situation. It made the score 3-0 Flyers as they were on their way to a 4-1 triumph.

"Fred Shero came into the locker room after the game," Watson remembers with a smile, "and he told me that I set the Russian hockey program back 20 years by scoring that goal.

"Gene Hart used to tell this great story about that goal. He used to say how he went to Moscow in 1992 and was there for about a week before he took a side trip to Siberia just to see what it was like there. He came across this prison where he saw five middle-aged guys in balls and chains. He asked the guard why those guys were being singled out and the guard told him, 'Oh, those guys were on the ice when Joe Watson scored back in 1976!'"

• • • • •

A gratifying aspect of Joe's tenure as a Flyer was the opportunity to play in the NHL with his younger brother, Jimmy. Just as Van Impe had helped him as a younger player, Joe looked after his kid brother. Actually, he might have been too good at it.

"I was so excited when I found out Jimmy was drafted by the Flyers," the elder Watson proudly reflects. "I told him that I would represent him and be his agent for his first contract. I went in and negotiated with Keith Allen and must have done a hell of a job. I knew that because when all was said and

**Joe Watson vs. the Soviets in 1976—a day that will live in infamy for Russian hockey.**

done, I had gotten my brother, the rookie, a better contract worth more money than I had myself. Something was wrong with this picture. He was making more money than I was, for crying out loud!"

All was forgotten, however, when the two Watson brothers from tiny Smithers became only the fourth brother combination to win the Stanley Cup together in NHL history.

• • • • •

By the 1977-78 season, Watson's role with the team was changing. It was becoming more common for the 34-year-old veteran to sit games out as he appeared in only 65 games that year. Younger defensemen like Behn Wilson and Rick Lapointe were expected to take on greater roles the following season.

With some reluctance, General Manager Allen had to offer his old warrior a proposition. He told Joe that there was still a place for him in Philly if he was willing to play 30 to 35 games and take a part-time role.

"I told Keith I thought I could still play a full schedule," recalls Watson. "His response was that it wouldn't be here. He asked me where I might want to go and I gave him Atlanta, Colorado, and a couple of other teams. It ended up being Colorado, and I wasn't too upset with that. I thought I would have some fun, do some skiing and enjoy myself.

"Still, it was very, very tough leaving Philadelphia after having been here to watch this team develop and become so successful and popular. I had been here 11 years and was one of the original guys."

But leave he did as he became the captain of the fledgling Rockies. In their third year since moving from Kansas City, the Rockies made the playoffs only to be eliminated in a preliminary-round playoff series by Watson and the Flyers. Just 15 games into the season the Flyers visited Denver for a game with Watson's new team.

That the old pro had to have some mixed feelings that night was obvious. That the game ended in a 2-2 tie was probably fitting. However, it was the next night in a game in St. Louis that Watson remembers painfully.

"During the second period, I was going back into our zone to get the puck," he remembers in great detail. "Our goalie, Michel Plasse, left the puck

**Big brother Joe (left) poses on the ice with little brother Jimmy Watson.**

behind the goal line for me to pick up. Just as I reached for it, Wayne Babych pushed me in the lower back. I crashed into the boards with my right leg taking the full brunt of the collision. I looked down and the leg was at a 90-degree angle and the bone was sticking out. I knew right then that my career was over. I never expected to go out that way."

What followed were 18 of the roughest months of Watson's life. His leg was broken all right. ... in *13* different places! Initially, there was some fear that he would never walk again. Six operations over the next year and a half helped allay those fears, although his damaged right leg was two and a half inches shorter than his left leg.

"They took bone from my hip and put it in my leg," he explains. "Then they took some wires and gave me electric shock every four hours so the bone would heal. I was in a huge cast up to my chest for ten or 11 months. I lost a lot of weight. I think I was down to 160 pounds at one point.

"It gave me a lot of time to think. You know, I always thought I was a pretty good Catholic boy to that point. I went to church. I went and prayed. How could the good Lord do this to me? I reasoned that I guess He has his own way of doing things. But it was so difficult because I loved to play the game, and all of the sudden it came to an abrupt halt. It was hard to accept. It took me a long time."

To this day, Watson harbors resentment about the manner in which his career ended.

"What bothered me more than anything else," he seethes, "was that Wayne Babych never acknowledged it or came to visit me in the hospital. Many of his Blues' teammates including Bernie Federko and Garry Unger were there. He never visited, though, and a couple of months after the incident he wrote me a letter indicating he was surprised some people thought it was a cheap shot that injured me. I wrote back and told him I thought it was a cheap shot! I wrote that the fact that he never came to see me seemed to show he felt there was something wrong there. That was it. I never heard anything more from him."

Thus with mental and physical scars, Watson was unexpectedly staring at life after hockey. It would figure that reconstructing his life would take him right back to Philadelphia.

•  •  •  •  •

After so much time in and out of hospitals, an offer in 1979 from Flyers head coach Pat Quinn proved to be a godsend to the recuperating Watson. Quinn wanted Watson to be an advance scout for the team. That, of course, entailed traveling from city to city to break down future opponents. What Watson could not have foreseen was the relevance his initial post-playing position would have.

"Wouldn't you know, the team goes on the longest unbeaten streak in the history of pro sports!" he laughs. "Pat had me running all over the place. I would go to the same city three times in one week. Or I would be in nine different cities over a ten-day period preparing all kinds of reports."

Those reports became very important because as October became November and then November turned into December, the Flyers did not lose. The entire sports world became focused on just how long the team would keep the run going. A win in Boston made it 29 consecutive games without a loss, a new NHL record. It would go on six more games. In all, the Flyers were 25-0-10, going without a defeat for 84 days! Everyone except maybe one tired advanced scout was thrilled that it had continued for so long.

"To be honest, I was kind of happy when the streak came to an end," admits Watson. "I was going all over the country. I was a bit travel-weary.

"In all seriousness, though, what those boys did was incredible, absolutely incredible. It will never be duplicated again in sports. Ever!"

The streak also brought Watson back into the game he loved. It was the perfect tonic for a guy trying to overcome the horrific end to his playing career. With all of his traveling, he never had enough time to lament. It was always full steam ahead, just the way Watson had always gone about things.

● ● ● ● ●

He was a scout and an unofficial assistant coach at times until 1984. Then another door opened. Ticket sales were lagging slightly and he was asked to get involved. Joe Watson the scout became Joe Watson the account executive. For the first couple of years, he sold tickets. Eventually, he moved into selling advertising.

"I always loved getting out to meet people and talking with them," he explains. "I just had to learn about the product and how to sell the product. I think I learned from the best. Ivan Shlichtman was the best, and he helped me out tremendously. He taught me the technology and the things to say and words to use. I used to go with him a lot on sales calls and learned how to make a sales presentation. Ivan was the best, the very best."

Shlichtman was a longtime Flyers sales person. His influence on Watson's sales career can be compared to Van Impe's effect on his playing career. He clearly had some type of positive influence. Watson has spent two decades in the field.

"I could get my foot in the door where a lot of salesman couldn't because of who I was," Watson points out. "It worked out very well because people wanted to talk hockey and talk sports and that was one thing I was always good at. As a result, I opened a lot of doors for myself and the sales staff."

One tool a good salesman needs is a nice, firm handshake. You know what they say about how much you can tell about a person from his handshake. Well, in this area, anyone who knows Joe Watson can verify he has nothing to worry about.

In fact, back when I first came to Philadelphia, I remember when I introduced Joe to my wife, Bernadette, on the steps of the Spectrum. I had warned her that Joe had the firmest handshake I had ever experienced. She told me not to worry.

After introducing them, we chatted for a minute or two. Joe, as usual, was gregarious and energetic, telling us how much we would enjoy the area.

Joe Watson was an "unofficial" assistant coach before heading into the sales ranks.

As we separated, I asked my wife why she had been so quiet. She said she was trying to get her breath back because she thought Joe's handshake had broken her hand!

I've noticed whenever my wife has seen Joe from that point on, she prefers and initiates a hug before a handshake even becomes a possibility. Imagine all of those sales calls over 20 years and all of those handshakes. It's become a Joe Watson staple.

* * * * *

Watson's professional life had truly rebounded in the years after his playing career ended. First as a scout and then in marketing, he had been able to stay associated with the sport and organization he loved.

In a cruel irony, while his professional life was revitalized, his personal life fell apart. Married since 1969, Watson and his wife, Marianne, decided to separate in 1991 and eventually divorced in 1996. The woman who had been at his side for his glorious Stanley Cup triumphs and his tragic career-ending injury was no longer there. The family, which included son Ryan and daughter Heidi, was together no more.

"It was the worst thing I've ever gone through in my life," Watson reflects now, his patented boyish grin disappearing with the mere mention of this subject. "Talk about depression. It was so painful. So many things go on in 26 years of marriage. Half of my life was spent with my wife. We had a lot of good days. I feel sorry for anyone that has to go through a marriage breakup. It was very painful."

Once Watson had shown his resolve recovering from a broken body. Now he was being called upon to recover from psychological trauma.

•  •  •  •  •

To the rescue came his relationship with hockey and in particular, the Flyers. Watson poured himself into his work and to his duties with the Flyers Alumni, which has become his pride and joy.

Watson is quick to point out that the Flyers Alumni has raised over $1.8 million for various local charities. Prominent among the fundraisers for the Alumni are the exhibition games involving former Flyers, many of them from the Stanley Cup teams, against other teams. Not surprisingly, Watson is the head coach of the group.

Now these games can get testy. Watson remembers some near-international incidents that developed.

"We were in Switzerland one year and playing this team from the former Czechoslovakia," he remembers with a chuckle. "Ed Hospodar [former Flyers defenseman] had broken a player's nose and cheekbone with an elbow. His name was Richard Farda. At the banquet that night, we invited Dave Schultz to the podium and Farda, standing in the back of the room, gives him the finger while he is talking. Well, wouldn't you know, Schultzy takes off after him. We nearly had a brawl right in the dining room. I had to remind Schultzy that we were in a neutral country. They don't care. He would have wound up in jail!"

In general, though, the alumni games are a lot of fun. The guys get together to play a little hockey, for sure. However, there is plenty of time for storytelling too.

"The camaraderie is beautiful," Watson confirms. "The guys relate stories that happened 20 years ago. Bob Kelly leads the way. He's one of our funniest guys, and I mean he will bust on anybody, it doesn't matter who you are."

Through it all, money is raised for some great charities. It is obvious that Watson takes it to heart.

"There aren't many sports organization alumni groups that can raise $1.8 million for charity to begin with," he states. "It bothers me that we get very little recognition for it."

He has a point.

•  •  •  •  •

Thirty-seven years and counting. Joe Watson and the city of Philadelphia in general and the Flyers, in particular, have forged a lasting union, despite his early protests. In fact, it has been in Philadelphia that Watson has rebuilt his life, not once, but twice.

In fact, after the ninth surgery on his right leg, his legs are once again the same length. He walks better today than he has at any time since that difficult night in St. Louis in 1978.

He continues as the senior member of the Flyers sales staff. He is now involved in selling not only Flyers products, but also the 76ers and other events that occur at the Wachovia Sports Complex. He continues with his enthusiastic involvement with the Flyers Alumni as well.

His personal life is different. He has not remarried but doesn't complain about the life of a bachelor.

"For the most part, I'm very independent," he explains. "I left home when I was 16 years old to play junior hockey so I've kind of grown up by myself in that way. I have a lot of nice friends in the Philadelphia area and a nice lady friend and we have a nice time together. That's what life's all about anyhow. We're only passing through, so we might as well enjoy the trip."

It's obvious Watson and his former teammates on the Cup teams have followed that motto.

"The way we lived," Watson admits, "I can't believe so many of us have lasted so long!"

He understands the love the people of Philadelphia have for the Broad Street Bullies. As part of his marketing duties, he gets out in the public a lot and he experiences how that admiration is still strong to this day.

"We gave a lot to this city," he points out, referring to the joy the two Cups brought a championship-starved city. "Ever since, the city has given a lot back to us."

This from a city he didn't want anything to do with back in 1967.

**Now the senior account executive with the Flyers, Joe Watson is entrenched in the Philadelphia area.**

# #15
# Terry Crisp

## Bitten by the Coaching Bug

Perhaps the most surprised person to become a Philadelphia Flyer back in the 1970s was one Terry Crisp. Approaching his 30th birthday, the journeyman center had become quite familiar with the Flyers as an opponent of theirs when he wore the jerseys of the Boston Bruins, St. Louis Blues, and New York Islanders. But just prior to the trade deadline in 1973, the Flyers sent Jean Potvin and future considerations to the Islanders in order to acquire his services.

Crisp was a 5'10", 180 pounder who had never accumulated more than 30 penalty minutes in any of his NHL seasons to that point. Thus news of his acquisition by a team at that point quickly gaining a reputation as a rough-and-tumble group, surprised even him.

"I had witnessed so many battles with the Flyers from my days in St. Louis," Crisp explains now. "My first reaction was, 'What the hell do the Flyers want with me?' Right about then they were just beginning their swashbuckling, 'us against them' approach. So I wondered what Fred Shero would want from Terry Crisp going to that kind of team."

He quickly found out. Shero was very good at finding roles for a player and then making that player appreciate and even strive to excel in that role. Shero was honest with him from the beginning. He told the veteran that the Flyers needed a third- or fourth-line center, depending on injuries, and a good penalty killer. Crisp, with aspirations to someday become a coach, understood the role and its significance.

"Freddy often told us there are no small roles on a team," Crisp reasons. "He was an absolute master at making everybody feel like their role was the most important. It didn't matter what it was, you were made to feel that your job was just as important as Bobby Clarke's or Bernie Parent's. He had a knack for giving accolades in the press to the little guys or the lesser lights. Of course, the big guns always got the attention, but Freddy made sure the rest of us got our moments in the sun, too."

Thus despite his initial surprise at coming to Philadelphia, Crisp settled into his role and contributed to the final stages of development of those teams into Stanley Cup material.

• • • • •

Terry Crisp has what could be considered the best piece of memorabilia from the Cup years. As time wound down in Game 6 against Boston in 1974, the Spectrum was, of course, bedlam. But give Crisp credit for keeping his wits about him.

"As the final seconds ticked off the clock, the puck was cleared down into our end on what should have been an icing call," recalls Crisp. "For some reason, they didn't call it. Joey Watson went back to play the puck and had it on his stick as the horn sounded. He got all caught up in the excitement of the moment and just left the puck sitting there. I raced over to pick it up and the linesman got to it just before me. I said, 'Hey, that puck means a hell of a lot more to me than it does to you.' He looked at me, thought for a second, and then said, 'Yeah, Crispy, you're right.' And he handed it to me."

**Terry Crisp found his role and fit in with improving Flyers.**

Crisp still has the most significant puck in Flyers history in a drawer in his home with the original tape around it as a label of the date of the event. Someday, he plans on putting it into a nice glass case, but for now it sits just as it was more than 30 years ago.

• • • • •

Crisp appeared in 71 games in each of the Flyers' Stanley Cup seasons. He indeed had thrived in the role Shero had envisioned for him. His penalty killing was outstanding and he often was out on the ice against some of the top offensive players for the opposition.

By the 1975-76 season, though, his ice time began to diminish. He was heading into his mid-30s, which back then signified the twilight of one's playing career. He would only see action in 38 games that season. By the next year he would play in only two contests all season.

"It was just my time," he recollects. "They had told me my ice time would decrease. They came to me and told me Minnesota was interested in trading for me, but I told them I would rather ride it out in Philadelphia. My career was coming to an end and I didn't want to start moving around again at that point. They even mentioned moving into coaching down the road, and I said that was fine."

He would dress for every single pregame warmup in 1976-77, despite actually playing in only the two games. After the skate, he would get into street clothes and go up to the press box and take part in the game broadcast.

"I played one game in Vancouver because Rick MacLeish's grandfather had died and they couldn't get a replacement out fast enough," Crisp remembers. "And I played one game in Pittsburgh because there had been a brawl the night before and a whole bunch of players had received game misconducts and they needed a body. That was it. Two games. I was under no illusions that it was my final year and that I was headed into coaching after that."

Crisp's coach was always aware of his playing time, or lack thereof. During his final two years as a player, Shero would give some subtle and some not-so-subtle acknowledgments of his awareness.

"One time after a stretch where I hadn't played for seven or eight games, I found one of his famous notes at my locker room stall," Crisp recalls. "It read, 'They also serve who sit and wait.' He was smart enough to see that I was a little down so he left me a little note."

One of Crisp's favorite stories came from a game in Chicago. The Flyers were protecting a one-goal lead late in the third period in a game that he had only played one or two shifts all night. Future Hall of Famer Stan Mikita was ready to take the draw for Chicago. Shero tapped Crisp on the back and told him to get out there. Crisp, pumped to be called upon for such an important face off strode out onto the ice and positioned himself across from Mikita.

"All of the sudden, I get a tap on the backside and it's Clarkie telling me to go back to the bench," Crisp explains. "At first, I told him no because Freddy had just sent me out there. But Clarkie insisted so I slowly made my way back to the bench. After the game, the press was all around Freddy. They asked him what he was thinking when he sent me out there at first to take that important face off. He thought about it for a second, and after telling them that he was stalling for time, he then added, 'The best part about it is that Crispy thinks he got a shift!'"

•  •  •  •  •

In his early years in the NHL as a St. Louis Blue, Crisp played for Scotty Bowman. Later on, of course, Fred Shero was his coach. It should be no wonder then that coaching became his passion. He had two of the best teachers a prospective bench boss could ever want.

Crisp became Shero's assistant in 1977-78 with the Flyers. Coupling what he learned from Bowman with his observations of Shero gave him a terrific coaching foundation.

"I learned from Scotty about discipline," Crisp explains. "One man runs the ship and only one man can run it. Scotty ruled with an iron fist. He ruled with no nonsense. He ruled with head games. So did Fred Shero, but their head games were different. Fred's were subtler. Scotty was right at you. Freddy found a way to put the onus on the players to come up with solutions. He knew the solution you wanted. But he didn't give that to us. He gave us the problem and then an avenue to attack it. Then he let the guys in the dressing room worry about it."

Shero was a willing mentor, although he might not have divulged all of his genius to Crisp. Take all of those famous quotations and sayings that he posted on the blackboard and handed out to the players. One of Crisp's first objectives when he got into coaching was to ask Shero about those clever quips and to get a look at all of them.

"Okay, Freddy, now that I'm no longer a player and now your assistant, let me see your book," Crisp said.

"What book?" responded Shero.

"Your book of quotations with all of those great sayings. I want to get a copy of your book of quotations so I can start building my own list."

"Do you drink tea?" Shero asked matter of factly.

"What?" shot back a puzzled Crisp.

"Do you drink tea?" Shero reiterated.

"Yeah, sometimes," Crisp answered with a confused tone.

"Buy a box of Red Rose tea. The little tags on the tea bags have a saying on them. That's where I got them!"

Crisp walked away in amazement. His first project as a coach, gathering some of the most influential messages he had come in contact with in his hockey career, and his mentor had just told him they were found on tea bags!

Of course, Shero was fibbing to some degree. It is now known that he spent a lot of time reading to find those great quotes. I guess the great coach wasn't willing to give his pupil every single one of his secrets.

Still, though, Crisp learned so much from the likes of Bowman and Shero.

"I used Scotty and Freddy's practice models throughout my coaching career," Crisp says now. "I just honed them to what a particular team needed and went from there."

After Shero departed for New York, Crisp assisted Bob McCammon as Flyers coach during the 1978-79 season. He was considered for Shero's replacement, but his lack of head coaching experience hurt his chances. He knew eventually he was going to have to get that type of experience on his resume. When McCammon did not last the entire season, Pat Quinn became the head coach and Crisp was moved to the position of special assignment scout, he knew it was time to search for a head coaching position.

His opportunity came in the junior ranks with the Sault St. Marie Greyhounds of the Ontario Hockey League. There were some early growing pains.

"Yeah, we started our first season 0-11!" Crisp remembers, albeit somewhat painfully. "We finished dead last in our division and I kept saying to myself, 'Geez, do I really want to be doing this?'"

Things would get better though. The Greyhounds surged to 47-19-2 in Crisp's second year. By the time his six-year run as head coach there had ended, he had guided Sault Ste. Marie to three league championships and an impressive 249-149-12 record. Future Flyer Rick Tocchet had been one of his captains. Crisp clearly had discovered the hang of this coaching thing, although he realizes it's the players who ultimately determine the coach's success.

"I chuckle when people ask me about my coaching style and its success," Crisp admits. "It's like asking me what kind of a horse jockey I would be. Put me up on Secretariat and I would be one hell of a jockey. Put me up on a plow horse, and I'm going to be a really bad jockey."

Crisp maintains his six years coaching junior hockey was the perfect springboard to an NHL head coaching career.

"I look back on my six years there and think it was the best grounding I could have had as a head coach," Crisp explains. "Those kids taught me more than I could have learned anywhere else. The hockey end of it was easy in terms of the Xs and Os. It's the social aspect of it that was the challenge.

"Maintaining curfews, looking after those kids, babysitting them at times were all part of it. Convincing 18 of your 21 kids that they won't play pro but that they can still have fun and get a good education and have a good career in junior hockey was a main objective. And then you had to convince the other three or four that if they were going pro, if they could survive me, then they would be able to survive anything down the road."

His coaching style, a mix of his two mentors, evolved during those years in the OHL.

• • • • •

Crisp entered the professional head coaching ranks with the Moncton Flames of the American Hockey League. He spent two years coaching in the minors and continued to hone his craft. Crisp felt that the mind games intensify once you coach players who are being paid to play. Since the players realized how close they were to the NHL, though, Crisp felt he had a hammer with them. Two years and a 77-65-19 record later, he was ready to get back to the NHL.

He replaced the late Bob Johnson as head coach of the Calgary Flames in 1987. He inherited a talented team that had only two years earlier been to the Stanley Cup Finals, only to lose to Montreal and a rookie goalie named Patrick Roy.

Crisp's first NHL team had a pair of 50-goal scorers in Hakan Loob and Joe Nieuwendyk, two more who topped the 40-goal mark (Mark Bullard and Joe Mullen), and a young Brett Hull, who chipped in with 26 before getting dealt to St. Louis. On defense, he had Al MacInnis, Rob Ramage, and Brad McCrimmon. In goal was the up-and-coming Mike Vernon. Great character players like Joel Otto, Gary Roberts, and Lanny McDonald provided leadership.

"Badger Bob Johnson had put together a super hockey club," Crisp reasons. "My mandate when I got there was to get a ring. They wanted a Stanley Cup. The owners had all the money they wanted. They didn't care about first place. They didn't care about sold-out buildings. They wanted a Stanley Cup, pure and simple.

"If you're going to make an omelet, you're going to crack some eggs. I stepped on a lot of toes. I bruised a lot of egos. But I could never lose sight of the fact that I had to win a Stanley Cup."

In his first season the Flames captured their first ever President's Trophy as the NHL's best regular-season team. However, they stumbled in the playoffs, losing to the Edmonton Oilers in the Smythe Division Finals. No Cup meant more pressure on Crisp for his second year.

His team rose to the occasion. Doug Gilmour had been added in a trade from St. Louis. Theo Fleury burst upon the scene bringing a whole bunch of energy with him and the Flames once again cruised to the President's Trophy. A seven-game opening-round classic with Vancouver put quite a scare into the Flames before Otto's dramatic overtime winner catapulted them into the second round. It took the Flames only nine games to dispatch Los Angeles and Chicago and make it to the Stanley Cup Finals against those same Montreal Canadiens.

At this point, Crisp decided to give his old mentor, Fred Shero, a call, hoping for some last minute inspiration.

"Hi Freddy, it's Crispy."

"Hi. How are you?" answered an emotionless Shero.

"We're in the Finals, starting tomorrow against Montreal," answered Crisp, expecting an upbeat response.

"Yeah, I read that," said a still placid sounding Shero.

"The Finals, Freddy! What do you think?" Crisp asked still looking for some sign of enthusiasm from his former coach.

"Yeah, that's good," Shero deadpanned.

Crisp was at a loss. He couldn't figure out why Shero seemed so unimpressed.

Finally, he offered this to his former pupil.

"The coach who works the hardest is going to win the Stanley Cup."

With that the conversation ended, and Crisp was left to ponder what that conversation was all about. Finally he figured it out.

"I started to think about it," Crisp recalls. "Freddy never said anything without there being some kind of message. Suddenly, it hit me like a bolt. He was telling me that I hadn't won anything. I still had a series to go. He was telling me not to pat myself on the back or to get puffed up like a big peacock. The coach who put his mind to it and grinded it out was going to win what counted. He was basically wondering why I called him when I hadn't won anything yet! That buckled me right back down. I went back in and started looking at video again and was driven to win that series."

It must have worked. The Flames defeated the Habs in six games and became the only team, other than the Canadiens, to ever lift Lord Stanley's Cup at the Montreal Forum. Crisp's mission was accomplished. He helped guide the Flames to their cherished championship. He had his third Stanley Cup ring.

**Terry Crisp was not afraid to hurt feelings in driving the Flames to the Cup in 1989.** *Photo by Brad Watson. Courtesy of Calgary Flames Hockey Club*

"You know the first Cup you can't top," Crisp says, referring to the Flyers' win in 1974. "When you win that thing, you have reached the pinnacle of what you chose to do when you were a little kid. When that day happens, whether you ever play again or are involved in a championship again, you can say you've been there. So the one in 1974 will always be the most memorable.

"However, from a satisfaction standpoint, it is the Cup I won as a coach that stands out. As a player all you worry about is yourself, your job and your responsibility. As a coach, you have to worry about 20 guys. You worry about your lineup, the team's attitude, the whole ballgame. That makes winning with that group very gratifying."

Crisp never made the call to his former coach after lifting the Cup as a coach. Shero would pass away just over a year later and to this day, Crisp regrets not having given the phone call to thank him for his pre-Finals message.

The next season, the Flames were once again outstanding, falling just a couple points shy of a third straight President's Trophy. However, they were shocked in the first round of the playoffs by Wayne Gretzky's Los Angeles Kings. Crisp would get fired shortly thereafter.

How can a coach who has had his team at or very near the top of the league for three straight years, including a Stanley Cup triumph, be let go so quickly? It goes back to Crisp's approach to the Calgary job. He was asked to win a Cup. In driving the team to that goal, he was tough on some players. In the end, that dictated a shorter term as head coach. General Manager Cliff Fletcher told him when he let him go that the first sign of trouble the following season would have led to an uprising against him.

"Every one wants to have respect," Crisp explains. "You want respect from your co-workers and those around you. Coaches are no different. But respect is a two-way road. It ticks me off when I hear a GM say, 'The players no longer respect the coach, so we had to fire him.' What do you mean, they lost respect for the coach? Because he was tough on them? Because he demanded they earn their pay? Because he demanded he get 60 minutes of hockey out of them? Well, you know what? There are a lot of players who I didn't always have a lot of respect for either. But I'm not allowed to say it. So as a coach you learn early on that it's not fair. Don't think you are going to go into a fair arena as a coach. You're not."

The fact that some of the players from his championship Calgary team probably, in his words, "hate his guts" is a difficult realization for Crisp. He would have loved to have them revere him the way the Flyers did Shero. However, it was a different situation in Calgary.

"Looking back at it, I wish some of the players that I pushed so hard back then had a better rapport with me now," he admits. "I don't feel bad about how I treated them. It was necessary to achieve what we did. I'm not sure to this day that we would have been able to win it all if I had worried about developing that rapport. You walk a fine line."

• • • • •

Crisp rebounded to have "one of the most enjoyable" years of his life in 1992 when he was an assistant coach to Dave King for the Canadian Olympic team. The team, led by the likes of Eric Lindros, Sean Burke, and Dave Tippett, captured a silver medal, the first medal won by the Canadians in the Olympics in more than two decades.

He was back in the NHL in 1992-93 as the head coach of the expansion Tampa Bay Lightning. This was an absolute 180-degree change from his experience in Calgary. Instead of a talent-laden team in a Canadian city, he was the boss of a team of castoffs in a virgin market in sunny Florida.

"It was totally different," Crisp relates. "There was no pressure for a while. When [general manager] Phil Esposito hired me, he told me we were going to build it and stay together and that's the way it was. He brought in a lot of veteran players and we added players from the draft. My experience in Tampa was great.

"It was fun coaching, yet tough coaching. We had a hodgepodge group of players and had to gain some respectability. We were in a market that had never had hockey, so we had to try and make the game happen. It's safe to say we were all wearing a lot of hats."

Crisp must have done something right. He ended up setting an NHL record (since broken by Nashville's Barry Trotz) for most games coached by an expansion head coach as he was behind the Lightning bench for their first 391 games. In 1996, he took them to their first playoff berth. Wouldn't you know it, their first-round opponent would be the Philadelphia Flyers.

It was a nasty series with venom being spewed on the ice by the players and even off it by some of the writers covering the match up. In fact, one Philadelphia writer had to have guards stand behind him for protection at a game in Tampa after he made some disparaging comments about the Lightning fans. The series set single-game records for attendance at the Thunderdome.

"For me, it was a lot of fun," Crisp recalls. "There was so much excitement down there with the attendance records and such. I still talk with Clarkie, and I buy the wine by the way, and tell him that we would have knocked the Flyers out that year had our goaltender Daren Puppa not gotten hurt. We would have had them!"

As it was, the Flyers outlasted the Lightning in six games. The next season, the Lightning sank to sixth in their division and missed the playoffs.

"What had been patience had turned to expectations," he reasons. "The pressure started to crank up. The fans started getting antsy. The owner started getting antsy. Then as coach, you start to do the hot plate dance as people take shots at you. After six years, it was time I suppose for some new blood for them and for me to move on with my life."

• • • • •

Fired in Tampa during the 1997-98 season, Terry Crisp would not be away from the game very long. He would, in fact, join on with another expansion team, this time in Nashville, and this time as a broadcaster. After a year as a broadcaster on network television, Crisp signed on with the Predators as their radio and television analyst.

"I had some experience from my days back in Philly when I worked with Gene Hart for that one year," Crisp reasons. "Then the one year at Fox. But it's more fun working with a team. When you are at a network, you can't cheer for anybody. With a team, you travel with the guys, so you feel much more a part of it."

He has witnessed the expansion Predators go through the same growing pains his Lightning once did. He has talked with Predators coach Barry Trotz about some of the coaching philosophies that enter into the equation while avoiding discussion of the Xs and Os.

In fact, while enjoying his stint alongside Pete Weber in the Nashville broadcast booth, Crisp does admit he hasn't completely closed the door on coaching again.

"I would love to get back into coaching and take one more shot at it," he admits. "I don't want to go back and babysit. I don't want to go back and

**Terry Crisp shares the broadcast booth with play-by-play man Pete Weber (left) in Nashville.**

have to deal with a bunch of prima donnas running around in the room. I would want to arrive on the scene and basically tell the players, 'I'm here to win the Cup, boys. I'm not here to make friends. I'm not here to lollygag with you. I'm here to win the Cup. That's my objective. It better damn well be your objective.' I would have maybe two years to get it done. I wouldn't have to mold a team. I just want to get on the buggy and take it over the finish line."

As he talked, I almost felt like a player. He clearly still has coaching in his blood.

• • • • •

Being involved in hockey, Crisp still has many opportunities to see his old Flyer teammates. He is a firm believer in the bond that exists among them.

"If I ever needed a favor, I would phone Bobby Clarke," Crisp claims. "He would be there in a heartbeat. Or Bobby Taylor. The Kindrachuks, and the Billy Barbers. There's a nice, quiet, unspoken bond there. If you're in trouble, they'll help you. At the next gathering, you are most definitely made to feel part of the group.

"The greatest thing about us is that while the Cups are beautiful and the rings are gorgeous, it's the memories that are forever and will never tarnish."

# #16
# Bob Clarke

*"It's All About Winning"*

During my first couple of months as the Flyers' radio play-by-play announcer in 1993, I resided in Ocean City, New Jersey, at the shore house of Bob Clarke. My wife and I were still looking for a house, and Clarke was gracious enough to allow me to stay at his place while that search went on. He was in Florida, at that time, working with the Panthers.

Being new to the organization, I spent much of my first months trying to engross myself in Flyers history. I wanted to find out as much as I could about where the Flyers had been and where they might be going. There just happened to be several Flyers videotapes at Clarke's place that were lying around. These were perfect for my research purposes, I thought.

On one of them there was a clip from a game in March 1981. In it Clarke, while standing at the side of the net, is hit in the head by a shot from Reggie Leach. Those were the days when helmets weren't mandatory. Blood began to stream down the side of Clarke's face and onto his jersey. He hardly seemed fazed. He simply skated up ice. It became quite appropriate that later in that game, with a blood-soaked jersey on, Clarke registered his 1,000th NHL point. Take a slapshot in the head. No problem. Clarke had things to do that night!

Of course, I had heard of and seen some of the examples of Clarke's determination prior to my arrival in Philadelphia. However, this particular example really drove the point home. Here was obviously one of the more driven and courageous players in NHL history. As I saw further illustrations on those tapes and heard from those who played with and against him, those characteristics only became easier to see.

Bob Clarke notched his 1,000th NHL point in a blood-stained jersey thanks to taking a Reggie Leach slap shot in the head earlier in the game.

Then as I interviewed people for this book, the unique qualities of Bob Clarke constantly came up when his former cohorts spoke of him. Here's just a sampling of their remarks concerning Clarke's drive and determination:

"He was an unusual package," says his general manager Keith Allen. "He made everybody around him better. And he was one of the great competitors of all time. I mean he never gave up. He was absolutely the total package."

"His leadership and his desire to succeed as a team were remarkable," assesses Ed Snider. "He was willing to sacrifice anything for the good of the team."

"The bottom line with Clarkie is all about winning," states Bob Kelly. "He sacrificed his family to win. We all did. It's what you had to do to win. Even as a general manager, he doesn't waver. It's all he knows. If there's any way, shape, or form that he can win, he will."

"He was, in my mind, the greatest leader in all of pro sports, bar none," says Bobby Taylor. "Clarkie simply refused to let us lose."

Time and again as I talked with his former teammates and those who were around the team when he was a player, leadership would come up. It's a quality sought after by general managers and coaches in sports, and yet so sparsely in supply. By those who witnessed his actions on and off the ice, Clarke would seem to have been the definition of a leader.

However, when you ask Clarke himself about leadership and his abilities in that area, you get a different interpretation. The guy they all considered the leader among all leaders never saw himself that way at all.

"I've tried to understand what they call leadership when it relates to me, and I really can't," he explains. "When I played, I just played. I didn't want to be captain. I didn't need to be captain. I didn't wake up one morning and say, 'I'm going to lead these guys.' There's no definition of what leadership is.

"I think from my standpoint, as an individual, I was extremely selfish. What I wanted was to win. I was willing to prod guys and push them with that in mind. Reggie Leach was a great player but had some problems off the ice. I was willing to room with him and look out for him. I was willing to talk to Rick MacLeish and get after him about playing better. It was all because I wanted to win. I knew that if the team was better, then we all win.

"I even took advantage of my own family if it meant helping us win. Every single thing I did was to try and win hockey games. My wife [Sandy] swears that I dropped her off at the hospital when she gave birth to our second child and left her just to take part in a practice, an OPTIONAL practice!"

The image of him playing on despite bleeding from the shot that hit him in the head dances through my head. Perhaps his was a leadership by example. Players saw how hard he worked and couldn't help but give everything they had. He doesn't buy that either.

"That's just the way I played," he retorts. "Again, I didn't wake up in the morning and think to myself, 'I'm going to work my ass off today so somebody else will, too.' The other players had the same drive to win as I did. Maybe some a little less, others a little more. I think Shero somehow brought it all together and brought it out in us. As far back as I can remember, I always had that desire to get out on the ice and to win. I couldn't get enough of it. Is that leadership? I don't think it is."

Perhaps it was just that Clarke's incredible will to win was very contagious to those around him, whether he was aware of it or not. It might not be leadership in his eyes, but it served the same purpose.

• • • • •

Winning in the sport of hockey, of course, ultimately means the Stanley Cup. It's intriguing that a player as synonymous with winning as Bob Clarke finds the whole fascination of Canadians with the Cup somewhat mysterious.

"I've never understood how kids in Canada just love hockey and just want to win the Stanley Cup," the Flin Flon, Manitoba native wonders. "It's passed from generation to generation. Why do all the kids get out on that ice when it's 20 below zero chasing that bloody puck around? What imbedded that into us? For me, for as long as I can remember in my life, I wanted to win the Stanley Cup. I have no idea why. It certainly wasn't from watching television, because we didn't have it. But it's there and always has been."

Fortunately for Clarke, and unlike many thousands of other Canadian kids who have that dream, he was able to live out the fantasy not once, but twice.

"I remember sitting on the bench watching Joe Watson behind the net as the seconds ticked down [toward the Cup in 1974]," Clarke recalls like it was yesterday. "All of the sudden the gloves and sticks were in the air. That's imprinted in my mind until I'm dead. It will never go away."

•   •   •   •   •

Simply put, Bob Clarke *is* the Philadelphia Flyers. With the exception of a brief period in the early 1990s, from the time he stepped on the ice as a fresh-faced rookie in September 1969 through his second stint as the team's general manager, he has been the fulcrum of the organization.

As a player, Clarke was involved in so many of the franchise's glorious moments. The climb from expansion neophytes to Stanley Cup Champions tops the list, of course. However, there was also the win over the Russians in 1976, which brought him an angry satisfaction, if you will.

"At the time, I hated the Russians," he admits. "I think hate is a great motivator when it is kept on the ice. All everyone wanted to talk about was how great the Russians skated, how great they passed, etc. For me, it was us saying, 'We'll show you.' It wasn't quite the same thrill as winning the Cup, but when we beat the crap out of them, I was so happy!"

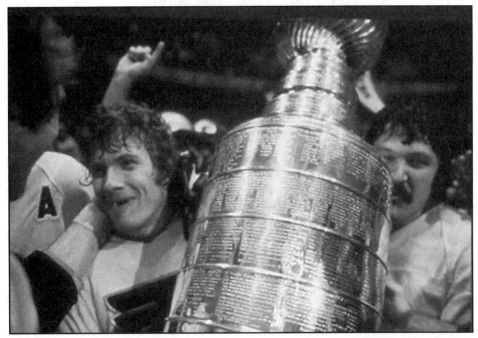

**A childhood dream becomes reality for Bob Clarke.**

He was one of the key veterans who went on the incredible ride in 1979-80 of 35 games in a row without a loss.

"We just kind of stumbled on that streak," he offers. "It's rolling along…seven games…15 games, and then we realized we were on quite a run. What I liked about that streak was that it wasn't about one goalie or one defenseman or forward. It was a different combination of people every game coming through. Veterans and rookies all took part. I can't visualize it ever happening again."

Then, of course, there was the heartbreak of the loss in the Finals that same year to the Islanders.

"We got some bad calls, but we had chances at other times in that series to make those bad breaks less damaging," Clarke reasons. "That's the way it works in a series. I do think if we had gotten them back to Philly for Game 7, our experience would have helped us. The Islanders were still up and coming. I think we would have won. But then why would I think any other way?!"

In all, Clarke played 15 seasons with the Flyers. This consisted of 1,144 games in the NHL, all in the orange and black. He is still their all-time leader with 852 assists and 1,210 points. Despite the many great offensive players who have suited up with the Flyers, Clarke remains 327 points ahead of the next highest point-getter. He won the Hart Trophy as the league's Most Valuable Player three times. He was named to play in the NHL All-Star Game 10 seasons in a row. He was a no-brainer selection for the Hockey Hall of Fame in 1987.

Yet no matter how impressive his statistical resume appears, it will be his approach to the game that most people remember about his playing career. He was a winner, pure and simple.

• • • • •

By the summer of 1984, Clarke was 35 years old but still certainly a contributing player to the Flyers' cause. In fact, he was just one year removed from winning the Selke Trophy as the NHL's best defensive forward. Many observers thought he had been one of the team's best players during the 1984 playoffs.

Perhaps then it came as a surprise to some that he was the choice of team management to replace the ousted Bob McCammon as the club's general manager that summer. The offer gave Clarke a very difficult decision. He could continue as a player, but then in all likelihood not have the managing opening available when he did choose to retire. Or he could take the GM job at that time and bid adieu to his playing days. He chose the latter.

"I still felt I could contribute as a player," Clarke recollects. "However, when Jay Snider offered me the job, I knew it was for the right reasons. I figured people a lot smarter than me thought it was the right move for the team, so I thought if that's what they wanted, then that's what I would do."

The decision ended the greatest single playing career that any Flyer has ever had. In retrospect Clarke does feel some regret about his choice.

"If any player asks me today, I tell them to play the game until you physically can't play it anymore," he laments. "There will be another life when you're done. In my case, had I stayed playing, I probably would have never ended up managing, but whether it's ego or pride or whatever, I still wish I had stuck around for at least a couple more years."

•   •   •   •   •

He went from Bobby Clarke, the Hall of Fame player, to Bob Clarke, the general manager with one decision. On the surface, it was a smooth transition. The Flyers would go to the Stanley Cup Finals in two of his first three years on the job, losing to the dynastic Edmonton Oilers each time. One could legitimately argue that if it weren't for timing their runs during the Oilers' era, the Flyers would have two more banners hanging from the rafters.

In any event, two trips to the finals in the first three seasons would seem to indicate Clarke handled the duties of GM with ease in his early years behind the desk. He, however, would say appearances could be deceiving.

"I didn't have any experience at managing anything, really," he says as he thinks back. "I mean I managed my own life to that point and that was about it. I remember I used to come home from work and sit down in a chair and have trouble keeping my eyes open I was so tired. I was amazed. As a player, I could practice and practice and never feel tired. Now, here I was sitting behind a desk all day, and I was exhausted. It took me quite a while to get used to the mental stress that job brings.

"Decisions were being made for things I was responsible for that I didn't even really know what was going on. The draft? How the hell could I know how to run a draft? I didn't have a clue. I couldn't tell you who was a good scout or who was a bad scout. And these were responsibilities that were mine."

In retrospect, Clarke says it was plain old good fortune that garnered him so much success in his first spin as a general manager.

"I lucked out," he admits. "Gary Darling, who was already there as the assistant GM and Jay Snider had already hunted down Mike Keenan and did all the background work. I didn't even know who Mike Keenan was. He had been coaching in Rochester. I hardly even knew where Rochester was to tell you the truth! I would have had no idea where to find a coach, but they had already brought him in.

"Keenan absolutely deserves most of the credit for those Cup runs. I know a lot of the players ended up disliking him for it, but he pushed them to some unbelievable limits. He made some people into great players. Guys like Rick Tocchet for one, and while he [Keenan] was abusive to Scott Mellanby, I think he made him a better player. If it wasn't for the Oilers being so good, we could have had a couple of more Cups. But the success we had was more luck [finding Keenan] than planning on my part."

Keenan's stay in Philadelphia was a volatile one. The team had some incredible success. However, some of the players fumed. As time went by it became impossible to overlook the discontent.

**GM Bob Clarke says he "lucked out" getting Mike Keenan as his first head coach.**

"Mike would take people like Thomas Eriksson, Pelle Eklund, and Illka Sinisalo and want them to be like Tocchet," Clarke recalls. "These were European players who came from a different background and culture. They were terrific people and terrific players. He would rip them and ride them. What worked on other guys didn't work on them. Too many guys got cast aside by Mike, and the organization paid a big price for that."

Keenan was fired after his fourth season at the helm of the Flyers. Clarke's first term as GM with the club lasted six seasons. He takes a very realistic approach when giving an overview of his first try at managing.

"I don't think it's possible to go into managing unless you take a few years to learn about it first," he offers. "Running a draft was so far beyond my imagination. It takes you years to learn how to do that. Yet these were the responsibilities of the job. When it started to fall apart, the responsibility was mine. I accepted that, but I was totally unprepared for the job. I had no chance."

• • • • •

April 16, 1990 will not go down as one of the high points for the Flyers franchise nor Bob Clarke. It was on that day that Clarke's 21-year run with the organization came to an end. Team president Jay Snider announced that "philosophical differences" had forced him to relieve Clarke of his general manager duties with the team.

"I was in shock," Clarke remembers. "Driving home from Jay's office that day I was in disbelief. It hit me that, for the first time in my life, really, I was going to have to go out and look for a job."

The Flyers had gone 66-75-19 during the previous season, missing the playoffs for the first time in 19 years. Jay Snider felt the time had come to move on. In retrospect, there probably was not enough communication between Snider and Clarke during the tough times following the Keenan years.

"I don't think philosophically my differences with Jay were that great," Clarke says now. "We probably just didn't talk enough about where the team was headed."

Well over a decade later, Clarke can look at that day differently. There's no more shock, obviously, and he can see both why the move occurred and how it might have turned out for the best in his case.

"It was the right thing to do," he explains. "I took responsibility for some of the things that went wrong. I also think Jay wanted it to be his team at that point. In the long run, it actually worked out well for me."

He didn't know it then, though. That's because for the first time since he had turned pro back in 1969, Bob Clarke was no longer a Flyer. He had been all that the organization stood for during a glorious two-decade period. But it was time to move on.

• • • • •

A four-year period in the early 1990s would take Clarke to Minnesota, back to Philadelphia, and then down to Miami, Florida. And while he was on the move, he looks back at that period as the time when he actually learned a tremendous amount about what it takes to be a good general manager.

His sojourn began in Minnesota where he was hired as the North Stars' GM. What he found when he got there was a paper-thin organization looking for direction.

"When the draft concluded, there were only three people left to run things," he recalls. "All that was left were the head scout, a secretary and me! That's when you find out if you can make decisions you have to make, do the homework you have to do, and pick the people you need to choose in order to get the job done. How the different responsibilities were assigned was up to me because I was basically the only one. I think the group we eventually had put together a hell of an organization. Much of the organization that was started then is still there today [although now in Dallas]."

Clarke's North Stars surprised many by making a run all the way to the Stanley Cup Finals in 1991 before Mario Lemieux and the Penguins knocked them off. The team would eventually move to Dallas in 1993 and become one of the NHL's most successful franchises. Clarke, however, had no desire to move to Texas so his tenure with the Stars lasted just two years.

He came back to Philadelphia as team president for the 1992-93 season but found there really wasn't that much for him to do. Russ Farwell was the general manager and Clarke didn't feel good about himself having so little responsibility. Thus, when the opportunity to run the expansion Florida Panthers came up, he jumped at it.

Clarke built the Panthers into instant playoff contenders by selecting a top-notch goaltender in John Vanbiesbrouck and surrounding him with a host of character players. It was this nucleus that would eventually go on a remarkable run to the finals in 1996, just the third year of the team's existence.

But rather than see those years for the accomplishments of the teams, Clarke thinks of them as a true learning experience.

"I learned so much from so many different people in all different walks of life," he explains. "When I went to Florida, we hired Chuck Fletcher [as an assistant manager]. He was only in his late 20s, but clearly one of the bright, young minds in the game. I was with my third team, but I still learned a lot from him, just watching and listening to him talk to people. He was intelligent and hard working. If you can keep your ego out of the way, you can learn from people like that and I did. Just as I learned from Bob Gainey in Minnesota and from Les Jackson about scouting. If you can apply what you learn to what you are trying to do, it at least gives you a chance to be successful."

By 1994, Clarke was a more accomplished general manager than he had been four years earlier. What better time to have the team from his glorious past come calling.

• • • • •

Clarke's former team had fallen on hard times. The Flyers had missed the playoffs in five consecutive seasons by 1994. They had engineered the huge Eric Lindros trade, but even that had not pushed them into the playoff mix. There was a need to find new leadership. Who better than Clarke, who was coming off being named Hockey News Executive of the Year for his work with Florida?

Ed Snider had made the decision to get back involved with the Flyers on a day-to-day basis. He knew Bob Clarke was the one to try to lead his team back out of the wilderness. Clarke agreed.

"I loved Florida," he says now. "I mean the climate was great. The people were great and the organization was great. But I always felt Philadelphia was my home. I wanted to get back there. It was where I raised my kids. It was where I needed to be."

So despite the feeling that he was deserting the Panthers somewhat because they had just completed their first ever season, Clarke went home. What he found wasn't exactly what he had remembered the Flyers being all about.

"It was a total mess, of the nature I had never seen let alone here with the Flyers," he remembers. "Players were bringing their dogs to practice and leaving dog dishes all over the locker room. It was unprofessional. There was a total lack of discipline. It was so bad players didn't even want to come here anymore. It had gone from at the top to being almost in disarray.

"Because I had experienced starting from the bottom in Minnesota and Florida, I knew what it was going to take to turn it around. We threw the dog dishes out, redid the entire practice facility locker room, and started changing things so the players knew this was going to be a professionally run outfit. We made simple rules that the players had to follow or they wouldn't be there anymore. When rules aren't followed, it can fall apart quickly on you."

As Clarke tried to reestablish the team's identity off the ice, he went about restructuring the club on the ice. One of his first objectives was to bolster the team's defense corps. Players such as Eric Desjardins, Kevin Haller, Peter Svoboda, and Chris Therien were added to the blue-line mix, and suddenly Philadelphia had a bigger, more mobile group of defensemen.

He also pulled off a trade that has gone down as one of the best in NHL history. The Flyers sent Mark Recchi and a draft pick to Montreal in exchange for Desjardins, John LeClair, and Gilbert Dionne. A stroke of genius, you say. Clarke confesses it was more good fortune.

"We lucked out," he says today. "There was no genius involved there. We had an idea how good Desjardins was and gave up a good player to get him. However, we had no idea how good John LeClair was going to be. It was flat out, straight luck!"

The trade proved to be the catalyst that sent the Flyers soaring into contention. They won the division title that season and defeated both Buffalo and the New York Rangers in the playoffs before losing in the conference finals to New Jersey. They have been in contention ever since, not having missed the playoffs for a full decade. Just as Clarke had helped them out of the wilderness as a player, he had brought them back as a manager. He was rewarded with his second consecutive Executive of the Year honor from the *The Hockey News* in 1994.

• • • • •

Clarke's second stint as the Flyers' general manager has been, by and large, successful. Each year the prognosticators select Philadelphia as one of the favorites to compete for the Stanley Cup. They've had some good runs, three times losing in the conference finals (1995, 2000 and 2004) and once losing in the Finals to Detroit (1997).

Still, it has not been a decade without challenges. The much talked about Eric Lindros saga dominated much of the franchise's fortunes during the 1990s. It ended in bitter fashion after Lindros had criticized the team's medical staff over his treatment for concussions and eventually forced a trade to the Rangers. Clarke has one regret about how the entire Lindros situation developed.

"We allowed a young player with a lot of ability to have different rules from the other players," Clarke laments in retrospect. "We allowed his parents to become too involved with the team. By the time we stood up to it, it was too late. We lost the player, and I think Eric has never gotten back to the player he should have been. It was a major loss for Eric, for our team, and for me."

Another challenge of a general manager is the handling of head coaches. The Flyers have had their fair share of coaches in recent years. The time comes when a move has to be made, and it's the general manager who carries the hammer.

"It's horrifying when you have to make that decision," Clarke explains. "You try to do it decently, but there's no such thing as firing somebody and doing it decently, I don't think.

Clarke has had to fire a close friend like Terry Murray and his longtime linemate and championship teammate Bill Barber.

**The Eric Lindros saga garnered much of Bob Clarke's attention as general manager in the 1990s.**

"Billy Barber was a Hall of Fame player with our club," he relates. "He had done so much for the organization. It was hard to make him go through that. We tried to help the situation as much as possible by offering him a position with the team and by giving him a long-term, well paid contract before he was let go. He deserved that for all he had done. Those kind of guys you have to take care of as best you can. You can't do it at the expense of the team, but you do the best you possibly can.

"My relationship with Billy is the same as it always was, even after the firing. It had nothing to do with liking or disliking anyone. I would like to think, or maybe I'm just hoping, that Bill saw it as almost a relief because things had gotten so out of hand and he had been through so much.

"Terry Murray was a tough one, too, because he is one of the better coaches and men you will ever meet. I mean he's solid and decent. My wife's still mad at me for firing him."

Such is the life of a general manager. His decisions will never make everyone happy. Over the course of a decade in the general manager's chair, there's a good chance you will anger just about everyone with one move at some point. The result is that general managers are rarely the most popular men in town.

In Clarke's case, it makes for an unusual dichotomy. In 1984, on Bobby Clarke Night at the Spectrum, the retiring star stood at center ice for 18 minutes, unable to begin his speech because the fans were giving him a raucous standing ovation. It went on and on. The love and devotion expressed that night symbolized the adoration heaped upon Bobby Clarke, the player.

Twenty years later Clarke rarely goes on ice to present the trophy in his name to the current Flyers Most Valuable Player because his appearance would inevitably generate at least some negative responses from the partisans. General manager Bob Clarke is seen in an entirely different light by the general public.

"We would all like to be tough enough to say getting criticized or booed doesn't bother you," Clarke admits. "But it definitely bothers you. Sure it bothers me. I don't want that to happen. I certainly haven't wanted to make decisions that would hurt this club, but I have. And so I will hear about them. The only thing you can do is be thick skinned enough to not let it affect your performance."

Criticism from the print media has been particularly acute at times in recent years. Clarke will not be affected by that.

"There isn't one newspaper writer who could do this job," he states. "They can criticize of course, but that's most often done in hindsight. I learned a long time ago that if you let what's written about you bother you, then you are giving the writer some ownership of you. Well, they ain't gonna own me!"

Perhaps the disgruntled fans and those critical in the media wouldn't be as harsh if they tried to understand what Bob Clarke is all about. Anyone who has coached him, played with him, or even just been close enough to observe him in action as a player or a manager over the long haul will come to understand that he is all about winning with a capital W.

"We're all here for one purpose and one purpose only," Clarke asserts. "That's to help the players in that locker room win hockey games. I never, ever wanted to part of anything that was rebuilding or going to be good in five years. That's all bull! If you're the guy sitting in that locker room, you don't want your management to think that way. You have to know that the people you are playing for want to win and win now. Not tomorrow. Organizations have been in the tank for years and years because they are always rebuilding. Around here we want to win. Ed Snider wants to win today. Keith Allen wants to win today. And I want to win today. It's never changed in that respect.

"Of course, you have to do it with a plan. But the only way I can survive in this business is if the players know I am trying to win just like they are...every day."

It has been his mission statement since the day he first hit the ice as a Flyer in 1969.

**GM Bob Clarke strikes a familiar pose these days from his booth in the Wachovia Center.**

# #17
# Simon Nolet

## Simon the Scout

There are four players whose names were on the Stanley Cup in 1974 that were gone by the time the Flyers lifted the treasured trophy in 1975. Among them was Simon Nolet, who first appeared with the Flyers in their very first year of existence, endured the building years, tasted champagne from the Cup in 1974 and then was off to the Kansas City Scouts via the expansion draft shortly thereafter.

But Nolet is remembered as a Flyer and in fact had his career go full circle when his hockey journey brought him back to the orange and black later in life. Despite enjoying just one of the Cup celebrations, Nolet is considered very much a part of the group that is still "walking together forever."

He came to the Flyers organization when the entire Quebec Aces minor league club was purchased just as the Flyers were getting their feet on the ground as an expansion team in 1967. In fact he appeared in four games with the first year Flyers after leading the American Hockey League in scoring that year.

Nolet would see his role with the big club increase during the ensuing five years. By 1971-72, he joined Bob Clarke as the only Flyers to be represented at the NHL All-Star Game. He finished that season with 23 goals and 43 points in 67 games. For some reason some remember Nolet as a spare part of those improving Flyer teams. The numbers and his teammates would seem to indicate otherwise.

In fact it is ironic that a guy whose NHL high for penalty minutes in a season was 47 is recalled for a fight as much as his all-around skill during the early years. You see during the 1970-71 season, Nolet found himself engaged in fisticuffs with one of the toughest players of that or any era, big John Ferguson.

"I used to score a lot against Montreal," recalls Nolet. "Their coach Claude Ruel must have figured if he sent Fergy after me, that will take care of that, because I was not known as a tough guy, and Fergy was certainly a lot tougher than I was.

"I was getting ticked off [from the harassment] and besides since the game was in Montreal, I had a lot of friends there so I figured I could either not say a word and keep turning the other way or I could fight. I kept telling myself that even if we fight, he's not going to kill me.

"So I decided to drop the gloves, and wouldn't you know it, I surprised him with four or five punches right off the bat. He came back and cut me with a punch at the end, but all that is remembered is that I got some punches in on big, bad John Ferguson.

"I think I earned a lot of respect that night and even I figured that if I could hold my own with Fergy, I suppose I could hold my own with anybody. Still, it was nice knowing that I had a lot of guys behind me that would have come to my aid if I got in trouble. That's what made those teams so special."

•   •   •   •   •

Nolet's fight with Ferguson was hardly the birth of the Broad Street Bullies. Still, it was an indication of the direction the team was going. Nolet knew he was part of a team that had a chance for greatness.

"Winning Game 2 in Boston (in the 1974 Finals) was the key," he says now. "We knew at that point that the Cup was ours as long as we did what we had to."

Nolet took part in the joyous celebration and parade, but at 32 years old, he had a feeling changes were on the way. The NHL was adding teams in Kansas City and Washington for the 1974-75 season, and Nolet fully realized he would be an attractive veteran pickup for an expansion club.

Sure enough, the Scouts selected Nolet on June 12, 1974. After spending seven years watching and taking part in the growth of the Flyers and experiencing the payoff with the Cup in 1974, Nolet had to say goodbye just like that.

"I sort of knew a little bit because of my age and because the Flyers had taken care of me with a four-year contract, that I might go," he says. "It was a disappointment to leave Philadelphia for sure, but I figured life has to go on. That's hockey. Better players than me had been traded before, that's for sure."

That attitude helped Nolet continue his fine play in Kansas City. He tallied a career-high 26 goals and 58 points with the Scouts in 1974-75 on his way to his second appearance at the All-Star Game. It was obvious that Nolet had been able to overcome the disappointment of leaving his buddies in Philadelphia.

Still when April rolled around, one had to wonder what went through his head as he watched those old friends march to their second Cup. Was he wistful because he couldn't be there? Or was he genuinely happy for his former teammates?

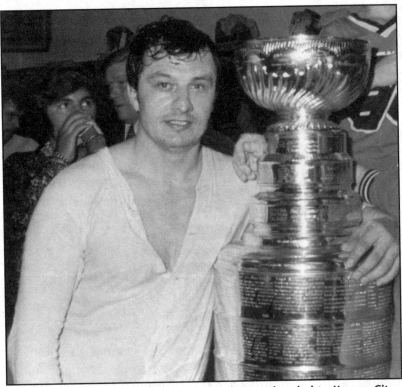

**Shortly after raising the Cup, Simon Nolet was headed to Kansas City.**

"I was cheering for them...they were my friends," he assures today. "I wish I would have been there, but that was past. I was happy for them."

•  •  •  •  •

Nolet's NHL career would last two more years as he moved on to Pittsburgh in a trade and then finished up with the Colorado Rockies (the Scouts had moved there in 1976). In his final season, he was off to a good start with 12 goals before Christmas when he suffered a knee injury that he never came back from. At 35, he knew his time as a player was up.

"It was time for me to retire," Nolet recollects. "I had a good opportunity to work as a sales representative for Labatt's Brewery up in Quebec, which I had done during the summers. I had really enjoyed it as a summer job, but when I began to do it full time, it was tough. There were some long nights and a lot of drinking. It was too much for me."

Eventually, as would seem to be the case with so many of the former Flyers, it was the lure of hockey that pulled him back. Nolet's ticket back into the sport came through the world of scouting.

**In Kansas City, he became Captain Nolet.** *Photo courtesy of Kansas City Scouts/New Jersey Devils*

"I got a chance to go work part time with Central Scouting in 1979," Nolet remembers. "Jim Gregory was running it, and a friend of mine, Martin Madden helped get me a spot. I watched five teams in Quebec that season and enjoyed it."

That was the beginning of over two decades (and running) of off-ice involvement in hockey for Nolet. The next year Madden signed on with the Quebec Nordiques and asked Nolet to join him with the second-year NHL franchise as a scout. Nolet agreed and began a ten-year run in that organization, but not always as a scout.

Nolet found himself chatting with Nordiques head coach Michel Bergeron often about the team. Bergeron took note and in 1982, asked Nolet to be his assistant. Nolet the scout became Nolet the coach. For five years he stayed behind the bench. He once again found himself part of a developing team. The Nordiques, led by the likes of Peter Stastny and Michel Goulet would climb from 80 points and fourth in the Adams Division in 1982-83 to 92 points and first in the division in 1985-86.

Nolet might have been tempted to compare those Nordiques teams to the ones he had been on in Philadelphia because of their regular-season improvement. However, Quebec could never get it going in the postseason. Ironically, their longest playoff run ended at the hands of the Flyers in the Eastern Conference Finals in 1985.

At one point, Nolet found himself in a position he never had anticipated, as an NHL head coach. Bergeron had a heart problem that forced him from the bench. In stepped Nolet, with absolutely no head coaching experience.

"I found it wasn't really for me," Nolet says in retrospect. "I don't really know why, but it wasn't for me."

His head coaching experience lasted all of a month and a half. He was soon headed back to a position he did like, one in the scouting department. Nolet became a pro scout with the Nordiques and was back to doing something he loved.

Three years later, though, the winds of change were blowing again. This time those winds would blow Nolet back to where his career began, back to Philadelphia.

"Pierre Page took over in Quebec [as general manager] in 1990 and while I suppose I was all set, there were changes being made," Nolet recalls. "I was already talking to Clarkie about coming back here [to Philadelphia], anyway. So, I figured it was time to make a move."

What better place to go than back to where he had constructed his best hockey moments. After 16 years that took him from Kansas City to Pittsburgh to Denver and then Quebec, Nolet was finally back where he felt he belonged, with one hitch.

"Two weeks after Clarkie hired me in 1990, he got fired!" Nolet remembers. "Fortunately, he assured me that the Flyers still wanted me and that I had a job."

It's a good thing. Nolet has been a part of the Flyers' scouting department ever since. He has helped the organization find such players as Simon Gagne and Justin Williams. Scouting has become his passion.

"I like everything about it," he beams. "I like being around the games, the whole atmosphere. I like the travel. It's quiet in a way. You go to the game, do your thing and that's it.

"Of course, like anything else, you need to do a good job. If you draft well, everything is fine, but if not, you do hear about it," he laughs. "But here in Philly, we have a great group of guys [in the scouting department] and there has not been a lot of change over the years. That makes it fun, too."

There is a perception in all sports that good scouts can spot talent when many people don't see it. There is this thought that they are almost mystical in that regard. Nolet thinks that is overstating the situation just a bit.

"There's no mystery at all," he confesses. "If you are around the game enough, it doesn't take an expert to determine if a guy can play well or skate well. It's just a matter of following standards when you watch a guy."

• • • • •

In any event, you can bet that Nolet is happy his scouting is being done for the Flyers. After all these years, he still considers himself a Flyer at heart.

"I suppose any time you win the Stanley Cup with another group of guys, there will be a bond," he says as if the three decades since the championship had not even occurred. "But the friendship with our group was special. The boys would like to have a beer now and then, but we would always go as a group. Everybody joking around with everybody, just great camaraderie.

"When Freddy wrote the 'walking together forever' line on the blackboard, some of us laughed, but you know, whenever I come to Philadelphia [usually for training camp as part of his scouting duties] and I see Dorny or any of the other guys, it's like seeing a brother, it really is. We all got along so well. It's amazing!"

**Back with the Flyers as a scout, Simon Nolet feels at home.**

# #18
# Ross Lonsberry

## *Mr. Dependable*

Trustworthy. Dependable. Reliable. Consistent.

Ask members of the Flyers' Cup teams about Ross Lonsberry and one of those four words inevitably comes up. He was a swift and sturdy winger for the all-important second line of the championship squads. As the years go by it seems his defensive accomplishments grow in stature almost at the expense of his offensive contributions.

Let the record show that Lonsberry scored 56 goals during the two title years. In fact, in 1973-74, his 32 goals trailed only Bobby Clarke and Bill Barber for the Flyers. It is clear Lonsberry was much more than a defensive specialist, but because of his prowess in killing penalties and his attention to detail in his team's zone, he is remembered more for his responsibility than other areas of his game.

"I always felt that I was a player who could be trusted," Lonsberry reflects. "I learned that very early in my career. Even though I had been a big scorer in junior hockey [he scored 67 goals in one junior season], it was always stressed to me to play both ends of the ice. When I came to the Flyers and Fred Shero's system, it felt like a perfect fit because I wouldn't take real reckless chances on offense.

"My whole goal was not to get our line trapped. I just felt I was the kind of guy you could trust to put on the ice in any situation, and I would play within the confines of the system. Billy Barber, Clarkie, and Reggie [Leach] could take chances. I felt I had to be the steadying influence on my line."

His line for the bulk of five seasons included Gary Dornhoefer and Rick MacLeish. They played in the shadow of the famed "LCB Line." However, their importance to the Flyers' cause was immeasurable. Dornhoefer always appreciated Lonsberry's reliability.

"Ross was very dependable," Dornhoefer states. "You always knew where he would be situated on the ice. He was very reliable defensively. He was, in short, a great guy to play with."

Just call him Mr. Dependable!

• • • • •

It's almost amazing that Lonsberry became such a vital cog in the Flyers' wheel when one looks at his initial days in the organization. How he lasted very long in the orange and black is something of a minor miracle.

Lonsberry was acquired in a huge seven-player trade with Bill Flett, Eddie Joyal, and Jean Potvin from the Los Angeles Kings in exchange for Bill Lesuk, Jim Johnson, and Serge Bernier in January of 1972. Lonsberry had been with the Kings for three seasons after beginning his NHL career with the Bruins. He had enjoyed life on the West Coast and even met his future wife in Los Angeles. His career had begun to take off with the Kings as evidenced by his selection to the NHL All-Star team just weeks before the trade.

However, the Flyers had demanded that the Kings include Lonsberry as part of the package, and so he was on his way to the Delaware Valley. He was less than thrilled.

"You have to remember it was the middle of winter," Lonsberry reflects. "I was going from sunny southern California to the cold northeast. The first thing you saw when you went over the bridge coming from the airport was a junkyard (the same one that had caught Joe Watson's attention some five years earlier). Plus there was the separation from my wife. It all added up to a degree of disappointment."

Perhaps such disappointment drives people to say things that they normally would not. Lonsberry remembers an incident shortly after his arrival that could have made his stay in Philadelphia a short one.

"We were at a fan club dinner and members of management attended as well," he recalls. "I approached Mr. Snider and relayed my disappointment about the trade. I told him that I thought I had left a better team in Los Angeles than I was playing with now!"

You have to understand this was the team owner that Lonsberry was talking to. Ed Snider was the man who had brought hockey to Philadelphia and had seen his team take some baby steps to that point toward respectability. For a newcomer such as Lonsberry to make such a statement had to be shocking.

"My wife said to me later that I was very lucky to still be with the Flyers," Lonsberry laughs now. "Mr. Snider thankfully was very calm and explained to me that there was a plan in place and things were on their way to getting better."

Obviously, things did get a lot better in the ensuing years. Lonsberry can thank Ed Snider for not reacting with fury to his frank assessment of the club on that night. As a result of that and Lonsberry eventually adjusting to life in

Philadelphia, he was able to enjoy and contribute to the two titles and all of the glory that accompanied them.

•   •   •   •   •

Take a look at any footage from the Flyers back in the mid-1970s and you will notice Lonsberry as one of the few members of the team wearing a helmet. It would be a nice story if he were some type of hockey pioneer, who was ahead of his time in seeing the danger of playing such a violent game without head protection. A nice story, but not the truth.

In reality, Lonsberry's helmet had more to do with appearance than it did safety. It all stemmed back to his days in Los Angeles.

"I was prematurely bald and had taken a terrible ribbing from players back in my minor league days," Lonsberry admits now. "So I figured I would wear a helmet. I wore it in some of the buildings where the fans were close to the ice. So when I went to camp with the Kings, I wasn't sure whether or not to put it back on. I was actually leaning against it when the general manager Larry Regan approached me and suggested I wear the helmet. I thought that was a little strange and then he told me that the team owner Jack Kent Cooke was going to be at practice and it was a good idea to wear the helmet."

Come to find out, Cooke had a certain image he wanted his players to uphold. One aspect of that image apparently was for lots of hair like Bill Flett and Eddie Joyal had. Poor Lonsberry was lacking in that area. So, he wore the helmet for that practice and then for the subsequent exhibition games.

"In one exhibition game, I scored a couple of goals and played real well," Lonsberry remembers. "After the game Mr. Cooke came down to the locker room and of course, I didn't have my helmet on anymore. When he came up to congratulate me on my performance in the game, I got the feeling he took one look at me and my head and was wondering if he wanted me representing his team at all!"

Given how this all transpired, it isn't surprising Lonsberry was a little preoccupied with his follicle challenges.

"The truth of the matter is that the real reason I wore a helmet wasn't that I was any smarter than anybody else," Lonsberry says now. "I was just vain and kept the helmet on my balding head!"

•   •   •   •   •

Thus, with his helmet in tow, Lonsberry spent parts of seven seasons as a Flyer. He simply went about his business quietly and efficiently, appearing in at least 75 games in each of his full seasons in Philadelphia. He reached at least 20 goals four times and continued to be a dependable player on some very good teams.

However, Lonsberry was also a guy who watched moves by management very closely and he could see changes were being made in the years after the Cups. Slowly but surely the members of the title clubs were leaving.

Ross Lonsberry dons his famous lid.

"It was obvious it was only a matter of time," he reflects. "We were breaking down. Wee, little things started to become larger breakdowns in following Freddy's system. Once Freddy left all bets were off."

On June 14, 1978, Keith Allen called Lonsberry with the news that he had been dealt along with Orest Kindrachuk and Tom Bladon, to Pittsburgh in exchange for the Penguins' first-round draft choice that year, which turned out to be Behn Wilson. As was the case with his reaction to his trade to Philadelphia, Lonsberry was less than enthused.

"Pittsburgh was a wonderful town, but from management on down, we had issues," he points out now. "There were ownership issues with rumors of moving the team to Dallas. Johnny Wilson was our coach and his approach was sort of old school and we didn't really have a strong system. I was disappointed because I had come from a team so dedicated to winning with the commitment of ownership and good people like Keith Allen. It was different in Pittsburgh."

Lonsberry remembers one particular incident that summed up the obvious philosophical differences between the two organizations.

"Our first year there we made the playoffs," he remembers. "The next summer they decided to trade our goaltender Denis Herron, who had played well for us, to Montreal for Pat Hughes and a backup goalie [Rob Holland]. I was at a golf tournament and the general manager Paul Martha was there and I asked him why he dealt our best goalie away. He told me that Montreal needed a goaltender. I responded by saying, 'And we don't?' It just didn't make sense to me."

Lonsberry spent three seasons in Pittsburgh. On a line with Kindrachuk and Rick Kehoe, he performed well and his numbers were pretty much the same as they had been in Philadelphia. What was lacking, of course, was the team success. It made for frustration for the ex-Flyers.

**Ross Lonsberry finished his NHL career with three seasons in Pittsburgh.** *Photo courtesy of the Pittsburgh Penguins*

• • • • •

So many of the Flyers were forced from the game of hockey by injury. You think of Bernie Parent's eye ailment, Bill Barber's knee, Gary Dornhoefer's various bumps and bruises, and Joe Watson's broken leg. In the case of Ross Lonsberry, health was not a factor.

Lonsberry was seriously hurt only once in his entire career, an eye injury as a Flyer which he made a full recovery from. During the 1980-81 season in Pittsburgh, he appeared in all 80 games. Despite being 34 years old, he never felt better. His contract had run out so it was time to approach the Penguins about a new deal.

"I went to Baz Bastien's [the Pittsburgh general manager] office and said I wanted to get things rolling on a new contract," he recalls. "Baz looked at me and told me they weren't going to offer me a new deal. He said they were going to look toward youth. I was in shock. It was like being in a street fight and having someone kick you in the gut and not being able to breathe."

Lonsberry was obviously unprepared for this news. He had not thought too much about his life after his playing career. He asked the Penguins if he could go down to the minors as a player-coach but was refused. He simply did not know what he was going to do. After nearly one thousand games as a dependable NHL performer, there no longer appeared to be a place for him in the game.

"I felt I had at least a couple of more years of hockey in me," he says now. "I had always foreseen my career winding down as a part-time player, playing 40 games or so and spending the rest of the time in the press box. That's when I figured I could make inroads to management for a job after my playing career, whether it be as a scout, coach or what have you. It just never materialized that way."

Lonsberry, through the advice of a family friend, looked into the life insurance business. Given that his wife, Wahnita, was from Los Angeles and could regain her job out there, and an opening with an insurance firm also existed there, the obvious move was back to the west, where Lonsberry has remained ever since. Not without regrets, however.

"I regret that I did not finish my career on my terms," he laments now. "I should have gotten my resume out there after the Penguins didn't re-sign me. At the time, though, I thought my kids were still young and I could actually spend more time with them and live a normal life. I thought it was time to make the split from the game. About ten years later, I started to wonder whether I had made that split too early. Had I panicked? Should I have contacted various teams back in 1981? By then, it was too late. Once you have been out of the game for ten years, it's gone."

• • • • •

Instead, Lonsberry has carved his own niche selling insurance in California. Overcoming the earthquakes, the wild fires and the carefree lifestyle, he has done well for himself and his family. He began in life insurance, moved to disability, and then finally progressed to property and casualty insurance along with workmen's compensation. He has moved through a couple of different companies before settling in for the last decade or so with one.

"I enjoy it," he says. "There are trying times like the last few years because of a lot of workmen's compensation issues. But I still enjoy it as a whole. You meet so many different people in so many different lines of work. It doesn't get boring because every place of business you go to is so different and their needs are so varied."

**Ross Lonsberry settled in sunny southern California and works in the insurance business.**

The guess is that most, if not all, of Lonsberry's clients find him to be a dependable, reliable, and trustworthy insurance agent.

•　•　•　•　•

Lonsberry hasn't lived in Philadelphia for just about a quarter century. Yet he says the bond that exists among members of the Flyers' championship teams is still very strong. He realized just how strong when he visited the Philadelphia for a roast of Bob Clarke in September 2002.

"We've all aged," he admits. "But we all want to go back to the times when we were most successful. We sat at the bar at Clarkie's roast until about 4 a.m. telling stories about our playing days. We've all gone our own way in life, and yet when we get together, it's so easy to feel like teammates again. The only thing that really seems to have changed is that we are all a little older."

*(Editor's Note: As this book was going to print, we learned Ross is battling a serious illness. Our thoughts and prayers are with Ross and his family.)*

# #19
# Rick MacLeish

## *Never Taking Life Too Seriously*

It is so easy in the world of sports to fall into the trap of considering those athletes with immense talent as nonchalant. For instance, think back to Mario Lemieux's early days in the NHL when scouts, coaches, writers, and broadcasters all used terms like "lazy" and "dispassionate" to describe his play. Of course, Lemieux went on to prove many of these detractors wrong by constructing a legendary career that included courageous comebacks from disease and back problems. I often think the Flyers' Rick MacLeish was in a similar situation. The man Keith Allen termed the "most talented player on our club" seemed to frequently be the subject of discussion about indifferent play. Even his own teammates felt they needed to give MacLeish a push from time to time.

Yet a look at his career in Philadelphia indicates MacLeish was an integral part of any success those great teams had. The numbers say he was perhaps the top clutch performer of the entire bunch. He led the Flyers with 13 goals in 17 playoff games in 1974 and again with 11 in 17 postseason contests in 1975. He scored the most significant goal in the Stanley Cup clincher against Boston. He got the game-winner against the Russians in 1976.

"He was the best player we had in every one of our playoff series," offers his former line mate Ross Lonsberry. "Part of that may have been because so much attention was paid to the Clarke line. However, Ricky was bigger and faster, and he scored so many big goals for us in the playoffs. He was so important to our success."

This hardly sounds like a lazy player. Actually, Rick MacLeish has always been a person who doesn't seem to take himself or life too seriously. Keith Allen used to laugh when MacLeish would ask him who the Flyers were playing that night. Bobby Clarke, Gary Dornhoefer, and others had to occasionally prod him into picking up the pace.

But the bottom line is that when the team needed him most, he delivered handsomely.

"I admit that at times during the regular season, I needed to get pushed once in a while," MacLeish reveals now. "Clarkie and my linemates certainly did. There would be times when I might be drifting back defensively and one of the guys would literally slap me on the butt with their stick. It hurt in some of those cold buildings.

"However, I think sometimes it was my skating that made it look like I wasn't pushing that hard. I had sort of an effortless stride. But when they tried to put somebody on me to catch me that was a little different. And I certainly never needed a push come playoff time. I was plenty hyped up then."

MacLeish's graceful skating motion actually symbolized the way he approached life. He simply cruised along, enjoying the ride. On one occasion in Boston, it almost cost him.

"I was out after curfew during the 1972-73 season," he recalls. "There were about seven of us in a club having a good time. It was about 11 o'clock and I got up to go to the bathroom. When I came back, there was nothing but seven empty glasses at the table. I look across the bar and there's Freddy! I got called in the next morning and assistant coach Mike Nykoluk told me that if I hadn't been having such a great year (he would go on to score a career-high 50 goals that season), I would have been on a plane headed to the minors. So, thank God I was hitting the net at the time!"

That would seem to sum up Rick MacLeish in a nutshell. He was casual in his approach, perhaps, but when he and his team needed him the most he produced.

● ● ● ● ●

Never did MacLeish come up larger than on that famous Saturday afternoon in May of 1974. In Game 6 of the Stanley Cup Finals, with the Flyers and Bruins locked in a spirited scoreless deadlock, MacLeish became the owner of the single most important goal in Flyers history.

"It was a simple play, really," he recollects. "I won the draw and went to the net. Moose took a regular wrist shot and I tried to tip it down just to change it up a bit, and wouldn't you know it went in. It's something we practiced hundreds of times. In truth, it was a lucky goal.

"What I remember most about it was that I never in a million years thought one goal would stand up as the game-winner. Not against the Boston Bruins. But Bernie was great and the defense really played well and that was it. There's no way I thought I was going to be part of history when that puck went in. It's funny how it works out. You just never know!"

"The goal."

•  •  •  •  •

When you survey the landscape of MacLeish's career, you wonder just how "lucky" it really was. He scored so many big goals. Seven times as a Flyer he surpassed the 30-goal mark in a season. In all, he would amass 328 regular-season goals in the orange and black. Add another 53 playoff markers, and you get the idea the man knew how to find the net.

A knee injury kept him out of the 1976 playoffs. I'm sure more than one Flyers fan has wondered if MacLeish had been there, perhaps one of his patented clutch goals here or there would have meant a different outcome against the Canadiens. We'll never know.

What we do know is that MacLeish put together one of the most productive careers in Flyers history. He was there for so much of their success in the 1970s and into the 1980s. But in the summer of 1981 MacLeish was a 31-year-old winger and the Flyers were looking to get younger. He was traded to Hartford in a deal that involved five players and five draft picks. Since he had spent 11 years as a Flyer, one might think the trade would have shocked MacLeish. Not quite.

"There had been rumors for several years about a trade involving me," he explains. "I was pretty much prepared for it. Keith called to apologize, but I wasn't startled at all."

That was obvious. In keeping with his mantra of not taking things too seriously, his reaction to the trade was to throw a party for his teammates at his home down on the Jersey shore.

"I invited everybody down," he laughs. "Clarkie came. Everybody came. It was a good time!"

What was not such a good time was his stay in Hartford in what he termed "a nothing organization." In fact, three weeks after having built a huge house in the area, he was on the move again, this time to Pittsburgh. In retrospect, the trade out of Philadelphia was the beginning of a journeyman-type existence for MacLeish.

He went from Hartford to Pittsburgh and then to Europe for a while before returning to Philadelphia for a 40-game tryout in 1983. A broken ankle knocked him out of action, and after 29 games and eight more goals and 22 points, he was told he was going to be released. The Red Wings were willing to let him finish the season in Detroit, and that's exactly what he did.

**Rick MacLeish skates in his second tour of duty in Philadelphia.**

By then though, the 34-year-old veteran was feeling the effects of his lengthy career. He had undergone five different knee surgeries and was having both of knees drained just about every other game. He realized the time had come to hang up the skates. "They were giving me shots of cortisone," he recalls. "I would wake up the next morning and wonder why in the world I was doing this."

To this day, MacLeish's knees give him problems. He says his medical cabinet at home is full of painkillers that he takes to get by. In his mid-50s, his doctors have told him he has the knees of a 75-year-old. But don't look for any remorse from him.

"I wish there was the technology then that there is now," he admits. "But I don't regret playing hockey all those years at all. I would absolutely do it all over again."

·   ·   ·   ·   ·

MacLeish found a business that suited him perfectly after his playing days concluded. Actually, he began working in the insurance business during his final season as a player.

"A friend of mine was working with Equitable so I took all of my tests when I got back from Europe," he recalls. "I decided to take the Flyers up on the tryout and played that last season, before actually getting into the insurance end.

"You can tell early on whether or not you will have success at it. By my third year, I could see it was going well. With my name, the companies used me to get in doors they might not have been able to get in. Everything worked out."

What has appealed to MacLeish about the insurance business that he has been a part of now for nearly two decades is the pace.

"It's not a hard job," he relates. "You have to know your products, but most of it is just striking up conversations with people and finding out what they might need. I'm more or less conservative. If we can beat what you got, then maybe there will be interest. I keep my own hours. I can work at my own pace. I like that."

He doesn't need a Clarke or a Dornhoefer to give him a push anymore. He works out of Lynwood, New Jersey, with a group of three other agents. He likes the fact that he can work a little harder in the winter to get time off in the summer.

As successful as he has been in insurance, he does still have a tinge of regret that he never revisited hockey after his playing career ended. "I was offered a radio position with the Flyers when I was let go as a player," he reflects. "I think now I probably should have spoken up and told them about my interest in getting in on the hockey end of things. I see coaches now like Craig Ramsay and John Paddock, and scouts like Al Hill and Ron Hextall, and I think I would have loved to have given it a shot. But I never wanted to move my family and that usually was part of it."

In the end, MacLeish found a situation that seems to suit his approach to life.

"What I do now is pretty easy," he admits. "I don't have to bust my behind all that much. It's my pace."

•   •   •   •   •

Throughout his life, Rick MacLeish has had a passion for horses. He grew up on a horse farm in Ontario, Canada, so it is basically in his blood. He began purchasing horses back in the 1970s and has had them off and on ever since.

"I bought a standard-bred horse named Doc Lindsey back when I turned pro as a player and he did pretty well for us," he recalls. "He made about $20,000, which wasn't bad for back then."

MacLeish quickly learned that the horse business could be profitable, while at the same time providing a certain degree of solitude.

"When you are with the horses, you are able to get away," he explains. "I enjoy it. It keeps me sane. Nobody can bother you. The other day I was out with the horses and six or seven deer came down and it was great."

Through the years, there are certain horses that MacLeish especially remembers.

**These days, Rick MacLeish is able to spend time with one of his passions—horses.**

He once bought a colt at a sale at Garden State Parkway for $9,000 that eventually made close to $100,000. What's surprising is that the horse was named "Damaged Goods," hardly a moniker that would inspire confidence.

"When I got him, he was this big black horse with a white mange on his shoulder," he remembers. "As it turned out, it was only dry skin. All we did was put some baby oil on it and it went away. People had thought he was damaged goods just because of some dry skin."

He went on to win races at Saratoga and Vernon Downs in the state of New York. Yes, MacLeish found out how the horse business can pay off. So much so that he does not have a problem with getting attached to the horses before selling them.

"Not with that kind of money coming in," he laughs.

• • • • •

The fact that MacLeish is still around and able to enjoy the horses or his insurance business is somewhat of a miracle. Befitting a man who has never taken life too seriously, he has had more than one flirtation with its conclusion.

In May 1977, MacLeish and Flyers defenseman Bob Dailey were on their way to dinner after a golf tournament in Burlington County, New Jersey. The highway was wet and the van they were riding in began to hydroplane before rolling over three times and landing on its roof. Neither MacLeish nor Dailey were wearing their seatbelts and both were thrown into the back of the van. Dailey fell on top of MacLeish.

"I got out of the van and went over to the guard rail and sat down," he recalls. "I had a headache, but felt all right, considering. The police finally arrived and after asking us some questions, they told us we had to go to the hospital. When I went to get up, I couldn't move."

MacLeish was taken to the hospital where it was determined he had broken the 13th vertebrae in his neck. While waiting to find out the prognosis, he had the misfortune of inadvertently letting Flyers team management know how banged up he was.

"Keith Allen and Ed Snider came to visit me just after they had given me a shot of dye to look inside of me," he recollects. "I warned the guys I wasn't feeling all that well. I'm lying there and they are standing beside me and I threw up all over both Keith's and Mr. Snider's shoes!"

MacLeish wound up in a body cast for three months. The doctors usually put a person in a cast that you can take off at night. However, they had an inkling MacLeish wouldn't keep the cast on even during the day, so they put him in a cast he could not get out of at any time. It made for a long three months. To get an idea of the depth of interest fans had in those Flyers, one fan bid $175 dollars at the Flyers' Wives Carnival for MacLeish's body cast after it was removed that fall!

Still, MacLeish realizes just how close the whole experience had taken him to his end.

"If we had been wearing our seat belts, neither of us would be here today," he claims. "The front of that van was completely smashed. What saved us was getting thrown into the back of it."

A twist of fate may have saved MacLeish again less than a year later. In the second period of a game in Los Angeles on April 1, 1978, MacLeish dove to try to knock the puck away from Marcel Dionne. He felt Dionne's skate boot bump into his neck but wasn't too concerned. He went back to the bench and sat down. He looked down and saw a pool of blood beneath him. He reached up and put his finger on where he thought the cut might be and the blood literally spouted out.

Every towel available was used as MacLeish was rushed back to the locker room. A Kings trainer recommended clamping the cut and then getting MacLeish to the hospital, which was 45 minutes away. Flyers doctor Everett Borghesani just happened to be on this trip and when he got to the room, he said the cut had to be stitched immediately.

"The Doc was only on the trip because he had some friends out in the LA area," MacLeish relates now. "If he was not there, and they had tried to clamp it and take me to the hospital 45 minutes away, I'm not sure I would have made it. There was a lot of blood. Getting it closed right away may have saved me. At the time, though, I didn't realize how serious it was until I took a drag of a cigarette and the smoke came out my neck!"

Humor in the face of near tragedy. It seems to be another MacLeish staple. There was another occasion when he was on a bridge going over 100 miles an hour in his red corvette and lost traction and spun out. If the car had touched the bridge, it would have most certainly exploded. It never touched a thing and just settled on the side of the road on the other side of the bridge.

"They say you have nine lives," he points out. "But I have been very lucky."

• • • • •

Rick MacLeish glided through much of his life just as he did on the ice surface back in his days as a player. There were bumps for sure, but he never let anything really bother him. Just as some perceived that as indifference in his playing performance, others have probably taken his overall approach to life as carefree, if not apathetic.

However, that approach was finally altered as he hit his 50s. He was playing in an alumni hockey game when he began to experience some back pain. It wasn't a sharp pain, more of an ache. However, he noticed as the game went along, the pain was spreading to his chest. "After the game, I went to one of the guys who I knew had previously had a heart attack, and asked him what it felt like," he recalls. "He explained some of the same types of pain I was having and then he put his finger on my neck and told me I might have been having one right then because my blood pressure seemed very high."

Without hesitating, some of the other players gave MacLeish a ride to the emergency room of a local hospital. It was full, so MacLeish decided they should just go to another one. About five minutes into the ride, the pain became very intense and MacLeish advised his friends that they better go back.

"At that point, I was rushed in," he remembers. "They told me I had been having a heart attack for the last two hours. They put a catheter in me and showed me on the screen where the blockage was. They knew right then they had to open me up."

MacLeish had his surgery on a Monday and was out of the hospital on Friday. But while his immediate recovery was relatively quick, his lifestyle would have to change forever.

"I've had a hard life in a way," he explains. "Through all of my surgeries involving my knees and the various accidents I've had, nothing really fazed me. But the heart attack woke me up. I think about Rick Lapointe [a former Flyers teammate] and how he dropped dead at 41.

"It's tough. I used to smoke a lot. I haven't had a single cigarette since the night of my heart attack. When I go to a place now where others are smoking, I feel like I've had a pack just from the second-hand smoke and I hate it. My diet is much better. I exercise more. I feel better now than I did before the operation, that is for sure."

Perhaps just as some of his teammates had given him a nudge back in his playing days, this was the guy upstairs giving MacLeish one last push to help him get his act together. If so, it seems to have worked.

•　•　•　•　•

Today Rick MacLeish is a different guy from the one who won the two Cups. Not only has he had to face mortality in the form of a heart attack, but he was also diagnosed with diabetes recently as well. His marriage ended back in the late 1990s. He remarried in 2000. He is now a grandfather, which puts everything into perspective.

"I go by his daycare facility about twice a week now," he explains. "It's nice to see the little one. It's almost like having another life. A lot of things have changed."

What hasn't changed is MacLeish's relationship with his former teammates. "When I had my heart attack, they were there for me," he relates. "A lot of guys came to see me. Others called. It was great. Everybody seems to pick each other up. I remember after Jenny Barber passed way, a bunch of us were down in Billy's basement actually trying to rejoice as a way of helping him. We are there for one another.

"On top of that, the bond with the fans will always be there. Twenty years from now I might be in a wheelchair, but these fans will recognize me. They remember what we did in this town when the sports teams were struggling. A bunch of guys from Canada got the championship roll going back in 1974. They will never forget that."

In the long run, Rick MacLeish was smooth, but hardly apathetic.

# #20
# Jimmy Watson

## *The Younger Watson*

When the subject of the best defensemen in Philadelphia Flyers history comes up, the names that are most often mentioned are those of the mercurial Mark Howe, the steady Eric Desjardins, and even the durable Joe Watson. For whatever, reason, not that many people consider Joe's younger brother, Jimmy, for that list.

The facts and those who performed with Jim Watson offer evidence that would indicate he should be. In nine seasons with the Flyers, the younger of the gregarious Watson brothers played in the NHL All-Star Game five times. He was selected to play for Team Canada in the 1976 Canada Cup where his teammates on defense included Bobby Orr, Denis Potvin, Larry Robinson, and Guy Lapointe. He appeared in more than 600 games for Philadelphia, bringing his smooth skating and reliable approach to the ice every night.

"Both of the Watsons were great competitors," explains their former general manager Keith Allen. "Jimmy though was the better skater. Hell, he went to play for Team Canada with the best of the best and he didn't look the least bit out of place."

In 1980, as a key member of a relatively inexperienced defense corps, he posted an incredible +53 to lead the NHL. Then again that was nothing compared to 1975-76 when he was +65. He never had a minus year in his career and finished +295. You have to be doing something right to be on ice for 295 more goals by your team in non-power play situations than those by the opposition.

So, the scenario begs the question, "Did Jimmy Watson feel underrated by hockey observers or underappreciated by the fans?"

"Actually I never really felt I was that good," admits the seemingly always frank Watson. "I mean I did all right, but I was always honored to be on a team with guys like Moose Dupont, Ed Van Impe, Tom Bladon, and my brother. In fact, I thought I got quite a bit of credit for our pair, when Moose was really the very good player.

"Also, if I ever did have any negative feelings once my career was done, I never had time to think about it because I got so involved with raising my family and helping my sons get on with their hockey careers. I would never say I had any bitterness."

Still, the numbers and evidence would suggest that the next time a discussion of the Flyers' best defensemen takes place, the name of Jimmy Watson should come up, whether he's worried about it or not.

•  •  •  •  •

Nine years separate the two Watson brothers. Thus, they didn't play a lot of hockey together in their native Smithers, British Columbia. Joe was already on his way to the NHL by the time Jimmy was able to lace 'em up and play competitively.

"I was only seven years old when Joe left home for good," Jimmy recalls. "I followed his career through newspaper articles and the radio and such. I even got to visit him once here in Philadelphia while I was playing [in the] juniors. It was then that I saw how great life at the NHL level was."

Still, before the two could realize their childhood dream of playing with each other in the NHL, there would have to be some last-minute maneuvering by the senior Watson. After being drafted by the Flyers, Jimmy actually entertained offers from the World Hockey Association to play in Calgary, where he had played his junior hockey.

"When I sat back and thought about it, though, I knew the decision I had to make," he admits now. "The fact that Joe was in Philadelphia and it was the NHL, which I had always dreamed of playing in, eventually I knew I had to pick Philly."

Thus his older brother negotiated his infamous contract, and the two Watsons were not only both in the NHL, but on the same team.

"It was a thrill and a half," he still beams to this day. "I mean I think I would have been all right even without my brother, but to be able to re-bond with him and get his advice, go to his place for dinner every once in a while, it was good for me, no question."

To add to the luster of their dream fulfillment, the two would celebrate back-to-back Stanley Cups in Jimmy's first two full seasons with the Flyers. Now that's maximizing a childhood dream!

•  •  •  •  •

Oh to be Jimmy Watson when he first entered the NHL. First, two Cups in his first two years. Then the following season he got to take part in what many people called Stanley Cup II and a half. The game against the touring

Russian Central Red Army team in January of 1976 represented a particular thrill for the younger Watson.

"I didn't sleep for two nights before that game," Jimmy recalls. "We were hated throughout the NHL for what they called our roughhouse tactics. Yet the other teams that had played this Russian team hadn't won, so here we were, suddenly the league's last hope.

"I'll never forget what happened just before the game. Scotty Morrison [at the time, the NHL's referee-in-chief] came into our locker room and told us, 'We're going to let you guys play!' We couldn't believe it! Some of our guys were licking their chops."

It's interesting how those roughhouse tactics seem to be okay when they were part of an international hockey war.

Anyway, the Flyers won handily as any hockey fan now knows. Watson revels in the event that it became.

"There was a banquet the day before the game that I will always remember," he recollects. "The Russian team was sitting at a table right next to ours. I'm telling you, there were some daggers being stared across the way that day. It was the free world versus the Communist bloc. It was NHL hockey versus European hockey. That was all a part of it, and it really built a lot of pressure. When we won the Spectrum went bonkers!"

You feel compelled to ask Jimmy the all-important question. "Did the win over the Russians match the feelings of winning the Cups?"

"Absolutely!" he responds without hesitating an instant.

• • • • •

By 1979, Watson was one of the veteran leaders of the Flyers' defense corps. He was in his seventh season on the back line, then 27 years old. His brother was now an advanced scout with the team so Jimmy had long since been establishing his own niche in the NHL. Still, even though he had seen so much already in his career, he did not foresee the remarkable season in store for that year's group of Flyers.

"I had no idea we had it in us," he says now. "In fact, we started a little slowly and got smoked in our first road game [by Atlanta 9-2]. I think that loss made us come together. It got us focused and made us realize we had some work to do. It flat out woke us up!

"Then we slowly and progressively started playing well together. Every game was almost methodical. It's amazing because we weren't necessarily the most talented group, but one thing led to another, and all of a sudden we had this streak going."

Watson helped anchor the defense corps made famous by the Killer Bs—Norm Barnes, Frank Bathe, and Mike Busniuk. None of this trio was playing in the NHL even three years later. But during that magical run in 1979-80, they played extremely well. Watson's leadership was a big part of it, as evidenced by his impressive plus/minus total.

"Our confidence just grew," he assesses now. "When we would play a home game, even if the score was tight, we just knew we were going to win. Our goaltending was strong with Pete Peeters and Phil Myre. Our guys knew their roles. It just all came together."

To the tune of 25-0-10 over a three-month stretch. Of course, any mention of that season is required to include a reference to how it ended. Thoughts of the 1980 Stanley Cup Finals still bring frustration to Watson.

"I think the Islanders had two more power plays per game than we did," he fumes. "Granted, we deserved most of them, but they deserved far more than they got, no question. As the series went along, we were getting better. We won Game 5 big [6-3] and felt good about our chances of forcing a Game 7 back in Philly where we weren't going to lose. And we played very well in Game 6. I mean very well. Then the two calls on Islander goals went against us. Leon Stickle flat out blew the offside call. It was too much to overcome."

The Islanders won the Cup with their 5-4 overtime victory that day. Now, you might think having already been part of two Cup winners that Watson wouldn't have necessarily been crushed by this disappointment. If so, you would have been dead wrong.

"It absolutely still sticks in my craw," he explains. "I was battling a shoulder injury during that series. I had been shot up with cortisone and novicaine for Game 6 and finally couldn't keep playing in the third period, leaving us with four or five defensemen. It was just a terrible way to have it end. When I lost at the end of the season, I would go into a funk for two or three weeks. I mean I was out of commission for a while. As competitive as I was, it was hard to accept the season ending. That year, with the way it ended and the shoulder problem too, I was miserable, just miserable."

As he speaks, you almost get the feeling his recollections of the events of May 24, 1980 still put him in a miserable mood over 20 years later.

· · · · ·

All things considered, though, one would think Watson still had a lot to look forward to in his hockey career after the 1980 disappointment. After all, he was only 28 years old as training camp dawned in September. Certainly, he had to be thinking he had several years as a player remaining to add to his already impressive NHL resume.

Unfortunately, he was cheated of most of those years by a painful back injury that had been bothering him for quite some time. In fact, he first injured his back when he was 18 years old working for a British Columbia water company. He tried to lift a heavy water pipe and strained his back. He got it adjusted to relieve the pain and discomfort, but his back was never the same.

"Later on doctors told me that the trauma from that injury was the beginning of chronic problems for my back," he relates. "It was a slow deterioration of the discs, a slow erosion. There was pain and I played through it. By 1980, it was frustrating because I always felt like I was about 75 percent of where I wanted to be. That's a tough way to play. It wears you down after a while."

Finally, after having played just 18 games in the 1980-81 season, Watson was forced to have surgery. This wasn't an average, everyday surgery. It's called spinal fusion. During the process, bone was removed from Watson's hip, ground into a sand-like substance, and then inserted into his lower spinal discs. The surgery was effective in that Watson was able to play the entire 1981-82 season, appearing in 76 games. However, once training camp arrived in September 1982, the pain was back, and Watson was not happy.

"I was starting to feel like a burden," he explains. "That's the last thing in the world I wanted to ever be. I did not want to be in and out of the line-up and that's what I saw happening. The doctors said maybe another surgery would have helped, but they mentioned the possibility of having to be in a body cast and losing a lot of blood, and I wasn't ready for that. So I decided to end it."

At just 30 years old, Watson walked away from hockey. With players almost routinely playing into their 40s these days, Watson now looks back with regret over having to leave the game at such a young age.

"Without the back problem, I could have played another five, six, or seven years," he points out. "I took good care of myself. I worked out and was

**By 1982, Jimmy Watson was playing through some severe pain.**

in great shape. I would have loved to have played longer, absolutely. That's probably one of the biggest regrets I've had in my life.

"But I just look at it as being a victim of circumstance. I wanted nothing to do with another surgery and besides, I had just begun a family. My first was a newborn. As it turned out, helping with my family turned out to fill the big void that would have been there after my playing career ended."

Thus, while his birth certificate might have indicated otherwise, Watson thought it was time to move on and begin a new chapter in his life. He had accomplished much in his nine NHL seasons, appearing in more than 600 games, making four trips to the Stanley Cup Finals, winning twice, playing with the best in the world in the Canada Cup, and participating in the victory over the Russians in 1976. That was one heck of a run for the younger Watson.

• • • • •

Upon retirement, every person has a plan. Watson's was to be there for his growing family, and if possible, to stay involved in the game of hockey. Eventually, he was hoping to move back to his native British Columbia. His first challenge came as a scout with the Flyers in 1982-83. He traveled throughout Canada trying to unearth talent that could eventually help in Philadelphia. On a scouting mission in Sault St. Marie, he was evaluating a guy by the name of Steve Smith when another player caught his attention.

"I was with the team for a week," he recalls. "I was around the team. I saw how the players were on and off the ice. There was this one kid who jumped out. He played real hard. He was mean and nasty and he was on all of his teammates when they weren't holding up their end of the bargain. I said this guy is a Flyer through and through."

On Watson's report, he made the necessary evaluations on Smith, but he indicated there was this other guy he really liked. His name was Rick Tocchet.

Despite finding a future Flyer star, though, scouting did not suit Watson.

"I didn't get a lot of fulfillment out of it," he admits now. "I'm a real hockey guy. I wanted to do more in the sport. I wanted to be more substantially involved. This isn't to slight anybody who scouts, because it is a valuable part of the entire process, but it got old for me. Every game was a road game of course, with all of the travel. I missed the excitement of the competition of having a win or a loss every night. I had a hard time dealing with that."

After one year scouring the amateur ranks for prospects, Watson decided to look in another direction.

• • • • •

Spend five minutes with Jim Watson and you recognize his intense sense of family and his desire to be closely involved with his children. He met his wife, Susan, while she was a flight attendant on one of the team charters. They were married in 1979 and had two sons and a daughter. Watson's focus has been those children ever since.

It is not surprising then that Watson's next endeavor evolved indirectly from taking care of that family. Shortly after retiring, he decided to do a complete renovation of his home in the Philadelphia area. He did it all himself.

"I did everything," he recollects. "I reframed an 800-square foot area, put a new roof on it, new siding, new windows, and a new kitchen. You name it. And I did all this work by myself. I did this to keep me engrossed in a physical activity while I was getting away from the scouting and getting away from the game. It was really good. It helped me to bridge from one career to another. By doing it, I saw that I could enjoy the construction side of things."

He soon bought a piece of land and built a new house for his family. It turned out to be the beginning of a long run in the business. He has been building homes ever since. Jim C. Watson, Inc. was established in 1984 and continues to this day as Watson's main form of income. He oversees custom-built dwellings as well as construction upon speculation. He admits that rising red-tape hassles are making it a more difficult business to enjoy, but building has always been in his blood.

"I always wanted to build a house," he reflects. "Once I did, I built another and then another. On thing led to another, and I've been building ever since."

• • • • •

Watson still needed to satisfy that hockey hunger of his. Once again, it was involvement with his family that opened another door. His sons were playing youth hockey in Valley Forge, and Watson wasn't happy with the conditions of the rinks and facilities, and rumors existed that it was about to be sold. He and a friend figured it might be a good idea to find a spot and build a rink themselves.

"We looked throughout the area," he recollects. "I mean we checked out Chester County, Montgomery County, all through Delaware County. We spent a year and a half trying to find an appropriate spot. Finally, my partner said he found a spot in Exton, Pennsylvania. The minute I saw the spot, I knew we had to jump all over it!"

They put an offer in on that day back in 1997. Several more partners were added, and a beautiful two-rink facility called Ice Works was born. Seven years later, it is now a sprawling four-rink complex bustling with activity.

"We feel like we are on the cutting edge," Watson says with obvious pride. "People can do so many things here. There's a huge health club that's part of the expansion. There are tremendous figure skating programs. And now we have the hockey academy."

Back in 2000, Watson began a thorough program in which kids, age 16 and up, spend the summer months in intense hockey instruction. The Jim Watson Hockey Academy has brought its namesake back into the game in a big way. "The Academy is here for a reason," he explains. "It's for kids to play at a high level and develop, but only if they want to play Division I collegiate or professional hockey. They have to want to do that. They have to want to make the sacrifice."

Watson takes his involvement a step further by representing some of his Academy graduates. By his count there were 12 of them playing either collegiately or in professional leagues in 2003. One was defenseman James Laux, who attended training camp with the Flyers and saw time with the American Hockey League's Phantoms. Two others are his two sons, Chase and Brett. The excitement Watson feels toward Ice Works, the Academy, and his participation in the development of young players is obvious.

"This has become my absolute pride and joy."

•   •   •   •   •

Obviously Jim Watson never made it back to British Columbia as originally planned. The Delaware Valley is very much home to him. His business interests and his kids are his sources of fulfillment. Unfortunately, he and Diane divorced just as his business endeavors were taking off.

"I didn't nurture the marriage as much as I could have," Watson confesses. "I was so engrossed with my kids and the business, that I just didn't give my wife enough time. She would ask for time alone and I wasn't there enough.

**His two-rink facility in Exton, Pennsylvania, is now Jim Watson's pride and joy.**

That was the mistake I made. When looking back on it, I should have taken her and we should have gone off on our own occasionally. We didn't, and we just grew apart.

"The good news is that we still get along quite well. She's still in the area and is a great mother to our kids. So we've kept the relationship pretty decent for people who are divorced."

Watson says he is so involved with Ice Works, his Academy, and his three children, that he doesn't have the time to get involved emotionally with another woman. For now, his life is full-speed ahead with his various interests. Those interests are very definitely in the Philadelphia area.

"I've become entrenched here," he explains. "It has become home. The family was the main reason to begin with. Now, of course, there are so many reasons. Being with my former teammates is a great benefit. A lot of the guys stayed here and also became entrenched. Look at the friendships I have with so many of them. Those are some of the tightest bonds you are going to have. They were there for me when I went through my divorce with a phone call or a word of encouragement. There's a lot of pain in that situation, but it was great to have that support."

That's a common thread throughout the members of the Cup teams. They were there for each other on the ice and they remain there for one another three decades later.

# #21
# Bill Flett

## *The Star Struck Cowboy*

With helmets now mandatory in the NHL and the buildings getting larger and larger, it is sometimes very difficult to differentiate one player from another down on the ice. Back in the mid-1970s, this was not a problem. Fans were generally in closer proximity to the action and their favorite players, with only a few exceptions, wore nothing on their heads.

The Flyers of that era were as recognizable as any team. There was Bob Kelly, with his blonde hair bouncing all round crashing and banging into opponents. And Rick MacLeish with his dark hair flowing as he effortlessly glided through enemy checking. Don't forget the lean and lanky Gary Dornhoefer, towering over many players and quite often camped out in the crease. Still, the player whose appearance was most distinctive was Bill Flett. The big winger sported a full beard, and there was no mistaking when he was on the ice. The beard was just one reminder that Flett saw himself as a cowboy and was aptly nicknamed as such.

His reputation as a cowboy stemmed from his childhood in western Canada. Flett spent his summers as a teenager riding in rodeos. The school year was saved for hockey and the other sports. But in the summer Flett and his cronies wrestled steers, rode broncos, and roped calves from quarter horses.

"I believe cowboys are the toughest athletes in the world," Flett said to Jack Chevalier in *The Broad Street Bullies*. "A cowboy has no guarantees, no contract. He rides healthy and he rides hurt. Rodeo cowboys have a pain tolerance that is hard to believe. I thought hockey players were tough until I rodeoed."

By the time Flett made a name for himself in junior hockey, his nickname as "Cowboy" was entrenched. During his two and a half seasons in Philadelphia, he was referred to more as Cowboy Flett than by his given name of Bill. And what a character he was!

"Here's a guy who was a real throwback," remembers Don Saleski. "Cowboy was an interesting guy. He knew how to enjoy life. We used to take a train to practice at the University of Pennsylvania rink and he used to buy a six-pack after practice and drink it up by the time we got home."

"He loved to be one of the boys," recalls Ross Lonsberry, Flett's teammate in Los Angeles as well as with the Flyers. "He did party and play very hard. But everybody liked Cowboy. As much as he partied, he was a tremendous teammate and somebody you knew would be behind you at all times."

Barry Cummins found that out in December 1973. He was a rookie defenseman for the California Golden Seals who took a full two-handed swing with his stick at Bobby Clarke's head, opening up a 20-stitch cut during a game. Flett was the first Flyer to get at Cummins, and he began pounding him into submission as did several of his teammates when they arrived on the scene. Cummins left the gathering a bloody mess.

"That bleepin' stupid fool," as Flett was quoted by Jay Greenberg in *Full Spectrum*. "You never hit a guy over the head with a two hander. It doesn't take much to kill a person."

Intense, at times, Flett was practically nonchalant at others. Saleski tells a story of a gathering in a bar in Vancouver in the middle of the summer when the "Vancouver Seven" as they were called were visiting, facing bogus charges from the brawl the previous season.

"Cowboy had the full beard really going because it was the off season," Saleski recollects. "We're sitting around with our attorney Gil Stein, having a beer, when Barry Ashbee lit a match, reached over, and set Cowboy's beard on fire! His beard went up in flames and Bill calmly lifted up his glass of beer, took a swig, and then took the beer with his hand and put the fire out. Gil Stein looked at us and said, 'You guys are absolutely crazy!'"

"He was a free spirit for sure," says Lonsberry. "But there wasn't anything that Billy wouldn't do for somebody. If you needed a dollar and he only had one left, he would give it to you and figure out something else for himself. There are very few people like that anymore in this world. He was one of them."

· · · · ·

In addition to being a great team guy, Bill Flett could also score goals. He was acquired by the Flyers from Los Angeles with Lonsberry in a seven-player swap in January 1972 to do just that. He would score 11 goals in 31 games with the Flyers after the trade that season before exploding for a career-high 43 tallies in 1972-73.

"In practice, both being right wings, we would line up next to one another on the shooting drills," recalls Saleski. "He could really shoot the puck. He used this little stick, but he could really fire it. Every time he would come back to the line after scoring, he would say, 'Well, kid. You've either got it or you don't.' He would say it every practice."

Oddly enough, Flett went into a deep scoring drought during the Flyers' first Stanley Cup year. He would light the lamp only 17 times as the Flyers charged toward the Cup. He would not score a single goal during the 17-game Stanley Cup playoff run. Flett contributed to the Cup with two key assists, including one on Clarke's game-winning goal in the pivotal Game 2 of the Finals. However, when a goal scorer stops scoring goals, change isn't far away.

General manager Keith Allen was fully aware of Flett's difficulties. Couple that with his desire to acquire Reggie Leach, and Cowboy's fate was sealed. Just a week after celebrating a championship, Flett was traded to Toronto for Dave Fortier and Randy Osburn.

"I was on vacation in Puerto Rico when I found out," Flett told the *Courier-Post* back in 1994. "I was disappointed. I really liked those guys."

Allen is matter of fact when analyzing why he decided to change the makeup of a team that had just won the Cup.

**A week after celebrating the Cup win, Bill Flett (left) was an ex-Flyer.**

"Cowboy got into the sauce pretty deep, and I just thought he was going to go downhill," Allen explains. "And with Clarkie and Leach having played in junior in Flin Flon together, the move seemed like a natural one."

With the trade began a sojourn through professional hockey for Flett. After one year with the Leafs, he was claimed on waivers by Atlanta. Halfway through his second year with the Flames, he was on the move again, this time to the World Hockey Association and the Edmonton Oilers. His career would experience a renaissance with the Oilers as he scored 103 goals in less than three full seasons in the WHA. In 1977-78, he eclipsed the 40-goal mark for the first time since his Flyers' days.

When the Oilers joined the NHL as part of the 1979 expansion, they brought Flett along. However, he was 36 years old during Edmonton's initial NHL season. He would appear in only 20 games, registering five goals and seven points. It would be the last pro hockey he would play. Fate had already conspired to make the game of hockey seem trivial to him.

**Bill Flett's career had some-what of a rebirth in the WHA with the Oilers.** *Photo courtesy of the Edmonton Oilers*

• • • • •

Even a cowboy can get knocked off of his horse on occasion. Flett's free spirit was shocked into reality while during his tenure in Edmonton, he and his oldest son Cody were involved in a horrific car accident. "It was about two in the afternoon," he said back in 1994. "I don't know how it happened, but the car went over a half-ton truck and through its tailgate. We flipped over and slid along the road before we stopped."

Flett turned the vehicle back over in a fit of panic and rage. He crawled in and pulled his 12-year old son out of the wreckage. Police and an ambulance arrived. Cody was rushed to the hospital, unconscious, as he would remain for the next eight weeks. He finally did regain consciousness, but when he did, his mental abilities had been affected, his leg needed to be rebroken, and skin grafts were needed to repair damage done by burns while the car was sliding. He would be in the hospital for more than a year.

"I feel so bad that he was in the car with me," Flett told the *Courier-Post*.

Cody would recover to the point that he would win the giant slalom and the downhill in the Special Olympics many years later. However, one has to wonder about what psychological damage that accident did to the Cowboy. He retired from hockey two years later, his life never to be the same.

• • • • •

Flett would do his best to move forward. Among his jobs out of hockey were working in the Alberta oil patch, renting machinery, working sales for a company called Digital Logging and selling seed oil for Cambra Foods. Another auto mishap in the late 1980s brought him more pain when he was hit head on by a car that was going 110 miles per hour. The engine of his car would up right beside him. He fractured his sternum and needed surgery to repair some damage to one of his eyes. But he survived.

In 1993 he was attending an Oilers' game when suddenly, he began throwing up blood. He eventually went to the hospital to get checked out and it was determined he had a bleeding ulcer. "The doctor told me I needed to stop drinking," said Flett. "I had been drinking every day, although I was never falling-down drunk."

Still, years of being the free spirit were beginning to catch up with him. Even he realized this and so he checked into the Betty Ford Center in Palm Springs, California, in March 1993. During this time he was in contact with the Flyers' alumni and they supported him in his efforts to recover. A month of treatment brought him to the realization that he had been running a lot of risks.

"You've got to realize it's a disease and live one day at a time," he said in 1994. "It can come up and grab you in a hurry."

•  •  •  •  •

It could be said the Cowboy learned these valuable lessons too late in life. Then again, people who knew him said he probably would have lived the same carefree existence even if he had known. But according to the website *www.hockeyresearch.com* in May 1999, he checked into the hospital with what he thought was severe heartburn. Instead, he was having a gall bladder attack. After two operations his condition stabilized but the gall bladder problem caused his liver to fail. He received a liver transplant soon thereafter, but complications developed and he became gravely ill.

"I called him on the telephone," recalls Saleski. "The nurse wasn't going to put me through but I told her I was one of his old teammates and she thought he would want to hear from me. He was so pleased that I called him. Before you knew it, we were telling old stories about our days in Philly. A couple of days later, he was gone."

Bill Flett died on July 12, 1999 from the complications after the liver transplant. He left his wife of more than 30 years, Doreen, and three sons. He was nine days shy of his 56th birthday. To one and all he was the "Cowboy," and while his life ended much too early, he spent his time on this earth getting as much out of it as he could. "He was a real personality," Saleski says. "He was a good guy, too. He had a heart of gold."

# #25
# Ted Harris

## The Unassuming Champion

When the 1974 and 1975 Stanley Cup Champion Flyers are mentioned, many of the names of the players quickly come to mind. There was Clarke, Parent, Barber, Leach, MacLeish, Dornhoefer, the Watsons, etc. Most every player from those teams has a recognizable name to Philadelphia sports fans. And then there is Ted Harris.

Only the most knowledgeable fans think of the name of Ted Harris when they harken back to the glory days. Part of the reason is that Harris spent a grand total of one season with the Flyers. The other is that despite settling in the Delaware Valley, Harris has kept a very low profile since retiring. The limelight is not what he seeks.

It is then ironic that Harris actually owns two distinctions that his fellow Flyer teammates do not. First of all, he played hockey professionally in Philadelphia before any of the other Flyers did. You see, he was a member of the old Philadelphia Ramblers of the Eastern Hockey League way back in 1957 and 1958. "I remember a couple of things about those days," he recalls. "I remember playing in the old arena [Philadelphia Arena at 46th and Market Streets], where you had to jump up to your bench from the ice surface. That was a different experience. I also recall the chain-linked fence that ran along the top of the boards. You didn't want catch yourself getting too close to that, I will tell you!"

Harris was a 20-year-old youngster then, just beginning what would become a 19 professional hockey career. It basically began and ended in Philadelphia, but there was so much in between.

In fact, the second distinction unique to Harris is that he is the only member of the Flyer Stanley Cup teams to have won a Cup elsewhere as a player. And he didn't win just one. He was a member of four Stanley Cup clubs with the Montreal Canadiens during the 1960s. Those were the Canadiens of Jean Beliveau, Henri Richard, Yvan Cournoyer, and John Ferguson. In three of the four seasons, they were coached by the legendary Toe Blake. Yes, Ted Harris was a member of *those* Canadiens!

**Ted Harris was a four-time champion as a member of the Montreal Canadiens.**

"You have to be lucky, and I got lucky going to the team that was the best in the league in those days," the exceedingly humble Harris explains. "They picked me up for my toughness, which they thought was a missing element. Not that I was a great fighter as my nose will attest, but I certainly wasn't afraid to get my nose in there.

"The saying they post in the Canadiens' locker room about passing the torch on is very accurate. We had a team that pulled together when it had to. I was part of a defense corps that basically used only four men so we just went out there every other shift and took care of business."

Indeed they did. Four Stanley Cups during a span of six years indicated they got the job done. About the only thing missing from those years was the symbol that all championship teams now have, rings for the players.

"The Canadiens did not give rings to their championship teams back then," he points out. "We got the small version of the Stanley Cup and a bonus, but no rings."

He would have to wait until the twilight of his career to get that.

•   •   •   •   •

By 1973-74, Harris had become a 37-year-old journeyman defenseman. The year that the Flyers won their first Cup he spent bouncing from the Minnesota North Stars to the Detroit Red Wings and then to the St. Louis Blues. He says this "year from hell" is one he chooses not to think about.

On the first day of the following season's training camp, his fortunes changed, although as he tells it, he almost didn't find out.

"I was at a restaurant over by the rink in St. Louis," he remembers. "The announcement over the PA system said, 'Will Ted Harris please report to the telephone area?' I saw a bunch of the younger players sitting at a table and thought they were pulling a practical joke. I wasn't going to let those little buggers get me to fall for that one! I didn't budge. Finally, one of the team scouts found me in the restaurant and told me I had been traded to Philadelphia."

The Flyers were searching for a defenseman to essentially take Barry Ashbee's place in the lineup after his career had ended due to the eye injury. Harris was only too happy to be the guy.

"St. Louis was rebuilding," he points out. "They weren't in need of a 38-year-old defenseman, that's for sure. When I found out it was Philadelphia, I knew I had lucked out. I also knew it was going to be a lot more fun playing with the likes of Schultz and Kelly than it had been playing against them!"

What Harris found once he arrived in Philadelphia was one tight-knit bunch. In fact, the togetherness surprised him some.

"The guys really hung together," he recollects. "We were always together whether we were on the road or at home. I don't think other teams had that, at least not as much as the Flyers. Freddy had a lot to do with that I think. I think he put in our minds that we would be together and stay that way for the rest of our lives."

Harris contributed his usual solid defensive effort during the 1974-75 season, helping the Flyers to their second Cup. He went through that season with a pretty good idea that it would be his last as a player in the National Hockey League. On the night the Flyers clinched the Cup in Buffalo, he became certain of it.

"I was to the point where the heart still said go, but the legs were saying no," he admits. "I was in the third year of a three-year contract and I certainly didn't expect a team to give an old guy like me another deal."

The first person to actually find out about Harris's retirement intentions was a young boy who asked Ted to autograph his program outside of the Buffalo Auditorium as Harris was making his way to the bus after the clincher in Game 6. The boy asked, "Are you happy Mr. Harris?" "Yes," replied Harris, "because that was the last hockey game I'll ever play."

**Ted Harris's one season in a Flyers uniform served as the perfect capper to his outstanding NHL playing career.**

Thus, 19 years after his pro hockey career, in essence, began in Philadelphia as a Rambler, it ended in the same city as a member of the Stanley Cup Champion Flyers.

• • • • •

Harris was done as a player but not done with hockey. The Minnesota North Stars had fallen on hard times and wanted their former captain and all-star defenseman back as head coach to lead the team out of the wilderness. "I had always hoped that maybe I could stay in the game," Harris explains. "I wasn't expecting to get a coaching chance right away like that, but I sure wasn't going to turn an opportunity like that down."

The North Stars were trying to rebuild. After having made the playoffs in five of their first six seasons in the league, they had missed the postseason in the two years prior to Harris becoming their bench boss. They had some solid veterans like Bill Goldsworthy and Dennis Hextall, and rookie Tim Young joined the team from the minors and eventually led the club in scoring. Cesare Maniago was the goaltender.

However, the club never really got going. The North Stars lost seven of their first eight games and went 3-13-0 in the first 16 contests and never recovered. The next season they improved slightly and made the playoffs before losing in the first round to the Buffalo Sabres.

"I had played with quite a few of the guys that I was then coaching," Harris reflects. "I think some of them resented the fact that I was giving orders instead of just being one of the guys. As I was going along, I was learning on the job how to handle things, but it was tough. Those are not days I choose to remember very often."

In 1977-78, the team lost its first six games and was only 5-12-2 when Harris was fired. He gave it one more try as head coach of Springfield in the American Hockey League the next season. That lasted less than a full year. As with just about everything in his life, Harris takes a matter-of-fact approach to his coaching experiences.

"It's one thing to make yourself go and have the desire to play the game and to know the game," he relates. "But it's an entirely different thing to teach somebody else and to motivate somebody else. In the end, I guess I wasn't a motivator."

The end of his coaching career also brought to an end his involvement in the sport of hockey. It was time for Ted Harris to face the real world.

• • • • •

So many of the former Flyers thought it was simply natural to return to Philadelphia once their hockey days were over. It is, quite obviously, one of the reasons why the bond among them is still so strong. However, in Ted Harris's case, the reasons were a little different. Here is a guy originally from Winnipeg, who spent six years as a player in Montreal and parts of seven seasons as a player and a coach in Minnesota. He was only in Philadelphia as an NHL player for one year. Granted, it was a great year, but still just one season. It begs the question, why settle here?

"I felt like I could probably make it here," he recalls. "I always liked Philadelphia, even from way back in my minor league days. I found the people here to be very close and very friendly. They still are. I think there is a lot to that 'brotherly love' stuff."

Adding to his reasons for being here was the breakup of his marriage. With his former wife in Minnesota, he thought it better to relocate to begin the next chapter of his life. That chapter began with five years in the insurance and investment business. It wasn't until 1987, though, that he found his true niche, managing a paint store in Westmont, New Jersey. For some ex-athletes, there is that desire to continue to be in the spotlight after retiring. For Harris, it was exactly the opposite.

"I am very satisfied with the accomplishments I had as a player," he explains. "For some guys there is the need to become even more accomplished after their playing careers are over. For others, like me, they are able to take what has come to them and have gone from there.

"I found that there was life after hockey. At one time, I didn't think there would be. I've enjoyed what I'm doing now. I enjoy coming to work every day. I guess as long as you do that, you are on the right track."

Harris remarried a local woman back in the mid-1980s and settled in as the manager of Conroy's Corner paint store. He prefers the low profile. So much so that even though I have lived in South Jersey for over a decade, now, I had no idea that a five-time Stanley Cup Champion and five-time NHL all-star actually lived right around the corner from me. I didn't find out until I sat down to interview him for this very book that Harris lives practically within view of my house! But that's Ted Harris, as unassuming as they come.

Ted Harris has run a paint store in south Jersey for years, out of the spotlight and not minding it at all.

# #26
# Orest Kindrachuk

## *Hockey Is His Magnet*

Even preceding Orest Kindrachuk's professional hockey career, it seemed as if the sport had some kind of irresistible influence on him. How he came to be a National Hockey League player is ample evidence.

Kindrachuk had an outstanding career in junior hockey. In his fourth and final year with the Saskatoon Blades of the WCJHL, he piled up 49 goals, a league-leading 100 assists, and 149 points. Yet he didn't get drafted. Surely with those impressive numbers some team would consider him draft-worthy. What was the problem?

"My draft year, for whatever reason, I decided I wanted to be a doctor," Kindrachuk recalls. "I thought my education was very important and at the University of Saskatchewan, they didn't care if you scored 1,000 points with your junior team, you couldn't miss class, labs or anything. So my draft year, I played in a local commercial league and was not selected."

The following year, in what would become a familiar pattern for him, he felt the lure of hockey.

"I had this thought that you know, I could always go back to school," he remembers. "However, I wasn't sure I could necessarily go back to playing hockey. They had an over-age rule back then, so I went back to the Blades."

His indecision, however, had caused him to slip right through the draft. The Flyers, though, had taken notice of the guy who was and always has been known as "Little O." Chief scout Gerry Melnyk had spotted Kindrachuk's talents and added him to Philadelphia's protected list. Thus, when he did decide to turn pro, he would be property of the Flyers.

"I think back now and maybe that was the way it was supposed to be," Kindrachuk says. "Maybe I wasn't supposed to play my draft year because I probably would have been drafted fairly high and maybe I would have never had an opportunity to play for a team that could win the Stanley Cup. I don't believe in destiny or fate too much, but maybe there was a little bit of that there."

His love of hockey had drawn him back. As it turned out, he was drawn right into a championship mix.

•  •  •  •  •

Kindrachuk's first year with the Flyers organization was 1972-73. He appeared in just two games with the big club, spending most of that season with the Richmond Robins of the American Hockey League, proving himself with 35 goals and 86 points in 72 games. That performance earned him his shot with the Flyers the next season. His timing could not have been better.

"It was obvious to me as soon as I got there that this team was on a mission," he recalls. "The dedication and desire of those players was so strong. There were no weak links in terms of motivation or work ethic. We felt, as a team, the way we played, that we would beat the opposing team, the referee,

**Orest Kindrachuk joined the Flyers just as they were joining the NHL's elite.**

and the league because they were always penalizing us. The league didn't seem to recognize this, but the Philadelphia Flyers, for about four or five years, were the best thing that happened to hockey.

"The three years we went to the finals, we couldn't wait to get to the rink each day. We couldn't wait to put the gear on. Freddy had us up at nine o'clock in the morning, too, so we were working like the rest of the world. We had so much fun playing the game."

As a rookie, he became a champion. And, then again, in his second season. Not a bad start to a career.

• • • • •

Kindrachuk would spend five full seasons as a member of the Flyers. He was a smallish center ice man (5'10", 175 lbs.), but hard-nosed and clever. The year after the two Cup wins, he tallied nearly a point a game with 26 goals and 75 points in 76 games. Members of the Cup teams though began to leave the team through trades and retirement as the years went by. Kindrachuk knew his time would come.

"I was on vacation with Bob Kelly in San Diego in the summer of 1978," Kindrachuk remembers. "When I heard that Keith Allen was on the phone, I knew he wasn't calling to see how my trip was going. When I found out I was going to Pittsburgh, I was pretty upset."

The Flyers had traded Kindrachuk, Ross Lonsberry, and Tom Bladon to the Penguins for a first-round draft pick (used to select defenseman Behn Wilson) and future considerations. The Penguins had missed the playoffs the year before and there were reports of financial turmoil within the organization.

Only 27 years old, Kindrachuk was going from a perennial contender in a successful market to a struggling team still trying to establish itself in its city. Still, he was understanding about bidding adieu.

"In order to stay competitive in any sport, you have to continually tweak the team," he reasons. "To see our Cup teams broken up hurt, but it was time. If you stand pat, like the Islanders did, you can end up being down for a long time. When I finally got dealt, I was devastated more by where I was going than by being traded."

• • • • •

Much to his surprise, Kindrachuk did not find the Steel City to be the hell he had heard about. To the contrary, his second NHL stop turned out to be a satisfying one for him personally. First of all, the three acquisitions from the Flyers were joined by other NHL veterans such as Randy Carlyle, George Ferguson, and Gregg Sheppard as new Penguins. A series of summer deals had added some serious quality to the Pittsburgh lineup.

Secondly, as his first training camp as a Penguin was drawing to a close, Kindrachuk learned that he was going to receive one of hockey's biggest honors.

"I was told by management that the players had voted me captain of the team," he says proudly. "That was a great feeling to know that your peers had voted you the leader of the team. It gave me the opportunity to help get a team started, and there's a great deal of satisfaction in that."

**Orest Kindrachuk wore the "C" with pride as a Penguin.** *Photo courtesy of the Pittsburgh Penguins*

He obviously thrived in the role. Kindrachuk led the Penguins with 42 assists and finished second on the club with 60 points as Pittsburgh finished second in the Norris Division. They set a franchise record for points on the road and surged toward the postseason with a ten-game unbeaten string in late March. Ferguson's overtime goal gave the Penguins a thrilling preliminary-round series victory over the Buffalo Sabres before the Boston Bruins finally ended the Pens' season of improvement in the second round.

All in all, though, Kindrachuk had turned his sojourn across Pennsylvania to Pittsburgh into a very positive experience.

•   •   •   •   •

In that first year in Pittsburgh, Kindrachuk played in a career-high 79 games. The next year, he appeared in only 52. By 1980-81, he would be in the lineup for only 13 contests. His decreasing activity had nothing to do with his performance.

"One night, I got hit about five feet from the boards," he recollects. "It was one of those cross checks in the back where you are just far enough away to cause some damage. Today the player would probably be suspended for a few games, but back then it was just part of the game. From that point on, I never really recovered the way I should have. We just didn't have the rehabilitation techniques that exist today."

He was in and out of the Pittsburgh lineup until February of 1981 when he finally decided surgery was necessary. He went back to his South Jersey home to rehab on his own after going under the knife. At the same time, he decided the Penguins weren't committed to winning long term so, as a free agent, he looked elsewhere.

"Washington general manager Max McNab had always liked my play," Kindrachuk recalls. "The Caps made me a nice deal, and so I decided to go there. The mistake we made was after a summer of rehab from the surgery, they took me overseas for training camp and I wasn't able to continue my workouts. That probably helped to end my career."

When the team returned to Washington, Kindrachuk's back began to ache again. He continued to try to play, although he only appeared in four games. The Caps wanted him to give it some time before making any decisions. Kindrachuk waited until Christmas but the pain was not subsiding.

"I was having to walk down steps backward the pain was so bad," he agonizes today. "I had had enough. I felt very comfortable leaving the game that from the age of six years old until I was 32 years old, I had accomplished all I could for a guy with my talent and ability. Being on two Cup winners and being captain of an NHL team, I just didn't think there was anything else left for me to risk damaging myself further for. Not only that, I also had to look in the mirror and realize I couldn't play at the level I wanted to anymore.

"The Caps wanted to have a retirement ceremony for me, but I declined. I told Max, 'I came into the league quietly and now I am going to leave quietly.'"

And so he did. "Little O" walked away from the game, at least for a while.

• • • • •

Soon after ending his playing career, Kindrachuk found himself with an offer to get right back into the game. The New Jersey Devils' organization offered him an assistant coaching spot.

"At that time, I had a three-year-old and another child on the way," Kindrachuk reflects. "I had been in hockey for 26 years, and after looking at the background of some of the coaches in the league, I just didn't think I would have the time to spend with my kids with all of the travel and time coaching would entail."

Instead Kindrachuk was interested in becoming his own boss. He had always been interested in finances and real estate. Enter the insurance business.

"I thought this is pretty good," he remembers. "I can be as big as I want to be. It's up to me and nobody else. Nobody can tell me I have to get out of bed in the morning. I was my own boss, which was the biggest thing. It's been over two decades, and I'm still doing it so I would say I made a good choice."

• • • • •

In the mid 1990s Kindrachuk decided to take a trip to Boston to watch the Flyers play their final game in the old Boston Garden. He was a little surprised at how strong his reaction was to being in that old barn again.

"When I walked into the old Garden, a flood of memories came back to me," he recollects. "For the first time in along time, I had the urge to get back into hockey. I suddenly felt it was time to get back in touch with the game."

Some 13 to 14 years removed from his days as a player, Kindrachuk was experiencing that almost magnetic pull of the sport of hockey once again.

"Hockey will always be in your blood," he admits. "It will always be there. So I remembered that I had noticed that some players were being taken advantage of when their careers were over, and I thought I might be of some help in that area. I kept reading stories where players after making good money throughout their careers would have nothing by the end of it. I felt I could have been someone they could trust to handle their finances. It really interested me."

Then he thought again. Being an agent involves a lot of traveling. In fact, one would have to make contact with the kids when they were very young. "I came to realize it was like starting all over again," Kindrachuk admits. "I would have had to travel to western Canada to get the kids when they were young. I had done enough traveling in my life so I closed the door on that. One thing I wasn't going to do was get on a bus. They say start your career on a bus, don't end it there."

• • • • •

One door closed, but another needed to open up in order to satisfy Kindrachuk's desire to return to hockey. That's when the Flyers' American Hockey League affiliate, first in Hershey and then as the Phantoms in Philadelphia, came into the picture. They needed a color analyst for their television broadcasts and who better than one of the former Flyers Cup winners to fill the bill?

"The first couple of years, I had the opportunity to work with Gene Hart [the Flyers' Hall of Fame announcer, who was working Phantoms games during the NHL Lockout in 1994]", he recalls. "That was probably the best thing to happen to me, being able to work with Gene as I got started.

"It was a perfect way for me to keep my finger in the game, too. Just to go to the rink and walk through the smelly dressing room, watching the players get their sticks ready. I looked at them and thought they don't know how good they've got it. Even at the AHL level. You're young and this is all you have to do. All you've got to do is play hockey, and play hockey to the best of your ability. What else could you want to do?! The players today...if they don't get that, then shame on them. You could have $80 million in the bank, but if when you're done playing you don't feel you've given it your all then you will live the rest of your life with a knot in your stomach."

That's one knot Orest Kindrachuk doesn't have to worry about.

• • • • •

Today Kindrachuk is a successful insurance salesman for the Equitable Financial Company in Cherry Hill, New Jersey. He is fully aware of the incredible love the people of Philadelphia and the surrounding area have for the members of the Flyers Cup teams. In fact, he believes it is the reason so many of the members of those teams still reside in the area.

"I can still envision walking into that locker room and seeing Freddy's quote about walking together forever," Kindrachuk recalls. "What a profound statement. When I see how many of the guys decided to stay here, I think that winning together is the reason. Also, when you win, let's face it, business opportunities are created. We all had to work after our careers were over, and there were better chances of finding good work here for us because we had won here.

"That being said, there is no denying the tremendous bond that exists among the players from those years. It will never be broken. We won together. We sacrificed for each other for whatever it took. Back in our day, when it came time to practice or to play a game or even to go have a beer together, you had better be there and do it at your best."

Successful in the insurance business, Orest Kindrachuk still finds ways to stay involved with hockey, too.

# #27
# Reggie Leach

## *Gaining a Different Perspective*

Wilhen people think of Reggie Leach, one of two images comes to mind. There's the guy on the ice, cruising into scoring position and then beating the goaltender with his blistering shot. And then there's the happy-go-lucky sort off the ice, never finding a party he didn't like.

Both images accurately portrayed Reggie Leach during his hockey playing days. He was at home back in those days, when the alcohol flowed frequently and yet his performance didn't seem to be affected. Leach will tell you, he rarely got sick from his drinking, other than what he calls an occasional booze-induced "concussion."

Fast-forward to today, and you might not recognize Reggie Leach. Oh, he's changed physically as have all of the former Flyers as they have reached middle age. But what is so different is his approach to life. This is clearly a man who has learned a lot of life's lessons the hard way. However, he used those lessons to create a different path for his post-hockey journey, one that is based largely in helping others not make the same mistakes he did.

His story is a fascinating one.

• • • • •

Before he was "The Rifle," gunning in goals by the bushel full, he was a young native, struggling to survive in Riverton, Manitoba. Born to three-quarters Indian heritage, he was raised largely by his grandparents and their 12 children, four of whom would die way before their time due to accidents or mental illness.

He developed a love for hockey but had few funds to support it. He would borrow skates from older friends and use crumpled newspapers to fill the spaces around his feet. In lieu of running water, he would carry buckets of water to places where he could create a rink. And then he would just shoot, and shoot, and shoot some more.

"I would practice for hours and hours at a time," Leach recalls. "It didn't matter whether I had a puck or something else, I would just keep shooting. I built up a lot of strength in my wrists that way. I would shoot things against buildings. Sometimes in arenas, even if it was dark, I would find a stick and a puck and fire it against the boards. I remember liking the sound of the puck against the boards."

The result was a player who would become one of the most dangerous offensive weapons of his era. After scoring 45 goals in his first year after being acquired by the Flyers in 1974-75, he lit up NHL goalies for a record 61 tallies the next season. Throw in 19 more goals on his way to the Conn Smythe Trophy in the playoffs, and Leach had registered the most prolific goal-scoring year the NHL had ever witnessed.

Part of his effectiveness was based in the size and shape of his stick.

"I found it easier to use a very light stick," Leach admits. "The blade on my stick was only nine inches. The total length of my stick from heel to top was only about 49 inches or so. And I used a big curve on my stick. It actually started from the shaft so that I got a lot more than a half-inch curve [the legal limit] when the entire stick was taken into consideration. I suppose you could say I cheated a little."

Leach was also adept at getting in position to make that uniquely configured stick work its magic. He would find a seam and then waste no time in firing the puck. On 381 regular-season occasions during his NHL career, that puck wound up in the back of the net.

•　•　•　•　•

Back when Reggie Leach first left his hometown of Riverton, Manitoba, he was considered a defenseman of all things. True, he was an offensive-minded defenseman, but he was a blue liner just the same. It was in his junior hockey destination of Flin Flon, Manitoba, where he would meet someone who would prominently affect his life.

"The coach took one look me on the ice and said I was too fast to be a defenseman," Leach remembers. "He decided to move me up front to play with a guy by the name of Bobby Clarke."

It was a sound decision. The two would play three seasons together in Flin Flon and produce some mind-boggling numbers. In the 1967-68 season, Clarke would score 51 goals and help Leach post an amazing 87. That's 87 goals in only 59 games! They obviously clicked on the ice. Just as important, they became friends off the ice, too.

"He was one of the first people I met in Flin Flon," explains Leach. "We hit it off right away and have been friends ever since. He's the one who actually pushed me to the limits all the time. One thing about Clarkie is that he had to work for everything he got. He couldn't shoot the puck. He couldn't skate. He was small. Meanwhile, I had everything come pretty naturally to me. So when he pushed himself so hard, he made me push right along with him."

Clarke was strongly in support of the Flyers acquiring Leach some five years after their junior partnership had ended. When Keith Allen pulled the trigger on the deal that sent Larry Wright, Al MacAdam, and a first-round pick to California, Leach and Clarke were reunited. Joined by Bill Barber on the famed LCB Line, the sparks flew, and one of the NHL's all-time most productive trios took off.

"I was surprised they made the trade just a week after winning the Cup," Leach reasons. "And then there was Clarkie and his big mouth telling everyone that I would score 45 goals in a bad year! When I had about five goals the first couple of months, people were ready to panic. But then I got used to the system they were playing and our line really came together.

"We were so effective because everybody knew their job. My role was basically just to shoot the puck and finish plays. Clarkie always knew where Billy and I were going to be. I just had to find the holes and be there at the right time. There weren't too many times he didn't get me the puck when I got there."

The LCB line would click as a unit for the better part of eight seasons. In its very first season together, of course, it was a huge part of a Stanley Cup championship. Leach cherishes the moment he had with his old junior buddy with the hallowed prize.

"I remember going into the locker room in Buffalo," Leach recollects. "I drank out of the Stanley Cup with Clarkie and his father. That was a special moment. I could remember Clarkie and I talking about dreams of the time we could be together after winning the Cup. And there we were living that dream."

Thirty years later, while they aren't in constant contact anymore, Leach still feels a closeness to his former junior teammate.

"To me, he will always be my best friend. He knows the way I am, and I know the way he is. We don't have to be together all the time. His lifestyle keeps him in the hockey world. Mine is somewhat separate from that, but that doesn't matter. He will always be my best friend."

●　●　●　●　●

Leach was still a productive player in the three seasons after his 1975-76 explosion. Still that production did slip some. He tallied 32, 24, and 34 goals respectively in those years. There were times when he appeared to clash with head coach Fred Shero, although he says now that was overblown.

"I think the press blew any of the problems I had with Freddy way out of proportion," Leach states. "I think he was a hell of a coach. There were times when he would make me stay out and skate after Clarkie and Billy had left the ice and he would tell me, 'Not all men are created equal.' I realize now that he was doing that to help me because I didn't work as hard as some of the other guys during games or practices. In general, I enjoyed him as a head coach."

It was, however, when Pat Quinn took over as the Flyers' bench boss in 1979 that Leach's game went through a resurrection. That, of course, was the year of the 35-game unbeaten streak. Leach would once again hit the 50-goal mark, this time as a veteran nearing his 30th birthday.

"As a player, that was the most gratifying year of my career," Leach says. "I even got to kill penalties for the first time. Pat Quinn was very good for me. He would always pull me aside and tell me man to man what was going on. I didn't have to hear it from anybody else. If it weren't for Pat, I probably would have been out of hockey by 1978 or so. Instead, I think in 1979-80, I was the most complete player I had ever been.

"The streak was unbelievable. Even if we were down two goals with two minutes to go, we just knew we were going to tie it up. I always thought I would get one or Ricky MacLeish or someone. We were a cocky bunch of guys. At the time, it was just one game after another, but then when you sit back after your career is done, you realize it was a pretty amazing stretch."

• • • • •

No account of Reggie Leach's career would be complete without reference to his legendary ability to party. It actually started when he was a youngster. When he was raised by his grandparents, drinking was not discouraged. Once he was involved with the travel and lifestyle the NHL provides, the opportunities to imbibe became that much more frequent.

Perhaps the greatest legend of Leach's career came from events surrounding Game 5 of the Flyers' Stanley Cup Semifinal Series with the Boston Bruins on May 6, 1976. Leach would tie an NHL record by pouring in five goals in a 6-3 Philadelphia victory. Of course that in and of itself was big news. However, circumstances surrounding the performance made it practically miraculous.

"We stayed at a hotel down in Valley Forge the night before that game," Leach recalls. "I got into a big argument that night with one of the coaches, so I got drunk and went home. I don't even remember going home. The next morning Clarkie found me passed out in the basement of my house and got me up. I had a couple of beers to revive me and told him to take me to the rink so I could play.

"When we got to the Spectrum, Freddy saw what shape I was in and he wasn't going to play me. Clarkie told him, 'Let him play. He will probably score a bunch of goals.' That's exactly what happened. I told Clarkie to just give me the puck and they'll go in. And they did!"

Leach beat Bruins' netminder Gilles Gilbert five times, three times with backhanders. Three times he had crossed over to the left wing and found a way to score. All while suffering from what he calls an alcohol-induced "concussion."

Reggie Leach's now legendary five-goal explosion in a game against Boston helped him gain the Conn Smythe Trophy as play-off MVP in 1976.

The players of the 1970s partied hard in general. Leach says it was simply part of the lifestyle, although he fully realizes he took it over the limit on occasion.

"When I drank, I was crazy," Leach admits now. "I didn't care about anybody but myself. When it came time to play the game, I did, but it didn't really matter to me whether or not I was in shape. I was lucky enough that God gave me the ability to play the game even when I wasn't in great shape."

Leach always thought he was singled out for his drinking, though. He believed just about every player drank and in many cases, drank often, back in those days. However, his feeling is that he was made an example of because of his heritage.

"I felt I was always pointed out no matter what team I played on," he asserts. "Natives are associated with being involved with alcohol and being crazy that way. So I always thought my drinking was made an issue of. If you switched that around and said that about all of the white players in the league who drank, you wouldn't have had enough players to play the games. They always said there was no prejudice in the league. That is a bunch of crap!"

Still, even Leach realizes the alcohol did have an effect on his career, although he might not have realized it at the time. After his 50-goal season in 1979-80, he would score 34 goals and then 26 the next two seasons. Late in the 1981-82 season, Pat Quinn was replaced as head coach by Bob McCammon. McCammon was looking to make a statement about discipline when Leach was 20 minutes late for the first practice under the new bench boss. The coach's statement was to give Leach his release.

"As an alcoholic, you always want to blame everybody else for your problems," Leach explains. "When the Flyers released me, I was three points shy of 50 points for the season which would have given me an automatic three-year contract extension. My reaction to getting let go was a bitter one, because in my mind it had nothing to do with being hung over and showing up late for practice and everything to do with the clause in my contract."

Leach would hook on with the Detroit Red Wings for the 1982-83 season and by this time his reputation preceded him. Red Wings head coach Nick Polano would hound him all season, attempting to curtail his drinking. After scoring 15 goals in 78 games that season, Leach was released again. He hoped to stay in the NHL but no team was willing to take a chance on a 33-year-old former sniper with a reported drinking problem.

As it turned out, Leach's final season in pro hockey was spent in Billings, Montana, of all places. He signed on with the Montana Magic of the old Central Hockey League. The two-time 50-goal NHL scorer would post 21 goals as a minor leaguer.

"There were a lot of former NHL players on that team," he recalls. "All it turned out to be was one big party all season long. It was like our last fling with hockey. We didn't win too many games but we had fun."

Leach's agent asked him if he wanted to get in shape the next year and give hockey another go. At that point, the guy who once stuffed crumpled up newspapers in his oversized skates just so he could skate, decided his hockey days were done.

"I didn't even think about getting back in the National Hockey League anymore," Leach remembers. "That's how goofy I was at that point. I didn't even want to play anymore. I figured I had had enough of everything."

Leach was blaming just about anyone he could find at that point. It wouldn't be long, though, before he would see the answer to many of his problems in the mirror.

• • • • •

For many people, change in their lives comes gradually, through the lessons learned with a variety of experiences. Others have that one, life-changing moment. Reggie Leach remembers his very clearly.

"At the end of August [in 1984], the Flyers Alumni scheduled a hockey tournament up in Canada," he recalls. "I was out drinking the night before and I showed up and just hopped on the bus we had rented and went to this tournament. I was drunk the whole time. I can't even remember the tournament at all.

"I came back from that tournament, and for the first time after drinking, I didn't feel well. I had the shakes and everything. I went to the hospital and the doctor told me I needed to stop drinking or I was going to be in serious trouble. My liver was starting to go. The doctor recommended a rehab program, and I started the very next morning."

This was not the first time Leach had tried to quit drinking. At the urging of teams he had played for or even his family, he had stopped drinking for short periods of time through the years. This time it was different.

"I had quit for two or three months at a time, but it was always because of someone else," Leach explains. "In 1984 I wanted to get help for myself, nobody else. In the end, that is the way it has to be in order for it to work. And it did. I spent six weeks in rehab and I learned about what my problems really had been and I finally understood a lot about what I had gone through. I learned more in those six weeks about myself than I had learned in my entire life up to that point."

It gave Leach an entirely new perspective on his life and on many of the things that had happened to him in the past. Even his release from the Flyers, an event that he had so much bitterness towards previously, took on a new light.

"I no longer saw my getting let go by the Flyers as something done against me," he reasons. "It was like the old saying about what one bad apple can do the whole bunch of them. It can ruin the group. At the time, they saw me as the one rotten apple."

Undergoing rehab was the first step in the drastic change that Leach's life took in 1984. He retired from hockey, stopped drinking, and got a divorce all during that calendar year. Clearly, his life was taking a different course.

• • • • •

At first Leach wasn't sure exactly what new direction his life would take. He tried selling cars, but he didn't like being inside so much. He tried selling insurance, but that didn't grab him either. Finally a friend suggested to him that he was very good at lawn care and landscaping. Perhaps that was an avenue he should explore.

"It was something I really enjoyed," Leach states. "I liked being outside and it reminded me of my youth when I used to work on a golf course. It's great. Even today, I'm still doing it."

Reggie Leach's tools of choice have gone from a hockey stick to a rake and other landscaping implements.

Leach does local work with his company called DeBran Landscaping. He has also signed on with Interstate Management Company that gives him work with Housing and Urban Development sites. While he admits working in some areas where safety could be a concern, he's happy to have consistent assignments.

In late 1990, Leach was asked to tell his story to a conference of natives in Manitoba, Canada. Not necessarily comfortable with speaking in front of an audience, Leach had no idea it would be the start of another very important aspect of his life.

"The first time, I read off of notes, and it was okay," he recalls. "But the next time I was asked, I just went and spoke from the heart and it was a lot better. I had nothing written down. I just went up there and talked. Now I go up to Canada a lot mainly to talk to the native youths about the dangers of drugs and alcohol. It's something I enjoy. I feel like I am being given a chance to give something back to the community. I hope some of these kids can learn from my mistakes."

Leach relates to the youngsters how he harmed his NHL career by making bad choices concerning alcohol. Occasionally he sees an example of his advice can pay off.

"This 15-year-old girl approached me after one of my speeches," Leach recalls. "I could tell she had been drinking. She asked me for help because her parents were always drunk and couldn't help her. I talked with her for a while and then we offered her the choice of rehab. She agreed and she hasn't had a drink since. I gave her my phone number and she called a couple of times for support. I ran into her girlfriend when I was up there recently and she told me that the girl is now married with a little girl and doing fine. That makes me feel so good."

With his business life rebuilt through landscaping and peace of mind achieved through his productive visits to Canada, Leach's home life rebounded when he remarried in the mid-1990s. His current wife, Deb, is his "biggest supporter." In fact, it has become her crusade to reacquire as much of Reggie's old hockey memorabilia as possible.

"She is my 100 percent backer," Leach says proudly. "I was drunk and stupid back when I played and gave away all of my sweaters and sticks. Well she is trying to get some of them back on the internet. We've gotten back a couple of my sticks, a jersey and a bunch of pictures I hadn't seen. She is so concerned about me getting all of my stuff back."

He is close to getting his 1975 jersey back from when he won his Cup. In a way, it would be a symbolic full circle for Leach. He has spent much of his life after hockey regaining much of what he tossed aside back then. Getting that jersey back might complete the journey in a figurative sense.

•　•　•　•　•

Perhaps no former Flyer champion has changed as much as Reggie Leach. As a player, he had trouble, at times, taking care of himself. Now, others, namely native youths in Canada, depend on him. Back in the 1970s, when something went wrong, Leach would find someone else to blame. Now, he has figured out one has to look inward at times when things go wrong.

Leach realizes the mistakes of his past cannot be completely washed away. There are two main areas of regret in his mind.

"I accomplished every goal in the National Hockey League that I wanted to, except one," he relates. "I did not make it into the Hall of Fame. I figured I cut my career short by at least a couple of years and that might very well have prevented me from getting in. As it was, I scored 381 goals. Who knows how many I could have scored if I hadn't made so many bad decisions?

"Alcohol also cost me my first marriage and my kids for many years. It wasn't until about four years ago [around 2000] when I started talking with them on a regular basis again. I didn't pay enough attention to my son Jamie's hockey career [he would make it to the NHL with Pittsburgh, Hartford, and Florida before spending several years playing in Europe] or my daughter Brandy's life either. I give my first wife all the credit in the world for raising those kids to become such good people. I wasn't around much at all when they were growing up."

"We've repaired a lot of the damage I did, but there's still a long way to go. There's still going to be that bit of mistrust. There are still times I don't feel like a father because I was away so long."

These are the hard lessons of life that Leach now passes on to the many Indian youths he speaks to. He understands that support during the tough times is vital.

"It took me years and years to conquer alcohol," he admits. "I still today thank some of my former teammates like Orest Kindrachuk, who helped me get through those times when I might have gone back to alcohol. At charity golf tournaments, they would get angry when people would offer me drinks. They really looked out for me.

"I'm happy with my life. I'm even happy about all of the experiences I went through back in the 1970s as an alcoholic. I think it all just made be a stronger person. I'm more giving now. I'm more understanding now. I think I've finally found a nice spot in my life."

A healthy perspective, indeed.

# #30
# Bobby Taylor

## "It's His Turn"

To look at the numbers, one would think goaltender Bobby Taylor did not play a significant role on the Stanley Cup teams. In 1973-74, he appeared in only eight games. The next season he would see action in only three games. Yet, all fans of those Cup teams clearly recognize the guy they call "The Chief" as more than just a spare part. Some of that recognition is because every single player on those teams played some kind of important role. Another part of it is that Taylor enhanced his recognition with the fans by spending nearly two decades describing Flyers' games on local television after his playing days.

Either way, Bobby Taylor was very definitely a part of the two-time Stanley Cup champion Philadelphia Flyers. In fact, if not for a cruel twist of fate, one never knows, Taylor might have been "the guy" between the pipes during the glory years.

"During the 1972-73 season, I was playing pretty well and battling Doug Favell for the number-one job," he recalls. "Then in Pittsburgh, I tore my hamstring real badly just after Freddy had finally said I had won the job. Timing is everything."

The Flyers would reacquire Bernie Parent during the next summer and of course, the rest is hockey history.

"It wasn't like I was going to complain about playing time," he explains. "After all, I was playing behind the best goalie in the world those two seasons!"

Still, as the backup Taylor did determine and fit into his role on the team.

"Freddy used to come in at the beginning of the year and flat out tell us that contrary to what we might believe, we were not all created equal," Taylor reflects. "Some guys were going to play more and make more money.

However, he was quick to point out that every guy was as important to the team as the guy who played the most. He felt once we recognized that, we would truly become a team.

"My whole idea was that we were all there for one reason and that was to win. Because Bernie played so many games, Freddy didn't like to practice him too much. So I took the attitude that I'm the guy who has to make the guys work in practice. If I screwed around in practice, I wouldn't be helping them. They wouldn't be sharpening their skills at all. So I took every practice like it was my game. If I didn't take this approach, I felt like I let everybody down."

NHL history is littered with examples of backup goalies who could not accept their role and proved to be a serious disruption for the team. Taylor never made that list. During the second Cup year, he did tell general manager Keith Allen that if there was a team interested in him, to pursue the deal. He did it quietly though, never letting his teammates or the media know. As it turned out, he's happy he wasn't moved until after the Cup years.

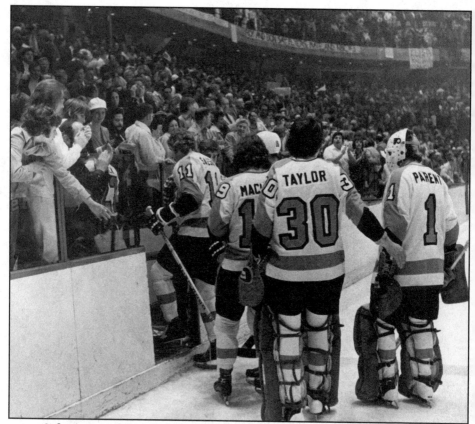

A frequent sight—Bobby Taylor greets Bernie Parent after another fine effort.

"I'm very happy. I got two rings," he states. "I don't think anyone on those teams begrudges me for getting the rings despite playing in just 11 games over the two years. I mean they joke around with me and all, calling me a cheerleader and so forth. But when it comes right down to it, they realize I was just a part of the team.

"There are great players who never get even a single ring, that never even come close to getting one. I played, what, six years in the National Hockey League, and I get two of them. It's incredible! I'm very, very proud of that."

$$\bullet \quad \bullet \quad \bullet \quad \bullet \quad \bullet$$

Those rare occasions that Taylor did get the nod to start became quite the event. None more than his start on Sunday afternoon, January 27, 1974 at the Boston Garden. It has become the stuff of legend.

"We were playing out west in California before traveling across country for a nationally televised game in Boston," Taylor recollects. "Freddy came up to me and told me I was going on Sunday in Boston. You have to remember I hadn't played in eight weeks. Eight full weeks! Now he tells me I'm going to play in Boston where we hardly ever used to win. All I could think about was Orr, and Espo, and Johnny Bucyk!"

The team flew east while NBC pushed the game heavily as a match up of Bernie Parent and the Flyers against the big bad Bruins in Boston! Tim Ryan, Ted Lindsay, Peter Puck, and the whole deal were ready for the showdown in Beantown. It was obvious Shero was not concerned with the potential theater of it all.

The morning of the game, word filtered out that Taylor, not Parent, would be getting the start. Near panic ensued!

"Ted Lindsay and Tim Ryan came out of the booth and went looking for Freddy," that day's starter remembers. "They were asking people around the locker room about what possible reasons there could be for me to be playing instead of Bernie. They couldn't find Freddy for quite a while. Finally, some reporters found him sitting up on the zamboni of all places. He's up there having a smoke as calm as could be. They surround him and asked him why in the hell I was playing. Freddy looked at them, took a long drag of his cigarette, blew out a big puff of smoke and nonchalantly said, 'It's his turn.'

"I tell everybody you know what? That's going to be on my tombstone. 'Here lies Robert Taylor. It's his turn!'"

$$\bullet \quad \bullet \quad \bullet \quad \bullet \quad \bullet$$

Going at times eight weeks between starts, it would have been easy for Taylor to become jealous of Bernie Parent and for some bitterness to develop. It never happened. In fact, Taylor and Parent had an outstanding relationship.

"Bernie was a great guy," Taylor explains. "You couldn't help but like Bernie. We worked hard and I tried to get out there before every period with him and just chat, try to relax him. He liked to talk about anything but hock-

**Bobby Taylor and Bernie Parent enjoyed a great relationship.**

ey in those situations. I remember before games, he would talk about his dog all the time. We would talk about anything, and I think it calmed him down."

In reality, though, Taylor proved to be the perfect complement to the extraordinary Parent.

"You want everybody in your corner," he explains. "The way our team was made up, it would have been hard for anybody to be a complainer anyway. You think about Bob Kelly, Simon Nolet, and Billy Clement, guys like that. They were rotated around on lines and didn't always get a lot of ice time and they never showed any jealousy."

Shortly after the Flyers won their first Cup, Parent, in his own way, let Taylor know he appreciated the support.

"He looked at me and said, 'You know, Chief. You and me, the next 10 years, we'll dominate this league.' It meant a lot that he said 'you and me.'

Even though I was gone two years later and he was forced out shortly after that with the eye injury, I still remember him saying that and how much it meant to me."

$$\bullet \quad \bullet \quad \bullet \quad \bullet \quad \bullet$$

Indeed Parent's "decade of dominance" for the two netminders never did transpire. On March 9, 1976, while on a reconditioning assignment in Richmond (AHL), Taylor got the call telling him he had been traded with Ed Van Impe to the Pittsburgh Penguins for goaltender Gary Inness.

"At the time, I was actually pretty pumped," Taylor says now. "I thought I was finally going to get the chance to play. As it turned out, I only stayed in Pittsburgh for 11 games, only getting to play twice. Six or seven times I was told I was playing and then as I was walking out the door to go on the ice for warmup, they would tell me the other guy was going. It was brutal."

He appeared in 23 games with Springfield (AHL) that season, and when it came time to discuss a contract for the next season, much of the talk centered on the minor leagues. For a guy whose career had begun with the New Jersey Devils of the old Eastern League and eventually peaked with the Cups in Philadelphia, time in the minors was not very appealing.

"I was not going to go back to the minors, possibly all the way back down to the Eastern League at that point. When they offered that, I basically told them to stick it where the sun doesn't shine! That was it."

Bobby Taylor's NHL career ended with a grand total of 46 games played. That works out to a Stanley Cup ring for every 23 games he appeared in. Not a bad ratio.

$$\bullet \quad \bullet \quad \bullet \quad \bullet \quad \bullet$$

The first months of retirement were not easy for "The Chief." He was 31 years old and had no idea what he wanted to do. He put on some weight as he carried a chip around on his shoulder. Not wanting to leave Philadelphia, he wasn't finding a lot of options. That's when his old pal Bob Clarke came to his aid.

"Clarkie and I were talking one day and he told me I should go see Mr. Snider and see if anything was available," Taylor recalls. "We went up to see him and he mentioned that they were just starting this regional television network called PRISM. It was perfect. The people were just starting things and thought my name might help from a credibility standpoint."

Just like that, Taylor's broadcasting career began. And what a beginning it turned out to be. In his first year with PRISM, Taylor teamed with long-time Philadelphia sportscaster Hugh Gannon as the network's first broadcasting duo and they covered a multitude of sports.

"That first year was so much fun," he remembers. "I did everything except baseball and basketball. I mean I got the opportunity to broadcast rodeo, boxing, track and field, and gymnastics. You name it. I was able to see people like Dwight Stones, Eammon Coughlin, Olga Korbut, Marvin Hagler and so many more. It was great experience."

One particular boxing match almost got Taylor a little too close to the action.

"Roberto Duran was fighting a kid from Philly," he recollects. "They decided to delay the decision until after the match, after the people had left because they were so worried there was going to be a riot. The Latino crowd and the African-American crowd were getting all riled up. The guys came out in the ring and told Hugh and I, 'If anything happens boys, you have to get under the ring.' We said, 'No kidding!'"

Taylor survived his various ordeals and his duties grew to include the marketing end of the business. He traveled throughout the Delaware Valley trying to sell potential subscribers on the concept of cable television. It all made for a hectic first year in the business.

"There were days where I might have to try and sell PRISM in Allentown before driving all the way to Atlantic City to call a fight that night," he explains. "I was only getting about $100 per event, so it was obvious I wasn't going to be able to raise three children doing that very long. But I did get to learn a lot about broadcasting."

•   •   •   •   •

Taylor's big break came in 1977 when Don Earle finished out his contract with the Flyers and Taylor was hired as the color analyst to team with play-by-play man, Gene Hart. It was the beginning of a long on-air partnership between the two. It also brought along new challenges for Taylor.

"You never realize how bad your English is until you hear yourself on the air," he relates. "The year before had helped, but I still had quite an adjustment to make. Trying to condense my thoughts and describe something in 10 seconds in what I normally might take 30 seconds to explain was very difficult.

"Ron Gold was the general manager for Channel 38 in town, and he gave me a tip that really helped. He had me carry a tape recorder in my car and when I saw something, I was to describe it in as few words as possible. When you see an item, it's easy to recognize it, but sometimes, it's hard to go from your eyes and your brain and have it come through the way you want to in your speech. That exercise really helped me."

In his more than a quarter of a century of broadcasting, he now passes that exercise along to prospective announcers at camps and seminars. Other than dealing with ribbing from his ex-teammates about having to wear make-up when he was on camera, there was only one other major obstacle he had to overcome in his early broadcasting days.

"It took a long time for me to criticize a player on the air," he recalls. "A lot of the guys still on the team in my first couple of years I had gone to war with as teammates. I wasn't comfortable criticizing them. But Ed Westfall gave me some good advice along those lines. He told me that if you always praise players, people won't listen to you. At the same time, if you always criticize, nobody will listen to you either. You have to find that fine line between praise and criticism and then people will look at you as a credible analyst. Ever since I heard that, I've tried to do that.

"In the early years, if I criticized a player during a game, I would do my best to find something positive about that player somewhere along the line in that game. Sometimes when guys get in slumps, the only time we are talking about them is when they are screwing up and that really isn't fair. We have to remember that if a player made it to the NHL level, under no circumstances is he a bad player. He has to be one of the best in the world to even get here. If we remember that, the tendency to get too negative isn't there."

Sounds like a sound broadcasting philosophy. And it must have worked. Taylor spent 16 years describing Flyers games. In so doing he became as recognizable to Philadelphia sports fans for his days in the booth than he did for his days, infrequent as they were, between the pipes as a goaltender.

•   •   •   •   •

In his days as a player, Bobby Taylor shared the Philadelphia net with a Hall of Famer in Bernie Parent. As a broadcaster, he shared the booth with another Hall of Famer in Gene Hart.

"In all sincerity, [Hart] was the most interesting guy I have met in my entire life," claims Taylor. "Here's a guy who could have signed a baseball contract with the Pittsburgh Pirates. He did a comedy diving routine on the Steel Pier at the shore. He was a classical music and opera nut. He was also a deadbeat race tracker with the horses. He even went to spy school at the Presidio. You talk about interesting. So many contradictions. What a full life he led!"

**Bobby Taylor called longtime broadcast partner, Gene Hart, the most interesting guy he ever met.**

Of course, what Hart is most remembered for is his eloquent description of Flyers hockey from the days of their inception through the two Cups, their Finals heartbreaks in the 1980s and then into the Lindros era of the 1990s. He passed away in 1999. Take it from the guy who followed him on the airwaves in Philadelphia, Hart had as large and loyal a following as a local play-by-play broadcaster could have, and deservedly so.

"The main thing that he really, really taught me was preparation," Taylor points out. "Many guys, and some still do it now, just show up. He taught me about getting to know the background of the players, finding out about some off the wall stats, and getting to know the personalities. He always said that you might only use three percent of what you have, but you never know what three percent it will be, so you have to be prepared. He drilled that into me and I'm forever grateful for that.

"He had such an enthusiasm for the game and the team. If you cut him, he probably would have bled orange."

• • • • •

Flyers fans grew accustomed to tuning in to Flyers games on television and then on radio and following their hometown hockey team through the descriptions of Gene and "The Chief." But by the early 1990s, team management decided to go in a new direction regarding its broadcast team, and Taylor decided to look for a new opportunity. Of course, his first thought was to join his old buddy Clarke, who was then in charge of the expansion Florida Panthers.

"My wife had been bugging me for two or three years to move to Florida," he explains. "My first thought was to go with Clarkie and the Panthers in Miami. He was interested but didn't have the final say on the broadcasters. The people who made those decisions kept putting me off. In the meantime, I saw in the paper that there was an opening in Tampa with the Lightning. I called Phil Esposito [then the Lightning General Manager] and sent a tape. Four days later, he called back and said the job was mine if I wanted it."

Taylor's decision was either the radio job in Florida, if he could get that offer formalized or the television position in Tampa. Current Flyers telecaster Steve Coates offered Taylor the advice that clinched the choice.

"Coatesy wanted me to take the Tampa job," Taylor remembers. "He told me that teams could always fire a voice, but it is much more difficult to fire a face. You think about that and it's true. If you fire a guy who's voice the fans hear, it's not as personal. However, if you fire a guy whose face they see all the time, it's much more personal to them."

Off to Tampa he went. After spending most of the previous two decades living in the Philadelphia area, Taylor was a Floridian. It was not an easy adjustment.

"It took me a long, long time to get used to it," he looks back. "At least five years, I would say. I missed Philly more than when I first moved away from home as a 15-year-old. I'm not kidding you. I was so homesick. I absolutely loved it in Philadelphia. It was a tough time."

Making matters more difficult, Taylor's twins were juniors in high school when the move took place. That is a very challenging time for a teen to leave all of his or her friends. In particular, Taylor's son Casey fought the move.

However, move they did, and 11 years later, Taylor *is* the voice of hockey to fans in Central Florida. The Lightning have had their ups and downs and Taylor misses the passion of Flyers fans, but in retrospect, he does see positives in his move there.

"I think it made me a better broadcaster," he relates. "You have to sell the game. Rick Peckham [his current broadcast partner in Tampa] and I always joke that we should be in Washington D.C. because we can put a twist on anything. Not only that, you learn how to temper everything you say on the air. You just approach the game differently."

**Bobby Taylor is now established as one of the voices of hockey to fans in Tampa Bay.**

Taylor also got the opportunity to broadcast some playoff games for ESPN because he was in Tampa and available at postseason time. All in all, it worked out pretty well for "the Chief."

"I still have a soft spot in my heart for Philly," he admits. "However, it's not like it was the first five years down in Tampa. I've gotten used to it. I've finally moved on."

In June 2004, Taylor enjoyed being part of another Cup experience as the Lightning became champions.

•  •  •  •  •

While all of the Broad Street Bullies seem appreciative and grateful about the opportunity to participate on those Flyers championship teams, one gets the feeling Bobby Taylor is perhaps, one of the most aware of his good fortune. When he discusses his time in Philadelphia, there is a gleam in his eye.

"My years in Philly with the Flyers, you just can't replace," he beams. "I've got two Stanley Cups. I have rings on my fingers. To this day, people remember me. I try to tell kids today that it doesn't matter if you score 800 goals, if you don't win, nobody remembers you. Who's the last guy you think of when you think of the NHL's all-time scoring leaders? It's Marcel Dionne, who was a fantastic player, but he never won. You think of Gretzky, Messier, and Gordie Howe and all those guys because they won Stanley Cups. But Marcel Dionne is the last guy you think of.

"I'm very proud of those rings, and let's face it, those years helped get me into the broadcasting business. The point of it is that I'm in the game still, doing something that I love and it's mainly because I was on those Stanley Cup teams."

His turn did eventually come.

# #35
# Wayne Stephenson

## The Independent Sort

Three players joined the Flyers after the team had already won a Stanley Cup. Reggie Leach felt quite at home having played junior hockey with Bob Clarke. Defenseman Ted Harris was a veteran player at the very end of his career, established in his ways. The third player was goaltender Wayne Stephenson. He was just emerging as an NHL performer when the Flyers acquired him in a trade with St. Louis. For Stephenson, joining such a close-knit group posed its challenges.

"It's tough when you come into a situation like that," Stephenson says now. "Number one, you don't really now anybody. You are the outsider coming in. My first little while in there was, let's just say, interesting. They were such a tight group. Being the outsider was tough."

Stephenson says the awkward feelings he had upon his arrival in the fall of 1974 were compounded by the fact that he was, in effect, taking Bobby Taylor's job as the Bernie Parent's backup. Taylor was a popular member of those teams. With Stephenson on hand it was obvious Taylor would see even less action than he did the season before and more than likely spend more time in the minors.

"Bobby Taylor is such a great guy," Stephenson explains. "We had known each other since we were 10 or 11 years old, playing against one another back in western Canada. But, I was obviously brought in for a reason."

Thus, Stephenson's tenure as a Flyer began with him feeling as an outsider. It gives him a different perspective than the rest of the players of what the team was all about. And yet, it didn't take him long to discover what made those teams tick.

"One of the first games I was in somebody hit one of our guys and then the fight started," Stephenson recalls. "Soon everybody was on the ice and there was a brawl. I couldn't believe it! I knew right then that when you fought one of them, you fought all of them. That was the mentality of that team."

That much even an outsider picked up on.

• • • • •

Outsider or not, Stephenson would become a vital member of the team before his first season as a Flyer was complete. After having appeared in only 12 games during the regular season, Stephenson became "the guy" just as the semifinal series with the up-and-coming New York Islanders was set to begin.

Gary Dornhoefer's warmup shot caught Bernie Parent just above the knee, sending him to the ice in pain. While x-rays proved negative, Parent would not be able to play in the next two games. Stephenson was thrust into the spotlight, even if he entered it reluctantly.

"When Bernie first went down, I was thinking, 'Get up Bernie, get up!'" Stephenson remembers. "But in reality, there was no reason for me to be caught off guard. That was my job. If Bernie went down, I had to go. There was no time to really think about it. I had to get myself mentally ready to play. That was the deal and my understanding of what I was to do. I just had to get going and get out there and do what I could."

He succeeded. Stephenson, in a script that would have been deemed too hokey for Hollywood, stepped in and stopped all 21 shots the Islanders sent his way propelling the Flyers to a 4-0 win in Game 1. He felt his time as a Canadian Olympian, facing the pressure of important games in brief stretches of time, had prepared him well. In Game 2, he was beaten four times, but his huge save in overtime allowed Bobby Clarke to win it, and the Flyers were on their way.

Parent was back in the net for Game 3 of a series that would eventually go seven contests. Just imagine, if the self-perceived outsider had not stepped in and done the job in the first two. It's possible the second Flyers Cup never would have happened.

• • • • •

It was during the following season, though, that Stephenson truly became an integral part of the team. Parent underwent cervical surgery to alleviate pain associated with a herniated disc. He would miss the bulk of the season. Stephenson would thrive on the activity. His numbers alone from that season jump out at you. He appeared in 66 games, going 40-10-13, with a miniscule 2.58 goals-against average. Even with Parent sidelined for much of the year, the Flyers were clearly still among the NHL's elite.

And so it was that when the Flyers represented all of North American against the vaunted Russians in February, 1976, it was Stephenson, and not Parent, between the pipes. Having faced the Russians on several preceding occasions as a member of the Canadian Olympic team, Stephenson did have a frame of reference going into the game. Still, it was a nerve-wracking time.

"I remember being so uptight the night before that game," Stephenson says now. "It felt like we had everything to lose and nothing to gain."

In actuality, the Flyers did gain something. They restored at least some semblance of pride to the NHL, whose teams have been unable to crack the Soviets to that point. The Flyers resounding 4-1 win proved North American hockey could still win out. Stephenson faced only 13 shots in gaining the victory.

"The guys came out and played one heck of a hockey game," Stephenson recollects. "I think you have to go back to Shero. I remember him telling us to stay with our man no matter what the Russians did in the first two minutes. Make them come to us. We threw them off right from the beginning. That was it."

The Flyers would, of course, make another run at a Stanley Cup that season. Parent tried to come back in the playoffs but eventually could not go. Stephenson took over and helped to get the team to the finals before the Canadiens prevailed. Many have said the Flyers might have taken a third Cup had Parent been healthy. Meant as a compliment to Parent, it could also hint at a lack of respect for what Stephenson had done that season.

• • • • •

Wayne Stephenson would remain with the Flyers until the end of the 1978-79 season. It would not always be a very smooth ride.

Prior to the 1976-77 season, he claimed to have been promised a contract renegotiation and refused to report to training camp. He would miss the first two months of the season before coming back on December 7.

**Wayne Stephenson was between the pipes when the Flyers beat the Russians in 1976.**

"There are some things I would like to do with my family," he said as quoted by Jay Greenberg in *Full Spectrum* upon his return. "If I wasn't going to continue to play hockey, I might have to wait until I was 55 or 60."

Today, he terms the holdout "stupidity" on both sides, something that shouldn't have happened, but did.

Similarly, during 1978-79 season, Stephenson made some comments about Flyers management that it's safe to say did not endear him to the organization. With the club holding several extra players on the roster to promote competition, Stephenson offered his own assessment.

"All the extra players have made the team tight," he said in a television interview. "The best thing that could happen would be for management to take a vacation in Florida."

Not surprisingly, the next summer, Stephenson became an ex-Flyer. He was dealt to the Washington Capitals for a third-round draft choice. Today he feels the trade was appropriate.

"It was time to move on," he says. "They had two young goalies in Pete Peeters and Rick St. Croix coming up, so that was the move to make there. I didn't have a future there."

His future was in Washington. But before moving on he looked back, and what he saw was a decent run in Philadelphia.

"Looking at the overview of it, I had to be happy with my time there," he said at the time of the trade. "The Flyers offered me a home for five years."

•　•　•　•　•

Stephenson, like so many of his former Flyer teammates, had moved from a consistent contender to a struggling also-ran. The Capitals were just emerging from their infant years as an expansion team. Their goal was simply for respectability. In 1979-80, after so many years as a backup, Stephenson was the starter from the beginning of training camp.

"They were starting to build their team in Washington," Stephenson recalls. "My first year we struggled early, but then we really started to play well. If we had gotten into the playoffs, it could have gotten interesting."

The Caps had Mike Gartner, Ryan Walter, and Bengt Gustafsson leading the offensive charge. Robert Picard was a promising defenseman. Gary Green, all of 26 years of age took over as head coach early in the season. After a miserable 5-20-5 start, the Caps started winning. They fell two points shy of a playoff berth.

The next season, Denis Maruk would pile up 50 goals, and Bob Kelly would arrive from Philadelphia to have his best season. Stephenson was hobbled by injuries and only appeared in 20 games. Mike Palmateer had been acquired and took over the bulk of the goaltending chores.

"I knew I had lost a step," Stephenson relates now. "When I got hurt in that last year, I knew it was time. When you lose a step in the position I played, you aren't going to last very long. It was time to move on."

He was 36 years old when he retired from hockey. He did so on his terms, a man of independence, and was now free to find another form of employment.

* * * * *

So many members of the Flyer Cup teams talk today of their difficulty staying away from the game of hockey upon retirement as a player. Not so with Wayne Stephenson. In fact, he had already gotten a taste of the "real world" before his NHL career had begun.

Stephenson quit hockey after graduating from University of Winnipeg and went into public accounting. As you would expect from a guy as independent as Stephenson is, his path to the NHL was unique. Eventually the St. Louis Blues would sign him, but the two years away from competitive hockey while in the business world evolved into a good training ground for him for his post-hockey life.

"I actually worked for two years," he reasons. "So I knew what I was going to get into when my playing days were over."

Once that day came, everything seemed to fall into place. A neighbor was senior vice president of Fidelity Bank in Philadelphia. He helped to get Stephenson an interview, and with a degree and two years' experience under his belt, he was hired. His career evolved after that. He spent several years in Philadelphia banking before moving his wife and four kids to Milwaukee to be closer to his ailing mother. Another eight years passed before a move back east, but not to Philadelphia. Instead he chose Cape Cod, where today he owns his own investment business with Cantella and Company out of Boston as his broker dealer. He also runs an insurance business separately.

When the time came for a move, Philadelphia was not on his list of desired locations, because he simply could not deal with the infamous Delaware Valley traffic. Once again, he marched to the beat of his own drummer. Whereas so many ex-Flyers wound up back in Philadelphia, or at least missed the area if they were transplanted, Stephenson does not appear to have any remorse along those lines. Truth be told, Stephenson seems very happy with his life now.

"I like having my own business," he explains. "I have my own office and I'm the only one in it. I get to go out and meet with people, try and solve their problems and then move on. I enjoy it. You have to work at it, of course. If you put the time in, it works for you. If you don't, it doesn't work. I still work 60 to 70 hours a week, but if I want to take a day or two off, I just do it."

He seems to be at his best when there is some freedom in the mix. An independent man would have it no other way.

* * * * *

Stephenson still makes it back to Philadelphia for a visit once or twice a year. He makes a point of playing in the Gene Hart Memorial Golf

Tournament because "Gene Hart was always good to me." He also makes it back for certain alumni functions and enjoys being back with his old teammates.

Yet there still seems to be this distance between him and the other championship members. He claims to not have time to get too involved with alumni events what with his business ventures. That is understandable.

However, from the day he became a Flyer, Stephenson felt somewhat like an outsider, and it seems he prefers to maintain at least some distance still today. It comes right back to his desire for independence.

"The best way to label me would be as independent," he admits. "I follow what I believe. I did what I was supposed to do as a Flyer and then I kind of went my own direction. I always do."

While keeping his distance, he still was able to respect the closeness of those teams. Even today, he sees how much they enjoy each other's company.

"They do so many things with each other to this day," Stephenson explains. "Many of them may have gone their own direction in their lives and yet they still get back together so often. Fred Shero was, and really still is, the key. He was the architect. He built the team concept. That is what it was all about. That is why they were so good and that is why they were so tight. That's why they stay together so much today. They enjoy each other and that's great!"

**Wayne Stephenson is now based in Cape Cod, although he makes it back to Philadelphia once or twice a year.**

# Together Forever

Barry Ashbee stood off to the side of the locker room as the other Flyers celebrated with vigor their first Stanley Cup in May 1974. After all that he had gone through, you could have excused him if had been feeling sorry for himself at that moment. But he chose instead to enjoy the thrill he saw in his teammates. He put things into perspective, too.

"I don't cry much, but I was in tears the last minute and a half," he told the *Daily News*. "I've never been so proud of a bunch of guys in my life. We've had so many setbacks. You might never see another bunch like this."

He was correct in so many ways. The Flyers teams were the last Stanley Cup champions to hail exclusively from Canada. In today's NHL, there are players from several different countries on each team and while the clubs can mesh together and deliver outstanding performances, it's doubtful the players will ever have that same kind of bond. Throw into the mix the frequent player movement of today, and such a connection becomes that much more difficult to achieve.

"I think it's a once-in-a-lifetime kind of group," Ed Snider says. "The fact that so many of them still live in the area is amazing. They are just great guys, the kind of guys that you want as friends forever. When we get together to this day, everybody is close and friendly and warm."

All of the players profiled in this book played at least one full season during the Flyers' Cup years. There were, of course, other participants. Bruce Cowick filled in for some injured forwards during the 1974 playoffs and picked up a ring. He would be selected by the Washington Capitals in the expansion draft a month later and would be out of hockey two years after that.

Al MacAdam appeared in five regular-season games in 1973-74 before getting into one playoff contest. After getting his name on the Stanley Cup he was packaged in a trade to California in exchange for Reggie Leach. He would go on to spend a productive 11 seasons in the NHL with California,

A gathering of several members of the Cup teams in September 2003 gave evidence that the bond is alive and well. Front row (left to right): Rick MacLeish, Ed Van Impe, Joe Watson, Ed Snider, Bob Clarke, Keith Allen, Bernie Parent. Back row (left to right): Jimmy Watson, Don Saleski, Dave Schultz, Wayne Stephenson, Larry Goodenough, Bob Kelly, Bill Clement, Bill Barber, Gary Dornhoefer, Orest Kindrachuk, Reggie Leach, Joe Kadlec. *Photo courtesy of Len Redkoles*

Cleveland, Minnesota, and Vancouver, before heading into the coaching ranks. He spent recent years as an assistant with the Chicago Blackhawks.

Defenseman Larry Goodenough was called up during the 1974-75 season and impressed enough in 20 games to earn a spot in the lineup during the playoffs. He saw action in five of those postseason matches, getting his ring. He would play in Philadelphia for parts of two more seasons before being dealt in the trade that brought Bob Dailey to the Flyers. Goodenough was with Vancouver for parts of four more seasons before experiencing minor league action for three more years. He settled in Philadelphia and is active with the Flyers Alumni.

Of course, there were countless number of support people like assistant coach Mike Nykoluk, trainers Frank Lewis and Jim McKenzie, director of player personnel Marcel Pelletier, and director of team services Joe Kadlec. All of these individuals contributed in their own way to the glory that this team experienced in 1974 and 1975.

After spending more than 10 years in the Philadelphia area and meeting and getting to know many of the members of the Flyers' Cup teams, I thought I had a pretty good idea of what they were all about. Then I decided to write this book. As it turns out, I've learned something about each and every guy that I wasn't aware of before.

During the course of researching material and interviewing these players, I have come to understand better the tremendous connection they have with one another. Obviously, it began with their playing days and all that they accomplished together and the way they accomplished it.

"When you go through what we went through together, there's a bond," explains Jimmy Watson. "It's probably like going to war with somebody in a fox hole. You would never forget that person. You would love that person. It's like that when you go into Boston Garden and you have guys playing beside you like that fighting and battling for each other. There's a bond formed there that will never, ever separate."

Winning adds to that chemistry. Or does that chemistry lead to the winning?

"It's the old 'chicken or the egg' argument," reasons Bobby Taylor. "We had a very close team to begin with. I mean winning the Cups helped make us closer I guess. But we were very close anyway. Freddy Shero had a knack for getting us to believe it was us against the world. That brought us closer together. Besides, we all liked one another."

General manager Keith Allen put the team together and watched it take off. He gives special credit to Shero for his ability to allow the team to grow on its own.

"He was a great coach and the guys really respected him," Allen says. He was never interested in stepping in and telling them he was the boss. Instead, he let them develop their own personality."

That personality took on a swashbuckling type of attitude both on and off the ice. Allen, for one, does not discount how much the team's off-ice demeanor worked hand in hand with their on-ice effectiveness.

"They played hard together on the ice, and they played hard together off the ice," Allen admits. "It's part of what made them such a close-knit group."

Those bonds that were formed have lasted three decades, through good times and bad. Bobby Clarke was the captain and leader of those teams. He's seen the friendships formed in the 1970s carry forth into the new millennium.

"I think it's a key part to being a great team," says the current general manager of the Flyers. "The enjoyment that you get from hanging around with people that you play with is important. The closeness doesn't come just because you win some hockey games together. I think the closeness comes from spending your off-ice time celebrating the good times, like the birth of children, as well as from being there when people have some of their tough times.

"As a group, over the years, this team has seen both ends of the spectrum with great joy and tremendous tragedy. When you think of Barry Ashbee, and Ed Van Impe's daughter, and Jenny Barber, there have been some very tough times. But, everybody still cares for each other. If one guy is in trouble, every one of those guys will come to his aid if they can help."

In tracing the paths of the lives of the Broad Street Bullies since their on-ice triumph, I found example after example of this interaction, which gives credence to the strength of their bond. A phone call from Don Saleski to an ailing Bill Flett days before his death. A call from Calgary head coach Terry Crisp to his old coach Fred Shero on the eve of his Flames going into the 1989

Stanley Cup Finals. Bob Clarke's ability to forgive Dave Schultz for comments about him in his book. And perhaps most striking is Bill Barber's continued love and respect for the Flyers even after being fired.

"Those guys were there for me during my darkest hour," Barber explains. "They always will be there. If I was in trouble tomorrow, I know the guys would be there for me."

• • • • •

When I gathered 17 members of the Cup teams for the picture that appears on the cover of this book, it was surreal. It was the night of a charity fundraiser put on by the Flyers in the form of a roast of former Flyer winger Rick Tocchet. As we assembled the guys for the picture, it was if we were back in the locker room 30 years ago. Jokes were flying left and right. Everyone seemed so comfortable. You could sense how much fun these guys have with one another.

That night was also a definitive indicator of the hold this team still has on the people of the Delaware Valley. When the announcement was made for members of the 1974 and 1975 Stanley Cup teams to assemble in the back of the ballroom, it became a true Kodak moment. Instead of just the photographer I had hired to take the shot, 50 or more people gathered to take hundreds of pictures of their heroes. It became a full-fledged photo shoot.

That night demonstrated the continued interaction the former Flyers have with the fans of the Delaware Valley. Those fans are very much a part of this bond, too. To this day, members of a team that won three decades ago are recognized around Philadelphia. This even though in some cases the players' appearances have changed quite a bit. When Dave Schultz appears on the jumbotron at the Wachovia Center, there's a noticeable buzz throughout the crowd. Bernie Parent is still an icon in the city.

"My next door neighbor isn't even a hockey fan, but she still remembers the day we won the first Cup," relates Joe Watson. "She remembers driving back into town at about 5 p.m. on that Sunday and seeing people all out and about in the streets, honking their horns. She had trouble getting back to her house because streets were blocked off. Thirty years later, she still describes it like it was yesterday! So many people can remember right where they were that day.

"We gave this area something they were in dire need of when we won a championship. So I guess you can say we gave a lot to this city and since then, the city has given many of us a lot back."

"It amazes me to this day how even young people know about the 'Broad Street Bullies,'" offers Terry Crisp. "That tag is going to live forever, ever, and a day in Philadelphia. No matter what other championships are won in football, baseball or any other sport. That one is what relates to the city of Philadelphia. The Broad Street Bullies. And I've got to tell you, they are proud of the tag!"